# Patterns Plus

Ninth Edition

# Patterns Plus

## *A Short Prose Reader with Argumentation*

Ninth Edition

**Mary Lou Conlin**
*Cuyahoga Community College*

**Houghton Mifflin Company**    Boston   New York

*Executive Publisher:* Patricia A. Coryell
*Editor in Chief:* Carrie Brandon
*Sponsoring Editor:* Joanne Kozyrev
*Senior Marketing Manager:* Tom Ziolkowski
*Senior Development Editor:* Kathy Sands-Boehmer
*Associate Project Editor:* Susan Miscio
*Cover Design Manager:* Anne S. Katzeff
*Composition Buyer:* Chuck Dutton
*New Title Project Manager:* Susan Peltier
*Editorial Assistant:* Daisuke Yasutake
*Marketing Assistant:* Bettina Chiu
*Editorial Assistant:* Anthony D'Aries

Cover image: © Jack Zehrt / Getty images

*Credits*

**Sue Hubbell:** Excerpt from *A Book of Bees* by Sue Hubbell. Copyright © 1988 by Sue Hubbell. Reprinted by permission of Houghton Mifflin Company. All rights reserved. **Mary Mebane:** From *Mary* by Mary E. Mebane, copyright © 1981 by Mary Elizabeth Mebane. Used by permission of Viking Penguin, a division of Penguin Group (USA) Inc. **Eliot Wigginton:** Excerpt from *The Foxfire Book* by Eliot Wigginton, copyright © 1968, 1969, 1970, 1971, 1972 by The Foxfire Fund, Inc. Used by permission of Doubleday, a division of Random House, Inc.

Credits continue on page 293.

Printed in the U.S.A.

Library of Congress Control Number: 2007921405

Instructor's examination copy
ISBN-10: 0-618-83302-1
ISBN-13: 978-0-618-83302-3

For orders, use student text ISBNs
ISBN-10: 0-618-77531-5
ISBN-13: 978-0-618-77531-6

23456789-MV-11 10 09 08

# Contents

Preface   *xxv*


**1   The Basics of Writing: Process and Strategies**   *1*

**2   Narration**   *13*

**PARAGRAPHS**

The Movie House   *John Updike*   *18*

> John Updike gives a lively description of the exhilaration of childhood terror and imagination.

The Hunt   *Lesley Stern*   *20*

> An addiction drives a woman to strange, middle-of-the-night behavior.

Why Harlem Is Not Manhattan   *John L. Jackson*   *22*

> A persistent young black man demands a ninety-nine-cent Big Mac in New York.

Geography   *Elizabeth Bishop*   *24*

> A geography lesson is remembered for its colors.

The Memorial Service   *Christopher Malinowski (student)*   *26*

> The writer and his brother share a favorite person's remembrance of her husband.

**ESSAYS**

Learning to Write   *Russell Baker*   28

> A renowned essayist remembers his first, bold answer to what would become his calling.

Daughter's Doll Teaches Mom Lesson on Race   *Connie Schultz*   32

> A mother learns that her daughter knows best when it comes to choosing the right doll.

The Story of My Ring   *Annie Reeves (student)*   35

> It's not just a ring—it has a story to tell.

A Little Nebraska   *Sarah Smith (student)*   38

> The whole state stands still on a football day at the University of Nebraska.

**3  Description**  *43*

**PARAGRAPHS**

A Perfect Dog   *John Grogan*   *49*

> Some dogs are easy to train—like this dog from the writer's childhood.

The Hiroshima Museum   *Barbara Kingsolver*   *51*

> The Hiroshima Museum shows us the horror of an atomic bomb explosion.

The Ravine   *Quincy Stott (student)*   *53*

> It was their favorite place to play and special because it drew them together.

The Wreck   *Richard Mack*   *55*

> The wreck was a horrible sight, but the writer felt the dead passenger seemed to say he was at peace.

Overindulgence   *Heidi Hall (student)*   *57*

> Hall describes, in delicious detail, her Aunt Helen's chicken and dumplings—and their after-effects.

**ESSAYS**

Hush Timmy—This is Like a Church   *Kurt Anderson*   *59*

> Bitterly opposed when it was first built, the Viet Nam Veterans Memorial in Washington, DC is now a revered and hallowed monument to the men and women who gave their lives in the Viet Nam War.

A Letter from the Desert   *Lt. Nicole A. Elwell and Jeff Elwell*   *63*

> A father shares a letter he received from his first lieutenant daughter serving in Iraq that describes the real life of the Iraqi people.

Regular Customer   *Gloria Garrison (student)*   *67*

> Just like the routine of the coffee shop, the customer comes every day to the coffee shop, orders the same food, and even says the same things.

Limbo   *Rhonda S. Lucas (student)*   *70*

> Seeing familiar objects in a new setting after her parents' divorce teaches this young woman a lesson about life

**4  Examples**  *73*

**PARAGRAPHS**

Distance Learning   *Mary Lord*   *77*

> It's a growing opportunity to learn—if you have a computer, just register for a class that's offered by distance learning!

The Digital Revolution   *Ellen Cobb Wade*   *79*

> Buying a cell phone, iPod, or any of the new digital devices is only the first step—then you have to program it! That's the challenge for even a digital alarm clock!

Boomtown, U.S.A.   *Jeff Glasser*   81

> A small town is radically changed by the discount-store, meatpacking, and trucking businesses.

Folk Art in the Barrios   *Eric Kroll*   83

> Wall paintings in Santa Fe, New Mexico, depict Chicanos as bold, strong figures.

My Suit   *Ricardo Galvez (student)*   85

> Galvez finds the way he is dressed makes a difference to others.

**ESSAYS**

The Social Meaning of T-Shirts   *Diana Crane*   87

> Your T-Shirt may say more about you than you think.

Foreign Flavors, Mainstream Taste   *Debra Aho Williamson*   90

> Those once "foreign foods" aren't foreign to us anymore.

Between Two Wars, 1913–1945   *Kathryn VanSpanckeren*   94

> The changes that took place in the United States between World War I and World War II have been described by F. Scott Fitzgerald, Ernest Hemingway, Gertrude Stein, and many other writers.

My Mother Never Worked   *Bonnie Smith-Yackel*   98

> A daughter details the boundless energy of her mother—a Great Depression–era farmer and mother of eight who, according to the federal government, "never worked."

## 5   Classification and Division   *103*

**PARAGRAPHS**

Chili   *Charles Kuralt*   107

> A quick look at some ways of preparing a popular meal, ranging from the ordinary to the exotic.

March of Science   *James K. Page Jr.*   109

> Three kinds of crispy foods make three kinds of crunchy noises, and they all make for happy eaters.

The Mad Dog's Hair: Alcoholism   *Gustave Simons*   111

> The writer explains the behavior of moderate, heavy, and alcoholic drinkers.

Fans   *Paul Gallico*   113

> Sports fans can be classified by the polite to rowdy ways they behave.

Brain Power   *Lester C. Thurow*   115

> We're not in an "information revolution," according to the writer, but an age of "skills and knowledge" as sources of wealth.

## ESSAYS

"Ever Et Raw Meat?"   *Stephen King*      117

> Readers can ask writers very strange questions, according to this horror-story writer.

Eggs, Twinkies, and Ethnic Stereotypes   *Jeanne Park*      122

> At first, intelligence set her apart in the classroom, and then it was her Asian-American heritage.

Secrets of Man's Unspoken Language   *Desmond Morris*      125

> You can tell a lot about people by the gestures they use.

Start Spreading the News: Seven Things You Should Know Before Moving to New York City   *Courtney Reimer*      130

> It isn't easy to live there, but. . .

## 6   Comparison and Contrast      *135*

### PARAGRAPHS

Happy Returns   *Sarah Bernard*      141

> How do you feel about returning gifts you don't like or can't use?

Good Girl, Bad Girl   *Anna Quindlen*      143

> Friends don't necessarily need common interests and qualities, as Quindlen demonstrates in the description of a boarding school friendship.

Dogs and Cats   *Konrad Lorenz*      145

> They are both favorite household pets, but that's about all a dog and a cat have in common.

Yin and Yang   *Mary Paumier Jones*      147

> Jones explains the meaning of the yin and yang movements in T'ai Chi, a Chinese form of exercise.

### ESSAYS

Neat People vs. Sloppy People   *Suzanne Britt*      149

> Tidiness is not the only difference between neat people and sloppy people. The writer claims that sloppy people are happier and nicer than neat people.

Conversational Ballgames   *Nancy Masterson Sakamoto*      152

> Sakamoto compares the difference between American and Japanese conversation to the difference between playing tennis and bowling.

Indy 500   *Chris Hanley (student)*      157

> It's not always the teenagers who are the most reckless drivers!

Shopping in Pajamas   *Francine Mercier (student)*      160

> By shopping online, you can avoid the crowds and the parking problems.

**7 Process**   *163*

**PARAGRAPHS**

The Supply Chain   *Thomas L. Friedman*   *166*

> Technology makes the supply chain move smoothly and efficiently to keep the shelves stocked at every Wal-Mart in the world.

How to Bathe a Cat   *The Dog*   *168*

> Only a dog would want to see this happen to a cat!

Brewing Beer   *Grace Lichtenstein*   *170*

> Making beer involves a more complicated and lengthy process than you might think.

The Right Way to Eat an Ice-Cream Cone   *L. Rust Hills*   *172*

> It takes a special technique to eat an ice-cream cone without having it drip on you.

The Cook   *Barbara Lewis (student)*   *174*

> Lewis describes her complicated and hectic two-hour job of preparing a dinner.

**ESSAYS**

A Guide to Proper Hand-Washing Technique   *Jennifer Traig*   *176*

> It's one thing to wash your hands; it's another challenge to shut off the faucets and still keep your hands really clean.

The Beekeeper   *Sue Hubbell*   *179*

> Hubbell shows us that a beekeeper has to become immune to bee stings, but that the process is painful.

Koto   *Edna Yano (student)*   *181*

> It's an exotic, thirteen-string instrument that is a challenge to play, but the writer struggled through the process and was successful.

The Art of Making Fimo Beads   *Julie Gifford (student)*   *184*

> It takes time and patience, but you can make fimo beads to fashion into necklaces.

**8 Cause and Effect**   *189*

**PARAGRAPHS**

Giving In   *Michelle Cottle*   *195*

> She didn't want to be the typical suburbanite, but two children and their paraphernalia made her give in and buy the car.

Why Eat Junk Food?   *Judith Wurtman*   *197*

> Junk food tastes good—but Judith Wurtman believes there's more to its appeal than its taste.

An Eyewitness Account   *Jack London*      199

The novelist describes the devastating effect of the 1906 earthquake on San Francisco.

A Momentous Arrest   *Martin Luther King Jr.*      201

A black seamstress makes history when she is arrested for not giving up her seat on a bus to a white man.

On Being Unemployed   *Nelliejean Smith (student)*      203

A young woman tells us from bitter experience what it means to be out of work.

**ESSAYS**

Global Warming in Canada   *Liz Sinclair (student)*      205

The rugged beauty of northern Canada is threatened by global warming, and the writer says the solution is not simple.

Racial Stereotypes Go Underground
*Cynthia Merriwether-deVries*      209

A teacher's research project tells us that we won't get rid of our racial stereotypes until we admit we have them.

The Thirsty Animal   *Brian Manning*      211

A recovering alcoholic remembers his plunge into alcohol abuse and describes the scars that will never go away.

More Than Words   *Victor Flores (student)*      215

A lesson is learned when the writer shirks his responsibility and disappoints his father.

**9   Definition**      217

**PARAGRAPHS**

Running with the Cardio-Bots   *Walter Kirn*      220

Drop into a gym or fitness center any time and you'll see them running on the treadmills!

The Ultimate Kitchen Gadget   *Robert Capon*      222

There is one gadget that has not yet been advertised on television.

Nostalgia   *Richard Shelton*      224

He doesn't define the word crepuscular, but you should be able to figure out its meaning.

What Does It Mean to Be Creative?   *S. I. Hayakawa*      226

An authority on semantics—the study of the development, structure, and changes in language—defines a creative person.

Grandparents   *Nancy Merrell (student)*      228

Merrell believes we take grandparents too much for granted and tells us how much they enrich our lives.

## ESSAYS

What Is Poverty?  *Jo Goodwin Parker*    230

> You may think it is just being poor or without enough money, but the writer makes us see what it really is.

What Is Intelligence, Anyway?  *Isaac Asimov*    235

> Perhaps intelligence should be defined by the practical ability to make things work and think things out, not by scores on standardized tests.

Total Eclipse of the Son  *Tiffany Kary*    238

> If a Japanese son no longer shows respect for his parents and elders, it's called hikikomori.

Earning Their Pinstripes  *Rick Reilly*    240

> If you think it would be fun to be a batboy for the New York Yankees, think again!

## 10  Argumentation and Persuasion    243

### PARAGRAPHS

Tax Junk Food? Yes  *Michael F. Jacobson*    250

> The writer says we should tax junk food and use the money to promote healthy habits.

Frightening—and Fantastic  *Anna Quindlen*    252

> There are scary people out there, and we need to teach our children to be wary. But we should teach them there are good people out there, too.

Drinking—What Age?  *Barrett Seaman*    254

> The writer claims that eighteen-year-olds may drink to excess initially, if the legal drinking age were lowered, but would soon put drinking in its proper place.

The Measure of Our Success  *Marian Wright Edelman*    256

> Edelman, founder of the Children's Defense League, encourages us to get involved in the problems of impoverished children and their families.

Flunking  *Mary Sherry*    258

> It's hard to believe, but that "F" grade, according to the writer, is an "expression of confidence" that the student can learn the material for the course.

## ESSAYS

Hang It Up  *Jesse Scaccia*    260

> A teacher tells how it feels to face a classroom full of students with cell phones in their hands.

Keep the Drinking Age at Twenty-One  *Robert Voas*    263

> A research scientist argues against lowering the drinking age.

Banning Smoking   *John Ruckdeschel*      *266*

The writer argues for a national ban on indoor smoking.

A Burning Issue   *Mary Boltz Chapman*      *268*

While Ruckdeschel argues for a national ban on smoking, some cities are still debating allowing versus banning smoking in restaurants.

**11  Combining the Strategies**      *271*

A Trip to Honduras   *Daniel Boehmer (student)*      *272*

A first-hand view of the needs of people in an impoverished country confirms a student's desire to seek a career where he can help others.

The Dare   *Roger Hoffmann*      *274*

The writer remembers that when he was young and confused about his identity, a dare turned into a dangerous rite of passage.

Poetry   *Kirsten Bauman (student)*      *277*

A student tells us her experiences with poetry and how she learned to appreciate it.

A Very Basic Decision   *Mary E. Mebane*      *279*

At an all-black college in the 1950s, a young woman struggles to overcome a surprising form of prejudice.

Time to Look and Listen   *Magdoline Asfahani (student)*      *282*

Asfahani recalls the pain she felt as a victim of discrimination.

**Glossary**   *285*

**Credits**   *293*

**Index**   *297*

# Thematic Table
# of Contents

 ## Animals and Humans

The following readings discuss animal and human behavior under different
    situations and challenges.

A Little Nebraska   *Sarah Smith (student)*   *38*

A Perfect Dog   *John Grogan*   *49*

Regular Customer   *Gloria Garrison (student)*   *67*

Fans   *Paul Gallico*   *113*

Secrets of Man's Unspoken Language   *Desmond Morris*   *125*

Dogs and Cats   *Konrad Lorenz*   *147*

How to Bathe a Cat   *The Dog*   *168*

 ## Childhood

In the following readings, the writers share their memories, lessons learned,
    risks taken in childhood and youth, and the significance of early parental
    involvement with one's children.

The Movie House   *John Updike*   *18*

Geography   *Elizabeth Bishop*   *24*

Daughter's Doll Teaches Mom Lesson on Race   *Connie Schultz*   *32*

Eggs, Twinkies and Ethnic Stereotypes   *Jeanne Park*   *122*

The Thirsty Animal   *Brian Manning*   *211*

Total Eclipse of the Son   *Tiffany Kary*   *238*

The Dare   *Roger Hoffmann*   *274*

 ## Communication

In the following readings, the writers consider the many ways we
    communicate and fail to communicate effectively.

Why Harlem Is Not Manhattan   *John L. Jackson*   *22*

Daughter's Doll Teaches Mom Lesson on Race   *Connie Schultz*   *32*

The Hiroshima Museum   *Barbara Kingsolver*   *51*

A Letter from the Desert   *Lt. Nicole A. Elwell and Jeff Elwell*   *63*

The Social Meaning of T-Shirts   *Diana Crane*   *87*

"Ever Et Raw Meat?"   *Stephen King*   *117*

Secrets of Man's Unspoken Language   *Desmond Morris*   125
Conversational Ballgames   *Nancy Masterson Sakamoto*   152
Racial Stereotypes Go Underground   *Cynthia Merriwether-deVries*   209
More Than Words   *Victor Flores (student)*   215
Total Eclipse of the Son   *Tiffany Kary*   238
Poetry   *Kirsten Bauman (student)*   277

 ## Education and Learning

What we've learned and what we have yet to learn are considered in the
  following selections.

Geography   *Elizabeth Bishop*   24
Learning to Write   *Russell Baker*   28
Distance Learning   *Mary Lord*   77
Racial Stereotypes Go Underground   *Cynthia Merriwether-deVries*   209
What Does It Mean to Be Creative?   *S. I. Hayakawa*   226
What is Intelligence, Anyway?   *Isaac Asimov*   235
Total Eclipse of the Son   *Tiffany Kary*   238
The Measure of Our Success   *Marian Wright Edelman*   256
Flunking   *Mary Sherry*   258
Hang It Up   *Jesse Scaccia*   260
A Very Basic Decision   *Mary E. Mebane*   279

 ## Expectations and Reality

In the following readings, the writers show us that expectations, whether
  positive or negative, may not be realized or may turn out differently
  than anticipated.

Geography   *Elizabeth Bishop*   24
Learning to Write   *Russell Baker*   28
Daughter's Doll Teaches Mom Lesson on Race   *Connie Schultz*   32
The Wreck   *Richard Mack*   55
Overindulgence   *Heidi Hall (student)*   57
A Letter from the Desert   *Lt. Nicole A. Elwell and Jeff Elwell*   63
Limbo   *Rhonda S. Lucas (student)*   70
The Digital Revolution   *Ellen Cobb Wade*   79
Boomtown, U.S.A.   *Jeff Glasser*   81
My Suit   *Ricardo Galvez (student)*   85
Foreign Flavors, Mainstream Taste   *Debra Aho Williamson*   90
My Mother Never Worked   *Bonnie Smith-Yackel*   98
Start Spreading the News: Seven Things You Should Know Before Moving to
New York City   *Courtney Reimer*   130
Good Girl, Bad Girl   *Anna Quindlen*   143
Yin and Yang   *Mary Paumier Jones*   147
Conversational Ballgames   *Nancy Masterston Sakamoto*   152

A Guide to Proper Hand-Washing Technique   *Jennifer Traig*   176
The Thirsty Animal   *Brian Manning*   211
What Is Intelligence, Anyway?   *Isaac Asimov*   235
Earning Their Pinstripes   *Rick Reilly*   240
Banning Smoking   *John Ruckdeschel*   266
A Burning Issue   *Mary Boltz Chapman*   268
The Dare   *Roger Hoffmann*   274
A Very Basic Decision   *Mary E. Mebane*   279
Time to Look and Listen   *Magdoline Asfahani (student)*   282

## The Family

The following readings consider the positive and not-so-positive aspects of
    family life.
The Story of My Ring   *Annie Reeves (student)*   35
Limbo   *Rhonda S. Lucas (student)*   70
My Mother Never Worked   *Bonnie Smith-Yackel*   98
Indy 500   *Chris Hanley (student)*   157
More Than Words   *Victor Flores (student)*   215
Grandparents   *Nancy Merrell (student)*   228
Total Eclipse of the Son   *Tiffany Kary*   238
The Measure of Our Success   *Marian Wright Edelman*   256

## Food for Thought

The following readings consider things we like to eat and drink, and
    things we maybe shouldn't eat or drink.
Overindulgence   *Heidi Hall (student)*   57
Foreign Flavors, Mainstream Taste   *Debra Aho Williamson*   90
Chili   *Charles Kuralt*   107
March of Science   *James K. Page Jr.*   109
The Mad Dog's Hair: Alcoholism   *Gustave Simons*   111
Brewing Beer   *Grace Lichtenstein*   170
The Thirsty Animal   *Brian Manning*   211
Tax Junk Food? Yes   *Michael F. Jacobson*   250

## The Individual in Society

The readings included in this section deal with the experiences, roles,
    and responsibilities of individuals and with the effect of society on
    their lives.
The Memorial Service   *Christopher Malinowski (student)*   26
A Letter from the Desert   *Lt. Nicole A. Elwell and Jeff Elwell*   63
Regular Customer   *Gloria Garrison (student)*   67
My Mother Never Worked   *Bonnie Smith-Yackel*   98

A Momentous Arrest   *Martin Luther King Jr.*   201
What Is Poverty?   *Jo Goodwin Parker*   230
Frightening—and Fantastic   *Anna Quindlen*   252
Drinking—What Age?   *Barrett Seaman*   254
The Measure of Our Success   *Marian Wright Edelman*   256
Keep the Drinking Age at Twenty-One   *Robert Voas*   263
A Trip to Honduras   *Daniel Boehmer (student)*   272
The Dare   *Roger Hoffmann*   274
A Very Basic Decision   *Mary E. Mebane*   279

 ## The Natural Environment

The following selections consider our impact on the environment and its
impact on us.

The Ravine   *Quincy Stott (student)*   53
Global Warming in Canada   *Liz Sinclair (student)*   205

 ## Progress

The memorable but sometimes questionable effects of discoveries, inventions,
and decisions made in the name of "progress," as well as our lack of
progress in solving some of society's problems, are considered in the
following readings.

Distance Learning   *Mary Lord*   77
The Digital Revolution   *Ellen Cobb Wade*   79
Boomtown, U.S.A.   *Jeff Glasser*   81
Between Two Wars, 1913–1945   *Kathryn VanSpanckeren*   94
Brain Power   *Lester C. Thurow*   115
The Supply Chain   *Thomas L. Friedman*   166
The Measure of Our Success   *Marian Wright Edelman*   256
Hang It Up   *Jesse Scaccia*   260

## Racial, Ethnic, and Cultural Issues

African-American, Italian, Japanese, Hispanic, Jewish, Chinese, and Muslim
issues as well as cultural and class concerns, are addressed in the
following selections.

Why Harlem Is Not Manhattan   *John L. Jackson*   22
Daughter's Doll Teaches Mom Lesson on Race   *Connie Schultz*   32
A Letter from the Desert   *Lt. Nicole A. Elwell and Jeff Elwell*   63
Folk Art in the Barrios   *Eric Kroll*   83
The Social Meaning of T-Shirts   *Diana Crane*   87
Foreign Flavors, Mainstream Taste   *Debra Aho Williamson*   90
Between Two Wars, 1913–1945   *Kathryn VanSpanckeren*   94
Eggs, Twinkies and Ethnic Stereotypes   *Jeanne Park*   122

Secrets of Man's Unspoken Language   *Desmond Morris*     125
Conversational Ballgames   *Nancy Masterson Sakamato*     152
Koto   *Edna Yano (student)*     181
The Art of Making Fimo Beads   *Julie Gifford (student)*     184
A Momentous Arrest   *Martin Luther King Jr.*     201
Racial Stereotypes Go Underground   *Cynthia Merriwether-deVries*     209
Total Eclipse of the Son   *Tiffany Kary*     238
A Very Basic Decision   *Mary E. Mebane*     279
Time to Look and Listen   *Magdoline Asfahani (student)*     282

▲ **Values**

Values associated with a particular culture, race, society, sight, food, piece of
   clothing, language, and even color are considered in the following readings.

The Hunt   *Lesley Stern*     20
Daughter's Doll Teaches Mom Lesson on Race   *Connie Schultz*     32
The Story of My Ring   *Annie Reeves (student)*     35
The Hiroshima Museum   *Barbara Kingsolver*     51
Hush, Timmy—This Is Like a Church   *Kurt Anderson*     59
A Letter from the Desert   *Lt. Nicole A. Elwell and Jeff Elwell*     63
Boomtown, U.S.A.   *Jeff Glasser*     81
Folk Art in the Barrios   *Eric Kroll*     83
My Suit   *Ricardo Galvez (student)*     85
The Social Meaning of T-Shirts   *Diana Crane*     87
Between Two Wars, 1913–1945   *Kathryn VanSpanckeren*     94
My Mother Never Worked   *Bonnie Smith-Yackel*     98
Brain Power   *Lester C. Thurow*     115
Eggs, Twinkies, and Ethnic Stereotypes   *Jeanne Park*     122
Happy Returns   *Sarah Bernard*     141
Neat People vs. Sloppy People   *Suzanne Britt*     149
Conversational Ballgames   *Nancy Masterson Sakamoto*     152
A Momentous Arrest   *Martin Luther King Jr.*     201
The Thirsty Animal   *Brian Manning*     211
Grandparents   *Nancy Merrell (student)*     228
Total Eclipse of the Son   *Tiffany Kary*     238
Drinking—What Age?   *Barrett Seaman*     254
Flunking   *Mary Sherry*     258
Keep the Drinking Age at Twenty-One   *Robert Voas*     263
Banning Smoking   *John Ruckdeschel*     266
A Burning Issue   *Mary Boltz Chapman*     268
A Trip to Honduras   *Daniel Boehmer (student)*     272
The Dare   *Roger Hoffmann*     274
A Very Basic Decision   *Mary E. Mebane*     279
Time to Look and Listen   *Magdoline Asfahani (student)*     282

▲  **The Working World**

The nature of work, the definition of work, and the effects of not working
are considered in the following readings.

Learning to Write   *Russell Baker*   28
Regular Customer   *Gloria Garrison (student)*   67
My Mother Never Worked   *Bonnie Smith-Yackel*   98
The Cook   *Barbara Lewis (student)*   174
The Beekeeper   *Sue Hubbell*   179
On Being Unemployed   *Nelliejean Smith (student)*   203
Earning Their Pinstripes   *Rick Reilly*   240
Tax Junk Food? Yes   *Michael F. Jacobson*   250
Banning Smoking   *John Ruckdeschel*   266
A Burning Issue   *Mary Boltz Chapman*   268

# Writing Across the Curriculum
# Table of Contents

## ▲ African-American Studies

The Social Meaning of T-Shirts   *Diana Crane*   87
A Momentous Arrest   *Martin Luther King Jr.*   201
Racial Stereotypes Go Underground   *Cynthia Merriwether-deVries*   209
A Very Basic Decision   *Mary E. Mebane*   279

## ▲ American Studies

The Story of My Ring   *Annie Reeves (student)*   35
Hush, Timmy—This Is Like a Church   *Kurt Anderson*   59
The Social Meaning of T-Shirts   *Diana Crane*   87
Foreign Flavors, Mainstream Taste   *Debra Aho Williamson*   90
Between Two Wars, 1913–1945   *Kathryn VanSpanckeren*   94
Chili   *Charles Kuralt*   107
Start Spreading the News: Seven Things You Should Know Before Moving to New York City   *Courtney Reimer*   130
Shopping in Pajamas   *Francine Mercier (student)*   160
A Momentous Arrest   *Martin Luther King Jr.*   201

## ▲ Anthropology

Secrets of Man's Unspoken Language   *Desmond Morris*   125

## ▲ Asian Studies

The Hiroshima Museum   *Barbara Kingsolver*   51
Eggs, Twinkies, and Ethnic Stereotypes   *Jeanne Park*   122
Yin and Yang   *Mary Paumier Jones*   147
Conversational Ballgames   *Nancy Masterson Sakamato*   152
Koto   *Edna Yano (student)*   181
Total Eclipse of the Son   *Tiffany Kary*   238

## ▲ Biology

A Perfect Dog   *John Grogan*   49
Dogs and Cats   *Konrad Lorenz*   145

How to Bathe a Cat   *The Dog*     168
The Beekeeper   *Sue Hubbell*     179

 **Business**

Boomtown, U.S.A.   *Jeff Glasser*     81
Foreign Flavors, Mainstream Taste   *Debra Aho Williamson*     90
The Supply Chain   *Thomas L. Friedman*     166
Global Warming in Canada   *Liz Sinclair (student)*     205
Tax Junk Food? Yes   *Michael F. Jacobson*     250
Banning Smoking   *John Ruckdeschel*     266
A Burning Issue   *Mary Boltz Chapman*     268

 **Communication**

Learning to Write   *Russell Baker*     28
Conversational Ballgames   *Nancy Masterson Sakamato*     152
More Than Words   *Victor Flores*     215
Hang It Up   *Jesse Scaccia*     260

 **Computer Science and Information Systems**

Distance Learning   *Mary Lord*     77
The Digital Revolution   *Ellen Cobb Wade*     79
Brain Power   *Lester C. Thurow*     115
Shopping in Pajamas   *Francine Mercier (student)*     160
Hang It Up   *Jesse Scaccia*     260

 **Economics**

Between Two Wars, 1913–1945   *Kathryn VanSpanckeren*     94
My Mother Never Worked   *Bonnie Smith-Yackel*     98
Brain Power   *Lester C. Thurow*     115
The Supply Chain   *Thomas L. Friedman*     166
On Being Unemployed   *Nelliejean Smith (student)*     203
Global Warming in Canada   *Liz Sinclair (student)*     205
What Is Poverty?   *Jo Goodwin Parker*     230
The Measure of Our Success   *Marian Wright Edelman*     256

**Education**

Geography   *Elizabeth Bishop*     24
Learning to Write   *Russell Baker*     28
Distance Learning   *Mary Lord*     77
Racial Stereotypes Go Underground   *Cynthia Merriwether-deVries*     209
What Does It Mean to Be Creative?   *S. I. Hayakawa*     226

What Is Intelligence, Anyway?   *Isaac Asimov*      235
Flunking   *Mary Sherry*      258
Hang It Up   *Jesse Scaccia*      260
A Very Basic Decision   *Mary E. Mebane*      279
Time to Look and Listen   *Magdoline Asfahani (student)*      282

## Geography and Geology

Geography   *Elizabeth Bishop*      24
An Eyewitness Account   *Jack London*      199
A Trip to Honduras   *Daniel Boehmer (student)*      272

## History

The Story of My Ring   *Annie Reeves (student)*      35
The Hiroshima Museum   *Barbara Kingsolver*      51
Hush, Timmy—This Is Like a Church   *Kurt Anderson*      59
Folk Art in the Barrios   *Eric Kroll*      83
The Social Meaning of T-Shirts   *Diana Crane*      87
Between Two Wars, 1913–1945   *Kathryn VanSpanckeren*      94
Brain Power   *Lester C. Thurow*      115
An Eyewitness Account   *Jack London*      199
A Momentous Arrest   *Martin Luther King Jr.*      201

## Law and Public Policy

Indy 500   *Chris Hanley (student)*      157
A Momentous Arrest   *Martin Luther King Jr.*      201
Tax Junk Food? Yes   *Michael F. Jacobson*      250
Drinking—What Age?   *Barrett Seaman*      254
Keep the Drinking Age at Twenty-One   *Robert Voas*      263
Banning Smoking   *John Ruckdeschel*      266
A Burning Issue   *Mary Boltz Chapman*      268

## Media Studies

The Movie House   *John Updike*      18
Distance Learning   *Mary Lord*      77

## Medical Science and Health

The Mad Dog's Hair: Alcoholism   *Gustave Simons*      111
Yin and Yang   *Mary Paumier Jones*      147
The Beekeeper   *Sue Hubbell*      179
The Thirsty Animal   *Brian Manning*      211
Running with the Cardio-Bots   *Walter Kirn*      220

Tax Junk Food? Yes   *Michael F. Jacobson*      *250*
Banning Smoking   *John Ruckdeschel*      *266*
A Burning Issue   *Mary Boltz Chapman*      *268*

   **Political Science**

The Social Meaning of T-Shirts   *Diana Crane*      *87*
Global Warming in Canada   *Liz Sinclair (student)*      *205*

   **Psychology**

The Movie House   *John Updike*      *18*
The Memorial Service   *Christopher Malinowski (student)*      *26*
The Wreck   *Richard Mack*      *55*
Hush, Timmy—This Is Like a Church   *Kurt Anderson*      *59*
Regular Customer   *Gloria Garrison (student)*      *67*
Limbo   *Rhonda S. Lucas (student)*      *70*
Folk Art in the Barrios   *Eric Kroll*      *83*
March of Science   *James K. Page Jr.*      *109*
Happy Returns   *Sarah Bernard*      *141*
A Guide to Proper Hand-Washing Technique   *Jennifer Traig*      *176*
Why Eat Junk Food?   *Judith Wurtman*      *197*
The Thirsty Animal   *Brian Manning*      *211*
What Does It Mean to Be Creative?   *S. I. Hayakawa*      *226*
Total Eclipse of the Son   *Tiffany Kary*      *238*

**Sociology**

Daughter's Doll Teaches Mom Lesson on Race   *Connie Schultz*      *32*
A Letter from the Desert   *Lt. Nicole A. Elwell and Jeff Elwell*      *63*
Regular Customer   *Gloria Garrison (student)*      *67*
Boomtown, U.S.A.   *Jeff Glasser*      *81*
My Suit   *Ricardo Galvez (student)*      *85*
The Social Meaning of T-Shirts   *Diana Crane*      *87*
Between Two Wars, 1913–1945   *Kathryn VanSpanckeren*      *94*
Fans   *Paul Gallico*      *113*
Eggs, Twinkies and Ethnic Stereotypes   *Jeanne Park*      *122*
Secrets of Man's Unspoken Language   *Desmond Morris*      *125*
Good Girl, Bad Girl   *Anna Quindlen*      *143*
A Momentous Arrest   *Martin Luther King Jr.*      *201*
On Being Unemployed   *Nelliejean Smith (student)*      *203*
Racial Stereotypes Go Underground   *Cynthia Merriwether-deVries*      *209*
Grandparents   *Nancy Merrell (student)*      *228*
What Is Poverty?   *Jo Goodwin Parker*      *230*
What Is Intelligence, Anyway?   *Isaac Asimov*      *235*

Total Eclipse of the Son   *Tiffany Kary*     238
The Measure of Our Success   *Marian Wright Edelman*     256
Banning Smoking   *John Ruckdeschel*     266
A Burning Issue   *Mary Boltz Chapman*     268
A Trip to Honduras   *Daniel Boehmer (student)*   272
The Dare   *Roger Hoffmann*     274
Time to Look and Listen   *Magdoline Asfahani (student)*     282

## ▲ Women's Studies

A Letter from the Desert   *Lt. Nicole A. Elwell and Jeff Elwell*     63
The Social Meaning of T-Shirts   *Diana Crane*     87
Between Two Wars, 1913–1945   *Kathryn VanSpanckeren*     94
My Mother Never Worked   *Bonnie Smith-Yackel*     98
Yin and Yang   *Mary Paumier Jones*     147
Indy 500   *Chris Hanley (student)*     157

# Preface

*Patterns Plus: A Short Prose Reader with Argumentation* provides students with an understanding of the thinking process, organizational principles, and rhetorical strategies involved in producing clear and effective writing. In this ninth edition, students are introduced to the uses of freewriting and brainstorming in defining ideas for their writing and to the process of collaborative writing. The study apparatus provides complete and clear explanations of the various rhetorical modes, and the paragraph and essay-length readings provide students with examples of how the modes can be used in organizing and developing their ideas.

## New to the Ninth Edition

*Patterns Plus,* ninth edition, provides students with a variety of models for their own writing and with readings that stimulate lively and thoughtful classroom discussions. Features of the new edition include

- Thirty-three new readings, including selections by such well-known writers as Sarah Bernard, Michelle Cottle, Tom Friedman, John Grogan, Walter Kirn, Anna Quindlen, and Jennifer Traig
- New student writers Daniel Boehmer, Traci Clark, Victor Flores, Gloria Garrison, Chris Hanley, Francine Mercier, Liz Sinclair, Sarah Smith, Quincy Stott, and Edna K. Yano to add to the popular selections by Magdoline Asfahani, Kirsten Bauman, Ricardo Galvez, Heidi Hall, and Nancy Merrell
- New collaborative writing assignments
- New Internet-based writing assignments (look for the globe icon)
- A revised Thematic Table of Contents
- A revised Writing Across the Curriculum Table of Contents

## An Overview of Patterns Plus

Chapter 1, an introductory chapter, describes the basics of the writing process and the construction of paragraphs and essays. In chapters 2 through 10, the various techniques used in developing the main idea of a paragraph and the thesis of an essay are explained: *narration, description,* and the expository modes of *examples, classification and division, comparison and contrast, process, cause and effect, definition,* and *argumentation and persuasion.* These are the traditional *rhetorical modes*—the strategies for development that have proved effective in providing starting points for student writers. Chapter 11, "Combining the Strategies," contains student and professional essays that illustrate the ways writers combine various modes of development within a single essay.

Professional and student selections in *Patterns Plus* were chosen specifically to build students' confidence by showing them that the writing of short, effective compositions is within their reach. Selections range from simple, accessible paragraphs to longer, more challenging essays. The student writings that are included throughout the text will make students aware of the level of skill they can realistically expect to achieve.

The breadth of reading selections also allows the instructor a wide choice of topics—from serious and timely discussions related to global warming, cell phones in the classroom, and the legal drinking age to the lighthearted challenges of washing your hands or bathing a cat.

## Apparatus

*Patterns Plus* offers a full range of study apparatus:

- *Headnotes* provide author information and a context for each reading selection to help students understand and enjoy the selection.
- *Words to Know* define unfamiliar words and clarify allusions that might be unfamiliar or regional.
- *Getting Started* questions prepare students to think critically about the topic presented in the reading selection or about topics for their own writing.
- Exercises promote comprehension and critical skills.
  *Questions About the Reading* are designed to stimulate thinking about the selection's meaning—expressed and implied—and to help students gain fuller understanding of the writer's message.
  *Questions About the Writer's Strategies* ask students to discuss the writer's *thesis statement, mode of development, point of view, figurative language*—or whatever strategy is particularly appropriate to a given selection—and thereby promote critical and analytical thinking.
  *Writing Assignments* are related to the topic and development mode of the reading selection and are designed to encourage

the student to generate ideas that can be developed into paragraphs and essays.

- The *Thematic Table of Contents* groups the readings in the text by such themes as "The Individual in Society," "Values," and "The Working World."
- The *Writing Across the Curriculum Table of Contents* arranges the readings by academic discipline, such as biology, education, and history.
- The *Glossary* provides definitions of all writing-process, rhetorical, and literary terms that are boldfaced throughout the chapter introductions and end-of-selection questions.

## Support for Instructors

The Instructor's Resource Manual for *Patterns Plus* offers instructors a wide variety of supplemental materials:

- Part One supplies teaching suggestions that will allow flexibility in determining course content and structure.
- Part Two contains questions and their answers about the content of each chapter. The questions can be used as quizzes or to generate class discussion.
- Part Three provides suggested answers to the reading comprehension and Writer's Strategies questions that appear at the end of each reading selection in chapters 2 through 10.
- Part Four offers suggested questions and answers for the extra readings in chapter 11.
- Part Five includes a list of the reading levels according to the Fry and Dale-Chall readability formulas. Reading levels are arranged by chapter and by grade.

## Acknowledgments

I would like to thank my good friends Ruth Silon, Cuyahoga Community College, for sharing her student's essay, "Students," and Kim Flachmann, California State University, Bakersfield, for providing "An Intruder in the House," by her student Carol Adams. My thanks also to Lynn Schubert, Los Angeles Harbor College, for "My Suit," a paragraph by her student Ricardo Galvez; George D. Gess, George Fox College, for "Overindulgence," a paragraph by his student Heidi Hall; and Kathryn Kemmerer, Pennsylvania State University, Hazelton, for "The Art of Making Fimo Beads," by her student Julie Gifford.

I am further indebted to the following persons for their helpful suggestions for revisions and new reading selections for this ninth edition of this text:

Patricia Arack, City College of San Francisco
Judy E. Harris, Tomball College
Patricia Malinowski, Finger Lakes Community College
Karen O'Donnell, Finger Lakes Community College
Everest Onuoha, Roxbury Community College

Finally, I again thank the people at Houghton Mifflin who worked with me on this, my twenty-third textbook with them: Joann Kozyrev, Kathy Sands-Boehmer, Daisuke Yasutake, and Annamarie Rice. I'd also like to thank Maggie Barbieri for her many suggestions on how to improve this edition.

My twenty-some years of working with the staff at Houghton Mifflin have always been a joy.

*Mary Lou Conlin*

# 1 The Basics of Writing: Process and Strategies

> The fondness for writing grows with writing.
>
> Erasmus, "Adagia" (1523)

THIS BOOK TELLS you about the process and strategies that you can use to produce effective writing. It includes many paragraphs and essays—by both student and professional writers—that you can read and study as models for your own writing. By understanding and following the process involved in writing, by learning the strategies writers use to communicate their ideas, and by practicing in paragraphs and essays of your own, you can develop the skill and confidence needed to write effectively on many different subjects.

## Purpose and Audience

It is important that you understand the writing process and learn a variety of writing strategies because you will need to write, in school and afterward, for different **purposes,** to different types of **audiences,** and for varied **occasions.** Your purpose might be to persuade (perhaps in a memo recommending a new procedure at work), to instruct (in a description of how to do a lab assignment), or to inform (in a note to your teacher explaining your absence from class). Your audience, or reader, may be fellow students or friends, and the occasion may be an informal activity; your audience may be your employer, and the occasion a formal report. In any case, you will need to make choices—as you work through the process of prewriting, drafting, rewriting, revising, and editing your work—about the writing strategies that will most effectively explain your ideas.

As a student, you will often have tests and assignments that require you to write either a **paragraph** or an **essay.** Although such compositions may differ in their length and content, a paragraph and an essay are alike in two important ways. First, each one should have a **main idea.** Second, the main idea should be fully explained or developed. In this book, you will learn the ways in which many writers go about finding a main idea and the strategies they use in explaining or developing it.

## Finding a Main Idea

If you are like most writers, you may find it difficult to come up with a main idea of your own. You may stare out the window, get something to eat, play a game on your computer, or in some other way put off starting to write. When you find yourself stalling, you may find it helpful to do some prewriting exercises to generate ideas. One method is to sit down and write without stopping for five or ten minutes. This is called **freewriting,** and its primary purpose is to get you started writing.

As the term implies, freewriting is often disorganized and lacks a clear focus. Your freewriting might look like this:

> Need to wash my car. May rain though. What to write about? Maybe last night's ball game. What's that guy doing in his yard? He just mowed it yesterday. Ball game was great—all those homers and extra innings— exciting. Glad I went. Need to go to the store. Out of bread. What'll I get for dinner?

When you look over your freewriting, you can see that you wrote about the baseball game you saw last night. You could write about the exciting game.

Sometimes your instructor will suggest a topic to focus your freewriting. For example, suppose your instructor asks you to write a paragraph describing the room you are in. Your freewriting might then look like this:

> Looks like rain. Wonder if I closed my bedroom windows. What can I say about this classroom except that it's pretty much like all college class-rooms. Seats with writing arms, blackboard, teacher's desk, tan walls with lots of dents in them. Have to pick Chad up from the day-care center at 4. Hope he won't be crabby like he was yesterday. What should I say about this classroom?

When you read over your freewriting, underline anything that strikes you as interesting or important. Your freewriting may trigger an idea that will focus your description. For example, you may notice that your classroom is like all classrooms, except that the walls have lots of dents. Choosing this as a main idea, you might then write a paragraph like this:

Main idea
> The classroom is like all college classrooms except for the many dents in its walls. Like all classrooms, it has thirty chairs with writing arms, lined up in five rows with six chairs in each row; a blackboard that still has the assignment on it from the previous class and needs a good washing; the professor's desk, with a podium on it to hold his oft-used lecture notes; and tan, finger-marked walls. But for some unknown reason, chairs have been shoved hard and often

Main idea
restated

against the walls, which have more and deeper dents than those in other classrooms. Only its dented walls make this classroom different from all college classrooms.

Suppose, however, that the assignment is to **collaborate** with one or more of your classmates in writing an essay about the environment. Collaboration means working with others on a project—in this case, writing an essay about the environment. Once the members of your collaborative group are determined, you will need to meet to discuss the assignment, determine each person's responsibilities, and schedule the project. One member of your group may emerge as the leader, or your group may elect a leader. The leader is responsible for coordinating the project and for seeing that each member of the group meets the schedule that is set for drafting, revising, and editing the assignment.

Next, each of you might want to do some freewriting in order to get started, but then you will want to do some **brainstorming** together. Brainstorming, like freewriting, is simply a way of putting your thoughts on paper to help you choose a main idea and develop supporting evidence for a paragraph or an essay. You will need to focus your thinking on words and ideas that relate to the environment, with one of you writing down what each person contributes. Your group's list might look like this:

| | |
|---|---|
| trees | water |
| pollution | diapers |
| landfills | food |
| harmful | resources |
| paper | waste disposal |
| flowers | cars, airplanes—noise |
| smog | cars, exhaust |
| plastics | wasting resources—oil, coal, water, land |

After your group finishes the brainstorming list, you will need to look for relationships among the words and ideas. For instance, your group could decide that the items can be clustered into two groups or categories: (1) things that the environment provides and (2) things that can harm or damage the environment.

| Environment provides: | Environment damaged by: |
|---|---|
| trees | waste disposal—diapers, plastics |
| flowers | cars—exhaust fumes, noise |
| food | airplanes—noise |
| resources—water, oil, coal | wasting resources—water, oil, coal, trees |

Based on these categories, your group may decide that the main idea for the group's essay could be "We depend on our environment for food, water, and other resources, but we are damaging our environment in several ways." Your group could then decide to **classify** the *ways* we are damaging our food, water, and other resources. After reviewing your brainstorming list and talking it over, your group might decide that the classifications could be *polluting, poisoning,* and *wasting.* You could say, "We are *polluting* the land and our water supply with waste disposal, *poisoning* the air with the exhaust from cars and airplanes, and *wasting* our resources by the overuse of paper and oil."

You might then decide to assign responsibility for providing supporting details for each of the classifications to different members of the group. Thus someone could be responsible for providing **examples** to support "polluting the land and our water supply with waste disposal"; someone else for "poisoning the air with the exhaust from cars and airplanes"; and someone else for "wasting our resources by the overuse of paper and oil."

## Stating the Main Idea

The main idea of a paragraph is called the **topic.** This topic is usually stated in a sentence, called a **topic sentence.** The topic sentence usually expresses a general rather than a specific idea, and it may be placed anywhere within the paragraph. However, you will find that it generally helps to keep your writing clear and focused if you state your main idea at the *beginning* of the paragraph. In the sample paragraph that follows, the main idea (or topic) of the paragraph is stated in the first sentence, followed by the supporting examples. This is called general-to-specific, or **deductive,** order.

Topic sentence

History does seem to repeat itself, even in the way college students behave. In the 1840s students protested and acted in violent ways. Students at Yale, for example, objected to their mathematics course and burned their books in the streets. Some captured their tutor and kept him tied up all night, and others shot a cannon through the tutor's bedroom window. In the 1940s and 1950s students were a fun-loving, game-happy lot. They swallowed live goldfish, took part in dance marathons, and held contests to see how many people could crowd into a phone booth. The more daring males broke into women's rooms in "panty-raids," then festooned their own rooms with the ill-gotten silks. Then, in the 1960s, students repeated the activities of the 1840s. They objected to their courses, littered the campuses with their books and papers, and locked teachers inside college buildings. They protested against all forms of social injustice, from war to the food in the cafeteria. The more violent threw rocks at the police, and a few planted bombs in college buildings. In the 1970s students repeated the fun and games of the forties and fifties. They held contests to see how many people could squeeze into a phone booth. They had dance marathons. The more daring ran naked across campuses, in a craze called "streaking." The slightly less daring did their streaking with brown

**Topic restated** — paper bags over their heads. Yes, history does seem to repeat itself, even in the sometimes violent and sometimes fun-and-games behavior of the students on college campuses.

In the following paragraph, the writer has stated the topic in the first and second sentences.

**Topic sentence** — In the nineties and the early 1900s, gold teeth were as much a part of the fashion scene as peg-top trousers, choker collars, and chatelaine watches. There were, of course, certain practical reasons for this popularity. From the viewpoint of the average dentist, gold-shell crowns provided a simple method of securely anchoring artificial teeth; at the same time they covered ugly, broken-down, and discolored natural teeth, as well as much inferior dental work. And to the patient, gold seemed to represent the most in value received.

Charles I. Stoloff, *Natural History* (February 1972)

As you become more experienced, you may sometimes find it effective to place the topic sentence at the *end* of the paragraph. In the following paragraph the writer has stated the topic in the last sentence. This is called specific-to-general, or **inductive,** order.

We think of an ideal society as being a community—whatever its size—in which the people, the environment, and the institutions are in harmony. No nation, ours included, has ever achieved such a society. In fact, most Americans would say it is not really possible to establish an ideal society. But strangely enough, we keep trying. Time after time, a group of people will drop out of the mainstream of American society to try another "life style" based on the group's concept of an ideal society. Most of these groups have believed in holding their property in common—that is, they believed in a communistic or communal concept of property. Most of the groups have also used the word *family* to refer to all members of the group, rather than to a mother, father, and their children as the family unit.

**Topic sentence** — But the groups have differed widely in their attitudes toward sex, marriage, and other values and seldom lasted for very long as a consequence.

As you study the student and professional writings that follow, you will find that writers do not always state the main idea of their paragraphs and essays outright. Instead, they may prefer to suggest or to **imply** the idea. Notice that the writer must provide enough clues to allow the careful reader to **infer** (determine) the main idea. In the following paragraph, for example, the writer implies the idea that the man saw the berries reflected rather than actually floating in the water. The writer provides the clues the reader needs to infer the main idea by saying that the man struck the bottom of the river when he dived in and that he then looked up and saw the berries hanging over him.

> While walking along the river, he saw some berries in the water. He dived down for them, but was stunned when he unexpectedly struck the bottom. There he lay for quite a while, and when he recovered consciousness and looked up, he saw the berries hanging on a tree just above him.
>
> Paul Radin,
> "Manbozho and the Berries"

If you experiment with implying your main idea, be sure to give the reader enough clues to determine your meaning.

In a longer piece of writing, such as an essay, the main idea is called the **thesis** (rather than the topic). The thesis is usually stated in one or more sentences called the **thesis statement.** Like the topic sentence of a paragraph, the thesis statement is often placed near the beginning of an essay. In the essay that follows, the thesis is stated in the opening sentence.

Thesis

A safe city street must have three main qualities.

Topic sentence

First, there must be a clear demarcation between what is public space and what is private space. Public and private spaces cannot ooze into each other as they do typically in suburban settings or in projects.

Topic sentence

Second, there must be eyes upon the street, eyes belonging to those we might call the natural proprietors of the street. The buildings on a street equipped to handle strangers and to insure the safety of both residents and strangers, must be oriented to the street. They cannot turn their backs or blank sides on it and leave it blind.

Topic sentence

And third, the sidewalk must have users on it fairly continuously, both to add to the number of effective eyes on the street and to induce the people in buildings along the street to watch the sidewalks in sufficient numbers. Nobody enjoys sitting on a stoop or looking out a window at an empty street. Almost nobody does such a thing. Large numbers of people entertain themselves, off and on, by watching street activity. . . .

Jane Jacobs, *Death and Life of Great American Cities*
(New York: Random House, 1961)

In addition to noting the thesis statement, notice that each paragraph has its own topic sentence. The topic sentences support and clarify the thesis. The topic sentences are supported, in turn, by the specifics in each paragraph.

Experienced writers may place the thesis statement in later paragraphs or at the end of the essay. They may, indeed, only imply the thesis. For your own writing, the important point to remember is that an effective essay has a clear thesis statement, just as a well-made paragraph has a topic sentence. When you are reading, your task is to discover the writer's thesis. When you are writing, your task is to make your own thesis as clear as possible to your reader. And your best strategy, initially, is to *state your thesis at or near the beginning of your essay.*

## Developing the Main Idea

The second important way in which paragraphs and essays are alike is that their main ideas must be explained or **developed** by the writer. The strategies used by writers to develop their ideas include

| | |
|---|---|
| narration | process |
| description | cause and effect |
| examples (illustrations) | definition |
| classification and division | argumentation and persuasion |
| comparison and contrast | |

These strategies for developing the main idea are called **modes of development.** Although they have different characteristics, the modes of development have a common purpose: to provide the reader with the specific information needed to **support** or clarify the main idea. As stated earlier, the main idea is a general statement; the development provides the details to support or explain the main idea.

In developing a paragraph, the writer usually (1) begins with a topic sentence, (2) develops the main idea (topic) by a series of related sentences that explain the idea fully, and (3) concludes with a sentence that restates or summarizes the main idea. Look at the following paragraph diagram and compare it with the example paragraph about the classroom on pages 2–3. Notice that the example paragraph begins with a topic sentence; develops the main idea (topic) with the sentences about the chairs, blackboard, desk, and walls; and then concludes by restating the topic sentence.

## Paragraph

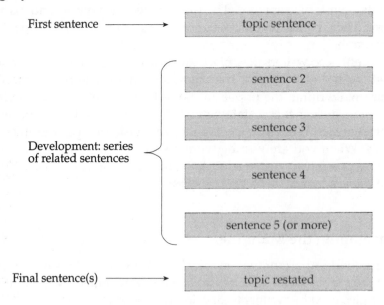

Next, compare the paragraph diagram with the essay diagram that follows. Notice that in developing the essay, the writer starts with a thesis statement, which is generally part of the introduction and may make up the whole first paragraph. Then the writer develops the thesis in a series of related paragraphs, called the **body** of the essay. Usually, each paragraph has its own topic sentence. The conclusion, which may restate the thesis or summarize the essay's important points, is usually found in the final paragraph.

## Essay

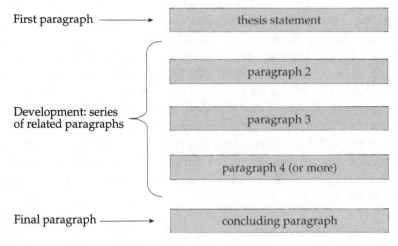

Now look at the following essay developed by a group of students for the environment assignment. Notice that the thesis is stated in the first paragraph, which is called the **introduction** of the essay. The thesis is developed, or supported, by the next three paragraphs that make up the body of the essay. In these paragraphs, each classification of the ways the environment is being damaged has been used as the topic for a body paragraph and items from the brainstorming lists (see page 3) have been used as examples to develop the topics. The final paragraph, called the **conclusion** or concluding paragraph, restates the thesis and sums up the main points of the essay.

Thesis statement
(introduction)

Modern conveniences have made our lives easier, but often at the expense of our environment. Science and society, which have been so quick to create and adopt new consumer goods, have been slow in creating and adopting practices to protect the environment from the same consumer goods. As a result, just through everyday living, we are damaging the environment we depend on and wasting our resources.

Development
(body paragraph)

For one thing, we pollute the land and our water supply with the by-products of modern life. We fill our garbage dumps and landfills with throwaway plastic products and "disposable" diapers that will not disintegrate for hundreds of years, if ever. Industries accidentally or willfully spill oil and chemicals into the ground or streams and pollute our water supply.

Development
(body paragraph)

For another thing, we poison the air with exhaust from the cars and airplanes that have become such an important part of our lives. In some areas, the exhaust from cars creates smog that poisons our lungs and causes respiratory ailments. Air pollution also causes acid rain that, in turn, destroys rivers, lakes, woods, and farm crops.

Development
(body paragraph)

Finally, we are wasting our resources shamefully. For example, we use far more water than we need to in brushing our teeth and taking showers. Even something as "harmless" as letting dripping faucets go unrepaired wastes a lot of valuable water. We water our lawns through automatic sprinkler systems that run even in rainstorms. We also waste oil by driving millions of cars hundreds of millions of needless miles each year and by keeping our houses warmer than we need to. We are even dangerously close to depleting our "renewable" resources. We cut down our forests with abandonment in order to eat from paper plates, drink from paper cups, and carry products home from the store.

Thesis and
important points
restated
(concluding
paragraph)

Yes, we have come to depend on technology to fulfill our needs, but we still need our natural environment. Unless we start developing technology to protect our natural world, it may soon pollute and poison us.

The essay has also been developed by using **classification, examples, cause and effect,** and **persuasion** as modes of development. The *classifications* are the *ways* we are damaging the environment: polluting, poisoning, wasting. *Examples* are plastics, diapers, and oil and chemical spills; exhaust fumes from cars and airplanes; using too much water to brush our teeth and water our lawns; driving needlessly; overheating our houses; and using paper products. In turn, the examples are *causes* of three *effects:* pollution, poisoning, and wasting. The smog created by car exhaust is also a *cause* of lung and respiratory ailments (*effects*). The essay also seeks to persuade readers to stop damaging the environment.

Notice, too, the use of the words *for one thing, for another thing,* and *finally* at the beginning of paragraphs 2, 3, and 4. These are called **transitional** words, and their purpose is to help the reader identify the connection among the ideas in a composition and to move the reader along from one idea to another.

Although the modes of development are often combined as they are in the students' collaborative essay, a single mode of development will often be dominant in a composition. For instance, if you are writing a **descriptive** essay, that does not mean you cannot use **examples** to illustrate your description, but it does mean that most of the paragraphs will be descriptive. Or you might write a **cause-and-effect** essay in which you **narrate** a series of events that constitute a cause and another event that is the effect. In general, however, you will learn to be comfortable with the modes of development if you first study them individually; and this text is organized so you can do that. You will see that chapters 2 through 10 deal with a single mode of development and bring together paragraphs and essays in which that mode dominates. Chapter 11 contains essays that combine the modes, even though one mode may still dominate.

Before each paragraph or essay, you will find a note that tells you something about the reading, definitions of words that might be unfamiliar to you, and a question that either will help you think about the reading or will provide a writing idea. Following each reading selection are questions about the reading, questions about the writer's strategies, and suggestions for your own writing assignments.

The Glossary at the back of the book defines and explains the technical terms you will learn to use. These terms are boldfaced throughout the text. If you encounter a boldfaced term and cannot recall what it means, turn to the Glossary to refresh your memory.

The ability to state an idea and to develop it so that it is clear to your reader is essential to all forms of composition. The writing strategies covered in this text will help you develop those abilities. However, to produce an effective piece of writing you will generally need to follow this process:

- **Prewriting** (freewriting, brainstorming), to get started and to define your idea
- **Drafting,** to learn what your idea is about
- **Rewriting,** to clarify your idea and to improve or add to the strategies used to develop it
- **Revising,** to improve the organization and content
- **Revising,** to polish the organization and content
- **Editing,** to improve word choices and sentences and to correct punctuation and spelling

Your instructor may also want you to keep a journal as a way to record your thoughts and experiences, to keep you writing, and perhaps to give you ideas for writing. Your instructor may also want you to compile a portfolio—a collection of all your drafts and revisions—as part of your course and to demonstrate your writing progress. Some instructors may want you to collaborate with your classmates on various writing assignments. Still other instructors may give you the option of submitting your drafts by computer and receiving their corrections and suggestions the same way. In any event, you should expect to draft, rewrite, revise, and edit all of your writing assignments until they are clear and convincing to your reader. You can then apply your skills to the many kinds of writing that will be required now, at school, and later, in your career.

# 2 Narration

HAVE YOU EVER seen a bad car accident, a fire, or a robbery? Have you had an especially sad or happy experience that made a lasting impression on you or made a difference in your life? If you later mention one of these **events** to friends, they will probably want to know more about it. What individual **incidents** made up the event? How did it happen? At what time? Where did it take place? On the spot, you become a narrator or storyteller and try to give a clear and lively account of the event. Thus you are already familiar with **narration,** one of the modes of development that writers frequently use to illustrate and explain their ideas. The purpose of narration is to interest the reader in a story that illustrates a particular idea clearly.

Narration is frequently used to tell about personal experiences. You have a variety of personal experiences every day. Your car won't start, you miss the bus, and then you are late for your class. Such experiences, although important to you, will not necessarily make for an effective narrative. For a narrative to be effective, the writer needs to describe an experience that has some unusual meaning or significance for both the writer and the reader. Usually, an experience is significant because it taught you—and may teach your reader—something new, something you never before realized about life. For example, in the following paragraph, the writer tells about a personal experience that taught him about being responsible, not only for making decisions but also for accepting the consequences of those decisions.

|  |  |
|---|---|
| | As I was growing up, my father and I often disagreed about how I should spend my time. He began telling me, "If you get yourself into it, you'll have to get yourself out." But |
| Topic sentence | I learned what it meant to be responsible for the consequences of my decisions only after I went to a weekend party |
| Incident 1 | when I should have studied for a math exam. I needed a good grade on the exam to stay eligible to play basketball. |
| Incident 2 | The consequences of my decision to go to the party were clear when I got my exam back with a notice that I was on academic probation. I spent two semesters of almost steady |

Incident 3

studying before I was back in good standing. Now, whenever I have a difficult decision to make, I remind myself, "If

Topic restated:
significance of
narrative

you get yourself into it, you'll have to get yourself out." It was a tough lesson, but I learned that making a decision means taking the responsibility for its consequences.

Effective narrative writing, like all good writing, is carefully organized. Since a narrative describes events, its organization must be governed by some form of time **order.** The writer often tells about events in the order in which they took place. This method of organization, called **chronological order,** ensures that the sequence of the incidents will be logical.

In the following sample paragraph, the writer uses narration to give a factual account of an event: the discovery of Wheaties. Notice that this writer has chosen to explain the different incidents in a simple chronological order.

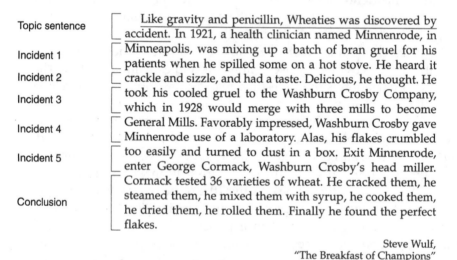

Topic sentence

Like gravity and penicillin, Wheaties was discovered by accident. In 1921, a health clinician named Minnenrode, in

Incident 1

Minneapolis, was mixing up a batch of bran gruel for his patients when he spilled some on a hot stove. He heard it

Incident 2

crackle and sizzle, and had a taste. Delicious, he thought. He

Incident 3

took his cooled gruel to the Washburn Crosby Company, which in 1928 would merge with three mills to become

Incident 4

General Mills. Favorably impressed, Washburn Crosby gave Minnenrode use of a laboratory. Alas, his flakes crumbled

Incident 5

too easily and turned to dust in a box. Exit Minnenrode, enter George Cormack, Washburn Crosby's head miller.

Conclusion

Cormack tested 36 varieties of wheat. He cracked them, he steamed them, he mixed them with syrup, he cooked them, he dried them, he rolled them. Finally he found the perfect flakes.

Steve Wulf,
"The Breakfast of Champions"

Notice the **details** in this paragraph. In addition to re-creating the incidents that are significant to his topic, the writer uses descriptive words to tell what happened. Minnenrode "spilled" the gruel, heard it "crackle" and "sizzle," and found that the flakes "turned to dust in a box." By using words that provide descriptive detail, the writer adds variety and interest to his narrative. (**Description,** a mode of development in its own right, is the subject of the next chapter.)

Notice, too, that this paragraph contains only the incidents or details that contribute directly to the story. Avoiding irrelevant incidents and details is essential to effective narrative writing. Perhaps you have heard some long-winded person tell a story and found yourself wishing that the person would skip some of the trivial details. You should keep this in mind when you are writing and limit yourself to the details that are *essential* to the main idea of your narrative. In the following essay, for example, the writer does not include any incidents that happened before the robbery. He concentrates on those incidents and details that explain his actions and reactions only during key moments. As you read the essay, think about the details the writer provides and try to form an image of the scene in your mind.

|  |  |  |
|---|---|---|
| **Thesis statement** | Recently I was unfortunate enough to be in a store when a robbery took place. I learned from that experience that a pointed gun makes people obey. | 1 |
| **Incidents arranged as they occurred in time** | I had stopped at the store on my way home from work to get a loaf of bread. I was at the check-out counter when a man standing nearby pulled out a gun and yelled, "Everyone on the floor and away from the cash register!" | 2 |
| **Frozen in place** | My first reaction was fear. Around me, people dropped to the floor. But I felt frozen where I stood. | 3 |
| **Gun pointed** | As I hesitated, the robber pointed his gun at me and yelled again, "On the floor!" Then I felt angry. I was bigger and stronger than he was. I was sure I could put *him* on the floor in a fair fight. | 4 |
| **Sank to the floor** | But the gun, small enough to be cradled in the palm of my hand, was bigger and stronger than I was. I sank obediently to the floor. | 5 |
| **Robbery took place** | All of us watched silently as the robber scooped money out of the cash register into a paper bag. Then he ran out the door, jumped into a car that was waiting, and the car raced away. | 6 |
| **After robbery** | Everyone stood up and started talking. A clerk called the police, who asked if anyone could describe the robber or the car. No one could. | 7 |
| **Dialogue Significance of narrative restated** | Then one man, blustering defensively, told the clerk just what I was thinking. "Listen. Tell them when a gun is pointed at me, it's all I'm looking at. One look and I'm going to do whatever I'm told." | 8 |

Look at each paragraph in this essay. The first paragraph is an introduction in which the main idea or thesis of the essay is stated. Each successive paragraph deals with an incident or a set of incidents in the narrative. Each incident contributes key information to the essay and moves the story forward in time. The final paragraph concludes the narrative by restating the main idea of the essay.

As you can see, the narrative mode is used for more than just retelling what happened. In addition to reporting the action, narrative writing often explains the *reactions*—emotions and thoughts—of the narrator and others involved. At other times, the writer may leave it to the reader to determine the narrator's feelings and reactions.

In this and other ways, the writer establishes a particular **point of view** for the essay. Point of view involves three elements: **person, time,** and

**tone.** The essay may be written in the **first person** (*I/we*), **second person** (*you*), or **third person** (*he/she/it/they*). The time in which the essay is set may be the past, present, or future. The tone is the attitude (serious, humorous, angry, sad) that the writer adopts.

In a narrative essay, the point of view creates the context for the incidents described: that is, who saw or experienced the events, when the events occurred, and how the writer felt about the events. Narration is generally written from the first- or third- person point of view—that is, from the point of view of the person who observed or was a party to the event. Usually, too, the person—the narrator—is kept consistent throughout the narrative, although writers may sometimes use different narrators to express another view or opinion of an event.

Because narration deals with an event or personal experience that already has happened, it is usually written in the past tense. Experienced writers may change the verb tense from the present to the past in what is called a "flashback"—but in general the tense should be kept consistent.

In narration and the other modes of development, an important factor in point of view is whether the writer is being objective or subjective. An **objective** essay presents the **facts**—the basics of what occurred or what is being described—without including the writer's own interpretations or personal opinions of those facts. The writer tries to portray the subject of the essay as truly as possible and does not try to influence how the reader will react. A **subjective** essay, by contrast, expresses how the writer feels and may try to get the reader to feel a certain way. It may state an opinion or reveal the writer's emotions, or it may present facts in such a way that the reader will draw a conclusion favored by the writer. The Wheaties story is an example of objective writing; it presents the facts without interpreting them. The other two examples are written more subjectively, expressing the writers' own feelings about and interpretations of the events described.

Often, writers give clues that indicate that they are being subjective. Phrases like "in my opinion" or "I felt" or "I learned" signal a subjective interpretation. (Just because an essay is written in the first person does not mean it is entirely subjective, however.) As you will see in some of the selections in this text, writers may not always tell you when they are being subjective. Some writers may even take an objective tone when they are being quite subjective—perhaps, for instance, by presenting certain facts about a subject but not others. No matter what mode of development is used in an essay, you should try to make sure just how subjective or objective the writer is being.

Narrative writing is called **nonfiction** if the story or event is true and actually happened. All of the preceding examples are nonfictional accounts. This kind of factual narrative is found in biography, history, and newspaper writing. Narrative is also the predominant mode used in short stories and novels. If a story is not true or did not actually occur, it is called **fiction.**

In fiction and nonfiction narrative writing, writers use **dialogue** as a "technique" to re-create what characters or people in the narrative said. In the essay on the store robbery, notice that the writer often tells you exactly what was said and encloses the statement using quotation marks to let you know he is quoting word-for-word conversation. Quoted dialogue can help the writer accurately express the incidents in a narrative and can add variety and color. To practice working with dialogue, listen to your friends talking with one another and see if you can reproduce something like their conversation in dialogue in your own narratives.

Writers use narration to tell about personal experiences, about other people's lives and experiences, and about factual or historical events, such as the discovery of Wheaties. Narration adds interest, suspense, and clarity to writing, as you will find in the reading selections that follow. Consequently, it is a writing skill well worth mastering.

The questions and assignments at the ends of the readings in this chapter will help you to recognize and apply the principles of narration. They will give you practice with the concepts of chronological order, narrative detail, subjective and objective writing, and dialogue.

# The Movie House

**John Updike**

*Our childhood memories are often laced with terror. This paragraph from John Updike's memoir of life in a small town is filled with details that provide a vivid description of just how exciting it is to be terrified.*

## Words to Know

**glowered**   scowled, stared angrily
**indulgent**   not strict, tolerant
**supersensory**   beyond or above awareness of senses, supernatural

## Getting Started

Can you recall a frightening incident from your childhood that haunts you to this day?

---

It was two blocks from my home; I began to go alone from the age of six. My mother, so strict about my kissing girls, was strangely indulgent about this. The theater ran three shows a week, for two days each, and was closed on Sundays. Many weeks I went three times. I remember a summer evening in our yard. Supper is over, the walnut tree throws a heavy shadow. The fireflies are not out yet. My father is off, my mother and her parents are turning the earth in our garden. Some burning sticks and paper on our ash heap fill the damp air with low smoke; I express a wish to go to the movies, expecting to be told no. Instead, my mother tells me to go into the house and clean up; I come into the yard again in clean shorts, the shadows slightly heavier, the dew a little wetter; I am given eleven cents and run down Philadelphia Avenue in my ironed shorts and fresh shirt, down past the running ice-plant water, the dime and the penny in my hand. I always ran to the movies. If it was not a movie with Adolphe Menjou, it was a horror picture. People turning into cats—fingers going stubby into paws and hair being blurred in with double exposure—and Egyptian tombs and English houses where doors creak and wind disturbs the curtains and dogs refuse to go into certain rooms because they sense something supersensory. I used to crouch down into the seat and hold my coat in front of my face when I sensed a frightening scene coming, peeking through the buttonhole to find out when it was over. Through the buttonhole Frankenstein's monster glowered; lightning flashed; sweat poured over the bolts that held his face together. On the way home, I ran again, in terror now. Darkness had come, the first show was from seven to nine, by nine even the longest summer day was ending. Each porch along the street seemed to be a tomb crammed with shadows, each shrub seemed to shelter a grasping arm. I ran with a frantic high step, trying to keep my ankles away from the reaching hands. The last and worst terror was our own porch; low brick walls on either side concealed possible cat people. Leaping high, I launched myself at the door and, if no one was in the front of the house, fled through suffocating halls past gaping doorways to the kitchen, where there was always someone working, and a light bulb burning. The icebox. The rickety worn table, oilcloth-covered, where we ate. The windows solid black and fortified by the interior brightness. But even then I kept my legs away from the dark space beneath the table.

## Questions About the Reading

1. Did the writer enjoy horror movies as a young boy? How can you tell?
2. What gives this paragraph a breathless, frightened quality? Try to identify specific **details** that contribute to this quality.
3. As a young boy, the writer spent many hours at the movies. Does he ever mention being there with friends? What does the writer **imply** about his social experiences in this paragraph?

## Questions About the Writer's Strategies

1. Is the **main idea** of the paragraph directly stated? If so, in which sentence(s)? If not, state the main idea in a sentence of your own.
2. What is the **point of view** in the narrative? Could another point of view be used? Using the first two sentences of the paragraph as an example, explain how you could change the point of view.
3. If you had never seen a horror movie, what **details** in the paragraph would give you an idea of what one would be like?
4. In what ways is this paragraph **subjective**? In what ways is it **objective**?

## Writing Assignments

1. Recall the most frightening episode from your childhood. Write a narrative paragraph describing the feelings you experienced.
2. Write a narrative paragraph that describes the neighborhood in which you grew up. Try to include details that will help the reader infer the size and type of town.
3. Think of an activity that you loved as a child. Write a narrative paragraph in the **third person** that describes a child participating in that activity.

# The Hunt

## Lesley Stern

*In this paragraph, the writer conveys the tension and suspense felt by the
narrator as he observes a prowler who enters his bedroom and ransacks
the closet. Lesley Stern is the author of* The Scorsese Connection *and*
The Smoking Book *and coeditor of* Falling for You: Essays on Cinema
and Performance.

### Words to Know

**accretions**   accumulations, collections
**dissipate**   ease, lessen
**voluminous**   large, huge

### Getting Started

How would you feel and what would you do if an intruder entered
your bedroom at night?

The door edges open and in the crack light flickers. A figure moves into
the room, a dark silhouette. The figure turns into the light and he sees: it
is her. Only her, a figure as familiar as his own body. The tension begins
to dissipate, but slowly, uneasily. It is as though knots have formed
through his being from tip to toe. He holds his breath and watches as she
moves across the room, easing the wardrobe door open, carefully trying
to avoid the habitual squeak. I must oil the hinges, he thinks. With her
back to the bed, shielding the flashlight beam, she scrambles among old
clothes piled at the back of the wardrobe; she burrows into the bottom of
voluminous coat pockets, turns shirts inside out, baggy jeans upside
down. He knows that she will already have gone through the house
searching in jars, behind books in the bookcase, at the back of untidy
drawers filled with junk. It happens once a year or so: the evil spirit
comes upon her in the night, and she invades her own house, excavating
the accretions of daily living, wanting desperately to find a remnant of
the past, a sign of life. "Not much to ask," she'd say if pushed, "a little
thing." That thing which is so simply and satisfyingly itself: a cigarette.

## Questions About the Reading

→ *BEDROOM* (handwritten)

1. Where is the narrator when the event takes place?
2. Who is the "intruder" who enters the room?
3. What does the "intruder" do?
4. Is this the first time the "intruder" has acted as she does?
5. Why does the intruder act this way?

## Questions About the Writer's Strategies

1. What is the main idea of the paragraph? *LOOKING FOR THE CIGARETTE* (handwritten)
2. Is the main idea stated or <u>implied</u>?
3. Is the paragraph objective, subjective, or both? *CHRONOLOGICAL* (handwritten)
4. What order does the writer use?
5. What is the point of view of the paragraph? Does it change? If so, where and why?

## Writing Assignments

1. Write a narrative paragraph about an experience you had that was scary.
2. Write a narrative paragraph about a happy event you are anticipating.
3. Use the Internet to find out more about the writer, and make an entry in your journal about Lesley Stern's birthplace, education, occupation, and honors.

# Why Harlem Is Not Manhattan

*John L. Jackson*

*A young black man insists that Harlem is not part of Manhattan.*

### Words to Know
**distinction**  difference
**Dominican**  a country (Dominican Republic in the West Indies)
**queue**  line or file of waiting people
**scissored**  cut

### Getting Started
Has anyone ever made you feel "different" or "left out" because of where you live?

---

Standing at the end of a too-long line of customers inside a too-crowded fast food restaurant in northern Manhattan, I listened attentively as Dexter, a twenty-three-year-old black man, argued across the shiny McDonald's countertop with the Dominican cashier who was trying patiently to take his order. Dressed in white, gray, and black fatigues, with neatly coifed dreadlocks down to his shoulders and two-summers-old Air Jordans on his feet, Dexter held up that queue by waving a colorful coupon in the palm of his right hand. Scissored out from an insert in that Sunday's local newspaper, the coupon redeemed a ninety-nine-cent Big Mac in every part of New York City (so read the fine print) "except the borough of Manhattan," where Big Macs, with this very same square of paper, were discounted to $1.39 instead. Well, hearing the cashier, Pam, make that borough-specific distinction several times, Dexter became increasingly annoyed. He crossed and uncrossed his arms with emphatic gestures. He sighed audibly and repeatedly. Squeezing a dollar bill and a dime in his outstretched left hand (the ten cents was "for tax," he declared numerous times), Dexter made his case: "This is Harlem," he stated with electrified finality, "not Manhattan! If they meant Harlem, if they meant Harlem, they should have written Harlem! Harlem is not Manhattan! So, I'm paying $1.10 for my Big Mac."

---

## Questions About the Reading

1. Where does the event take place? MC - D
2. Who is the person the event is about? DEXTER.
3. What does he look like? 23 / BLACK MAN.
4. What does he want?
5. Do you think his demand is justified? Why or why not?

## Questions About the Writer's Strategies

1. What is the point of view of the narrative? 1ST PERSON
2. Is the narrative objective or subjective?
3. What order does the writer use in the narrative?
4. What "technique" does the writer use to clarify Dexter's demand and emphasize his frustration?

## Writing Assignments

1. Write a narrative paragraph about an experience you or an acquaintance has had redeeming a coupon at the grocery store.
2. Write a narrative paragraph about an unusual or exciting event that happened in your city or neighborhood.

# Geography

## *Elizabeth Bishop*

*It is often obvious when a writer is using narration as a mode of develop-
ment. But narration can also be subtle. In this paragraph, notice how
Elizabeth Bishop uses sensory details—what she sees, hears, and feels—
to add appeal and color to an unspectacular event.*

### Words to Know

**recitation**   a student's oral delivery of prepared materials

### Getting Started

What was your favorite or least favorite subject in grade school?

O nly the third and fourth grades studied geography. On their side of
the room, over the blackboard, were two rolled-up maps, one of Canada
and one of the whole world. When they had a geography lesson, Miss
Morash pulled down one or both of these maps, like window shades.
They were on cloth, very limp, with a shiny surface, and in pale colors—
tan, pink, yellow, and green—surrounded by the blue that was the ocean.
The light coming in from their windows, falling on the glazed, crackly
surface, made it hard for me to see them properly from where I sat. On the
world map, all of Canada was pink; on the Canadian, the provinces were
different colors. I was so taken with the pull-down maps that I wanted to
snap them up, and pull them down again, and touch all the countries
and provinces with my own hands. Only dimly did I hear the pupils'
recitations of capital cities and islands and bays. But I got the general impression that Canada was the same size as the world, which somehow or
other fitted into it, or the other way around, and that in the world and
Canada the sun was always shining and everything was dry and glitter-
ing. At the same time, I knew perfectly well that this was not true.

## Questions About the Reading

1. Was the writer herself in the third or fourth grade? How do you know?
2. Was the writer paying attention to the geography lesson? Explain
   your answer.

3. What type of essay do you think this paragraph comes from? What do you think the writer's purpose was in composing the essay?

## Questions About the Writer's Strategies

1. What is the **main idea** of this paragraph? Is there a **topic sentence**? If so, where is it located? If not, where is the main idea expressed?
2. What makes this a narration paragraph? What are the incidents? What is the main event?
3. What else does the writer do besides narrate what happened?

## Writing Assignments

1. Recall a situation from your childhood, or even from later years, in which you used your imagination to keep yourself interested during what might seem a boring event. Write a narrative paragraph describing the situation and your mental reaction.
2. Pick an event that you think *nobody* would be interested in. In a paragraph, try to narrate the event in a way that will hold your reader's interest. Try to think of active, colorful words to enhance your narrative, and feel free to use humor if you like.
3. Write a paragraph about your favorite or least favorite subject in grade school and tell why it was your favorite or least favorite subject.

# The Memorial Service

### Christopher Malinowski (student)

*In his essay, Christopher Malinowski gives us a picture of a traditional memorial service and of the people who are there to light a candle in memory of a deceased loved one. One person in particular, in contrast to the others, speaks the name of her deceased loved one clearly and moves quickly to light her candle.*

### Words to Know
**stammers**   speaks hesitantly
**stricken**   struck, affected

### Getting Started
Do you have a tradition that you follow related to the birth of a child, a marriage, a graduation, or some other event?

---

**A**s my brother and I sit in the church pew, we watch people slowly file into the church for the All Souls Day Memorial Service. After a brief opening blessing, we see a microphone being passed slowly through the trembling hands of people. They say the name of a deceased person whom they wish others to pray for and light their candles in the flame of the burning Easter Candle, but they are stricken with so much grief that saying the name through choking tears is a struggle. As we listen, another gentleman stammers out the name of one person who had been dear to him during life. As he moves slowly to the candle, he stumbles as if the person he had loved mattered more than where he walked. As he walks back, I try following him with my eyes but lose sight as he moves behind a crowd of people. I soon realize that I am like the people in the congregation who try to follow the person throughout their lives, but lose sight of him or her when they least expect to. Then the microphone passes to an elderly woman whom my brother and I recognize instantly as my mother's secretary, Mary. However, she has become more than a mere secretary to my brother, our parents, and me. She has been a dear friend to all of us, someone to count on, my Confirmation Sponsor, and my former loving babysitter, who lost her husband during the past year from sickness and old age. She says his name into the microphone clearly. After finishing, she strides to light her candle. She doesn't see my brother and me as she reaches up to touch her candlewick to the large Easter Candle. Unknowingly, she lights our lives also.

## Questions About the Reading

1. What is the event that the writer and his brother are attending?
2. What is the procedure that is followed during the event? Why?
3. What does the writer means when he says he's "like the people in the congregation who try to follow the person throughout their lives, but lose sight of him or her when they least expect to."?
4. Who is the person who makes the greatest impression on the writer? Why?

## Questions About the Writer's Strategies

1. What is the main idea of the paragraph?
2. What is the point of view of the paragraph?
3. What order does the writer use?

## Writing Assignments

1. Write a narrative paragraph in which you explain a tradition you follow in observing some holiday.
2. Write a narrative paragraph about learning to drive a car, registering for classes, taking a bus to school, or asking someone for a date.

# Learning to Write

## *Russell Baker*

*Russell Baker is a Pulitzer Prize winner noted for his humorous writing. Although this passage from his autobiographical book* Growing Up *is lighthearted, we learn in the end that Baker is earnestly describing an event of serious, almost touching, personal importance.*

### Words to Know

**antecedent**   the word to which a pronoun refers
**listless**   without energy, boring
**prim**   formal and neat, lacking humor
**reminiscence**   memory of a past experience

### Getting Started

Can you describe an experience that changed the way you thought about yourself?

---

When our class was assigned to Mr. Fleagle for third-year English I 1 anticipated another grim year in that dreariest of subjects. Mr. Fleagle was notorious among City students for dullness and inability to inspire. He was said to be stuffy, dull, and hopelessly out of date. To me he looked to be sixty or seventy and prim to a fault. He wore primly severe eyeglasses, his wavy hair was primly cut and primly combed. He wore prim vested suits with neckties blocked primly against the collar buttons of his primly starched white shirts. He had a primly pointed jaw, a primly straight nose, and a prim manner of speaking that was so correct, so gentlemanly, that he seemed a comic antique.

I anticipated a listless, unfruitful year with Mr. Fleagle and for a long 2 time was not disappointed. We read *Macbeth*. Mr. Fleagle loved *Macbeth* and wanted us to love it too, but he lacked the gift of infecting others with his own passion. He tried to convey the murderous ferocity of Lady Macbeth one day by reading aloud the passage that concludes

> . . . I have given suck, and know
> How tender 'tis to love the babe that milks me.
> I would, while it was smiling in my face,
> Have plucked my nipple from his boneless gums. . . .

The idea of prim Mr. Fleagle plucking his nipple from boneless gums was too much for the class. We burst into gasps of irrepressible snickering. Mr. Fleagle stopped.

"There is nothing funny, boys, about giving suck to a babe. It is the— the very essence of motherhood, don't you see." 3

He constantly sprinkled his sentences with "don't you see." It wasn't a question but an exclamation of mild surprise at our ignorance. "Your pronoun needs an antecedent, don't you see," he would say, very primly. "The purpose of the Porter's scene, boys, is to provide comic relief from the horror, don't you see." 4

Late in the year we tackled the informal essay. "The essay, don't you see, is the . . ." My mind went numb. Of all forms of writing, none seemed so boring as the essay. Naturally we would have to write informal essays. Mr. Fleagle distributed a homework sheet offering us a choice of topics. None was quite so simpleminded as "What I Did on My Summer Vacation," but most seemed to be almost as dull. I took the list home and dawdled until the night before the essay was due. Sprawled on the sofa, I finally faced up to the grim task, took the list out of my notebook, and scanned it. The topic on which my eye stopped was "The Art of Eating Spaghetti." 5

This title produced an extraordinary sequence of mental images. Surging up out of the depths of memory came a vivid recollection of a night in Belleville when all of us were seated around the supper table—Uncle Allen, my mother, Uncle Charlie, Doris, Uncle Hal—and Aunt Pat served spaghetti for supper. Spaghetti was an exotic treat in those days. Neither Doris nor I had ever eaten spaghetti, and none of the adults had enough experience to be good at it. All the good humor of Uncle Allen's house reawoke in my mind as I recalled the laughing arguments we had that night about the socially respectable method for moving spaghetti from plate to mouth. 6

Suddenly I wanted to write about that, about the warmth and good feeling of it, but I wanted to put it down simply for my own joy, not for Mr. Fleagle. It was a moment I wanted to recapture and hold for myself. I wanted to relive the pleasure of an evening at New Street. To write it as I wanted, however, would violate all the rules of formal composition I'd learned in school, and Mr. Fleagle would surely give it a failing grade. Never mind. I would write something else for Mr. Fleagle after I had written this thing for myself. 7

When I finished it the night was half gone and there was no time left to compose a proper, respectable essay for Mr. Fleagle. There was no choice next morning but to turn in my private reminiscence of Belleville. 8

Two days passed before Mr. Fleagle returned the graded papers, and he returned everyone's but mine. I was bracing myself for a command to report to Mr. Fleagle immediately after school for discipline when I saw him lift my paper from his desk and rap for the class's attention.

"Now boys," he said, "I want to read you an essay. This is titled 'The   9 Art of Eating Spaghetti.'"

And he started to read. My words! He was reading *my words* out loud 10 to the entire class. What's more, the entire class was listening. Listening attentively. Then somebody laughed, then the entire class was laughing, and not in contempt and ridicule, but with openhearted enjoyment. Even Mr. Fleagle stopped two or three times to repress a small prim smile.

I did my best to avoid showing pleasure, but what I was feeling was 11 pure ecstasy at this startling demonstration that my words had the power to make people laugh. In the eleventh grade, at the eleventh hour as it were, I had discovered a calling. It was the happiest moment of my entire school career. When Mr. Fleagle finished he put the final seal on my happiness by saying, "Now that, boys, is an essay, don't you see. It's—don't you see—it's of the very essence of the essay, don't you see. Congratulations, Mr. Baker."

## Questions About the Reading

1. Why did the writer not want to write an essay? What discovery changed his mind?
2. Why did eating spaghetti so delight the people at the supper table?
3. What comment does the writer make on the role of formal rules in writing?
4. What is your opinion of Mr. Fleagle? How did it change during the course of reading the essay?
5. What was the significance of the essay's main event for the writer?

## Questions About the Writer's Strategies

1. What is the **main idea** of this essay?
2. At what point in the essay did you begin to figure out what the main idea would be?
3. What **order** does the writer use in describing the **incidents** in his narrative?
4. Is this essay written **objectively** or **subjectively**? Cite examples from the essay to help explain your answer.

## Writing Assignments

1. Write a narrative essay about the most important event you experienced in grade or middle school. Use **chronological order** to describe the event and the incidents leading up to it.
2. Write a narrative essay on one of the following events in your own life: leaving high school, learning to read a novel, using a computer for the first time, learning to have confidence, learning not to jump to conclusions, or controlling your temper. Try to indicate the significance that the event has had for you since it took place.

# Daughter's Doll Teaches Mom Lesson on Race

### Connie Schultz

### Words to Know

**balked**   refused
**furrowed**   wrinkled, rutted
**nuzzling**   caressing with the nose
**venue**   location, site

### Getting Started

What was your favorite plaything as a child, and why did you like it?

1   **S**ometimes our kids teach us lessons we thought we were teaching them.

2   That's how Addy made her way into our family's life five years ago.

3   Addy is an American Girl doll. She is based on the main character in a series of books about a slave girl whose family escaped to freedom in the 1800s.

4   Addy is black. My daughter is white. But from the moment Cait read her first sentence about Addy, she was convinced she and that slave girl were practically twins. And since her father and I had recently separated, it didn't take much lobbying on Cait's part to get exactly what she wanted from this mother steeped up to her furrowed brow in guilt: An Addy doll. An almost-$100 Addy doll, to be precise.

5   That Christmas morning, my then 8-year-old daughter greeted her new friend with squeals of delight. Not only did she get Addy, she and Addy got matching nightgowns, which Cait quickly snatched up before running off to her bedroom.

6   A few minutes later, there they were: Addy and Cait, cheek to cheek and dressed in matching white, ruffly nightgowns. "Don't we look alike, Mommy?" Cait said, her face beaming as she wrapped her arms around her doll.

I looked at my blue-eyed daughter, as pale as a calla lily, squeezing her 7
doll with the creamy brown skin and big dark eyes, and wondered what
she could be thinking. Tread gently here, I told myself.

"How do you and Addy look alike?" I asked.     8

Cait just smiled as she brushed back Addy's hair. "Oh, you know," she 9
said, nuzzling the doll's cheek. But I didn't know, and I felt left out,
blinded to the bigger picture only my daughter seemed to see.

For the next two months, Cait took Addy everywhere she went. You 10
can learn a lot about strangers by their reaction to a pretty black doll in a
white girl's arms. One woman, who was white, glared at me as we stood
in line at a McDonald's. "You *made* her buy that, didn't you?" she hissed,
shaking her head as she looked at Cait clutching Addy to her chest. "There
is no way she would have asked for a doll like that."

A young black woman working at a local drugstore stared at Cait and 11
Addy and then politely leaned in to whisper to me. "Did she want that
doll?" When I nodded my head, she winced. "Why?"

"We're a lot alike," piped up Cait. I looked at the bewildered woman, 12
shrugged my shoulders and smiled.

I thought of Addy recently after talking to a mother with two adopted 13
sons from Korea. For years, Linda has sent her boys to a camp for Korean
children adopted by Americans. "I thought it was a good idea," she said.
"All year long they are with kids who don't look like them, who didn't
come from Korea, and everything I had heard and read said this is a good
thing to do."

One of her sons, however, balked last year, announcing he did not want 14
to go to that camp again. Her 10-year-old did this in what is all children's
venue of choice for serious conversations: In the car, while his mother
was driving.

Linda was surprised, but undeterred. "Don't you like to be some place 15
where everyone is like you?" Her son's response so startled her she nearly
ended up on a tree lawn: "Isn't the important thing supposed to be liking
who you are and not being like everyone else?"

Linda smacked her forehead in recounting this conversation. "You know, 16
you raise them to believe certain things, to get beyond the issues of race and
gender and all that, but then you're blown away when you realize they're
there, all your lessons took, and *you're* the one who isn't getting it."

At that point I was required to welcome Linda into the Clueless Mothers 17
Club, of which I am president. Then I told her about Addy, and how I finally found out why Cait wanted the doll in the first place.

"Addy and I are so alike," Cait said yet again as I tucked them into bed 18
one night. "How so?" I asked. Cait reached up and touched my face.
"Addy had to leave with her mom, just like you and me."

I froze. For eight years I had been teaching my daughter that it's what's 19
on the inside that counts. Obviously, only one of us had been listening.

And you know what? Cait was right. She and Addy, they're so alike. 20
They're practically twins.

---

## Questions About the Reading

1. When did Cait get Addy, the black doll? CHRISTMAS MORNING
2. Why did Cait want Addy? SIMILAR TO HER
3. How did people react to Cait having Addy? OFFENDED/CONFUSED
4. What did Linda's Korean son tell her when she asked why he didn't want to go back to camp?
5. What is the lesson the writer learned?

## Questions About the Writer's Strategies

1. Where is the main idea (thesis) of the essay? Is it stated more than once? If so, where?
2. What is the order the writer uses in the essay?
3. What technique does the writer use to re-create what Addy, Linda, and the writer said?
4. Is the essay objective or subjective?

## Writing Assignments

1. Write a narrative essay telling about your favorite plaything as a child and explaining why it was your favorite.
2. Write a narrative essay telling about why you wanted to learn to drive a car and the first time you drove someplace by yourself.

# The Story of My Ring

**Annie Reeves (student)**

*In her essay, Annie Reeves, a student at Georgia College and State University, tells us that the ring she wears is not just a ring—it has a special story to tell.*

## Words to Know

**shrouded**  wrapped in a cloth
**significant**  important, impressive, having meaning
**symbolism**  representing the meaning of an object or relationship

## Getting Started

Do you have something that has been in your family for a long time, that has a special meaning for you?

---

I'm not sure if it's true or not, but there's a popular story that the wedding ring is on the third finger of the left hand because there is a vein that runs straight from it to the heart. The popularity of the engagement ring dates back to the Egyptian Empire and since has been used as the basis for engagement to marriage in Egypt, America, and the rest of the civilized world. For their engagement, my Grandfather Louis gave my Grandmother Marianne a silver ring with a large diamond and two smaller ones on either side. At my graduation they gave me a ring with the same setting but different stones. It's just a simple white gold hoop hugging my middle finger. But then there are the stones set in the middle, two white sapphires and one blue. What is significant about this ring is not the symbolism or the look of the ring, but rather the story of how my grandfather came to possess the stones in World War II.

In 1943, deep in the jungles of Burma, Louis and his best friend Thomas decided to fly a small fighter plane across the mountains into India. From the air two young men saw a huge sign that read "MA PHONG RUBY MINES." Their interest aroused, Louis and Thomas landed their plane in a field and hiked to the mine. The two men walked into a small one-room shack that served as the Ma Phong dealing house. A small Burmese man greeted them in a language they did not understand. But after a few minutes it became obvious to them that this mine was shutting down because of the war. Louis and Thomas decided to take advantage of the situation and trade everything they had in the plane for jewels. The Burmese man

35

was poor and wanted basic items, so they traded coffee pots, collared shirts, shoes, and underwear. In return they received star rubies, tiger eyes, white sapphires, blue sapphires, red rubies, and opals.

The picture Thomas took of the trade is in my grandmother's scrap-  3
book. In the picture, light is easing in through a window with four panes, casting a shadow from my twenty-one-year-old grandfather seated on a dirt floor. He is thin, still shaped like a boy, camouflaged by his khaki uniform. The Ma Phong worker, shrouded in a pale cloth hiding his feet and torso, pushes star rubies or sapphires across an upturned crate to my grandfather's eager hands.

That day as my grandfather flew his plane over the ancient Indian  4
mountains, what were his thoughts? Could he have known that these precious stones would go to a granddaughter whose mother and father had not even been born yet?

The Burmese man in the photograph exists in the memory of my  5
grandfather and in the imagination of everyone who reads his story. He carved a spot in history without doing anything noble or trying to earn respect. I know he could not have been content with life. A world war was raging around him. His village, temple, and mine had been destroyed. This poor man was trading thousands of dollars of jewels for clothing and kitchenware. Is the small man still alive in a northern jungle of India? Does his granddaughter have a bent and beaten coffee pot from 1943 hanging in her kitchen in New Delhi? Is there a family story about the two young airmen whose shirts her grandfather still wears?

The stones on my hand have been through war, across oceans and con-  6
tinents, and deep in the earth. On my hand they have felt the wetness of tears, kisses, and sweat. They are the silent witnesses of my life. They will sit next to my wedding band, and glitter as I stroke my children's faces. They will be on my hand when I hug my mother for the last time and on my hand when I close my eyes for the last time. The ring itself is not so important as the stones are and where they came from. These stones will forever link me to my grandfather, and my grandfather to a small Burmese man who wanted to survive.

## Questions About the Reading

1. Who gave the writer the ring?
2. Why was the writer given the ring?
3. Where did the stones come from that were in the writer's ring?
4. What is the significance of the writer wearing the ring on her middle finger instead of the third finger of her left hand?

## Questions About the Writer's Strategies

1. What is the thesis of the essay? Is it stated or implied? State the thesis in your own words.
2. What order does the writer use in paragraph 2 of the essay?
3. What are the details the writer uses to describe the condition of the Ma Phong worker and his surroundings?
4. What is the point of view in the essay? Is it consistent or does it change? If it changes, is the change justified?
5. Is the essay objective or subjective? Explain your answer.

## Writing Assignments

1. Think of something you have that is especially important to you. Write an essay in which you explain why that thing is important to you.
2. Ask a parent, grandparent, or someone you know who has served in one of the military services to tell you about an experience he or she had with a person of a different nationality or heritage. Write a narrative essay about their experience.

# A Little Nebraska

**Sarah Smith (student)**

*On a football game Saturday, the population of Lincoln, Nebraska, doubles. People come from all over the state to fill the University of Nebraska stadium to overflowing, and throughout the state, work comes to a stop while the rest of the population watches the game on television.*

### Words to Know

**falter**   hesitate, stumble
**irreplaceable**   cannot be replaced
**pretentious**   showy, false

### Getting Started

Have you ever arranged your work or school schedule around some favorite activity or television program?

T he small town of Imperial, Nebraska, has one grocery store. The store    1
has four carts, three baskets, and two checkout lanes manned by one
checker and one bag-boy. On this particular Saturday afternoon, four
people can be found inside. Walking slowly down each aisle is a grandmother and a 13-year-old girl. The grandmother's age shows in her face
and her walk, leaning on the cart for support. Her cotton white hair is
held neatly in place with an old hair pin; she is wearing a lovely flower-
patterned summer dress and a pair of comfortable white sneakers. In the
same way, the girl's youth is evident in her walk and manner, she takes
long strides down the aisles. The girl's hair is held up in a high ponytail
and covered with a baseball cap. She is wearing a red Huskers T-shirt and
holey jeans. She listens to her grandmother's instructions and gathers all
items that are dictated. She is becoming more and more anxious as time
ticks on.

Far across the state in the capital city of Lincoln, 78,000 people stand    2
singing the national anthem in Memorial Stadium. As the marching band
sounds out "Hail Varsity," the Huskers rush the field. The roar of the stadium becomes almost deafening, as team members feed on the crowd's
energy. The game begins with a kickoff to the visiting team and the
Huskers stopping them at the 20-yard line. On the sideline stands a
nineteen-year-old boy from Imperial, Nebraska. He is wearing a team
jersey, an issued pair of white pants, and an ankle brace on his left leg.

He stands watching the plays intently. He holds his breath at kickoff, and cheers for his friends and teammates.

In Imperial, the girl and grandmother walk slowly to their car. The girl's arms carry two big, brown bags. Her patience is almost gone now, and it is visible in her manner that her grandmother is holding her hostage. She had tried to explain earlier that day that this is the opening game of the season. It is the first chance she has to see the local small town boy, her cousin, in play, and she can't miss a moment of the game. The entire town is indoors glued to their TV screens, and here she is carrying groceries. Seemingly unaware of the dire situation, the grandmother slowly unlocks the car doors, "Place the bags in the back seat, Sweetie. Mind the eggs, now." Their house is approximately two miles in distance from the store. However, at the speed the grandmother drives they will arrive in ten minutes. She can barely see over the steering wheel and believes in stopping at every intersection. The possibility of being hit on this day is almost impossible, yet her driving continues as normal.    3

In the stadium the sea of red is on its feet cheering the winning team. The Huskers have stopped the opposing team from scoring and have run the ball for a touchdown. The boy watches as the kicker stands poised for the snap. He questions how many times back home he had done the same thing. He begins to think of his small town and the people in it. He knows today they will all be focused on the game. There will be fewer cars than usual on the streets and the local bar will be filled to the brim with customers who have no satellite dish to pick the game up at home. He hopes that one girl in particular is watching, his favorite 13-year-old cousin. Her admiration for him inspired him to come as far as he had, and he knew, whether he had played today or not, she would still be his biggest fan.    4

The girl is now running to the TV set to find the correct station. The groceries are sitting on the kitchen counter and the grandmother is carefully placing each item in its proper place. "Don't sit so close to the television," calls out the grandmother. "So much fuss over one little game." The grandmother does not understand the obsession with football. The girl's parents had been the same way before they died and she seemed to have it in her blood. After her parents died three years ago, the girl had come to live with her grandmother. The grandmother knew how to deal with the loss of her daughter. She had lost her husband ten years ago. "It's a part of life," she always said. Somehow the two of them had made it this far. Today she just was not in a football mood. The idea of rearranging one's day to fit a football schedule seemed a little pretentious. She felt assured that the game would turn out the way all Husker games do, with a win, so why the fuss about catching every moment?    5

Three years ago the boy had almost lost his chance to be at this game.  6
That was his junior year in high school, and he started for the varsity
team. He played defense on the opening game and in the last quarter he
almost lost his carrier. He landed on the bottom of a tackle and felt his
ankle pop. The doctors told him the injury was serious. The ankle was
broken, and if he did not give it time to heal, he might never play again.
It seemed like the end of the world, until his cousin moved in with his
grandmother. A car accident had claimed the life of her parents. Spending
time with her made a busted ankle seem minor. She was ten years old and
full of energy. She knew she had lost something irreplaceable and yet it
did not stop her. If she could continue, he knew he could too.

The girl does not hear her grandmother's instructions to move from the  7
set. She is looking intently for a glimpse of her cousin. He had been her
comfort and her friend when her parents died. Her grandmother helped,
but her cousin was never too busy for her and never made her feel like a
little kid. She felt needed when she visited him and told him no busted
ankle could stop him. She felt special just knowing he was her friend.

The boy's thoughts return to the game when it suddenly takes a major  8
twist. Something goes wrong in the play. The snap is dropped. There is a
mad dash to recover the fumble. In all of the confusion the kicker goes
down hard on his right knee. He is injured. The boy is now the only
kicker. The coach approaches him, "I hope you're ready, Son. You better
get warmed up."

The girl watches it all and begins to jump and cheer with the news.  9
She will see her hero play today. He is all the world to her and now the
world can see how great he is. "Grandma," she calls out. "He's going to
play." She is disappointed in the first half. The opposing team's defense
does not allow the Huskers to cross the 50-yard line. The girl does not
lose hope, and during half-time she says a prayer for her hero to have the
courage to do his job.

The boy's chance arrives in the third quarter. The Huskers come in 10
with new energy and run the ball for a touchdown in the first three minutes of the game. The boy's heart is pounding as he runs in to take his
turn at the extra point. The world around him seems to hold its breath.
He signals for the snap and is shocked as the ball flies above the setter's
head. The timing is off and the kick goes to the left. It hits the goal post
and bounces off into the stands. The band plays on and the crowd seems
to ignore the disaster.

In Imperial the girl is yelling at the TV, "Get rid of the snapper. I could 11
do better than that guy." The grandmother's interest has been sparked
and she joins the girl on the couch. The girl reminds her of the boy's high
school stats and the many times he has come through for his team in a
tight situation. He will not falter now.

The feel of the game has become urgent in the fourth quarter. The 12 Huskers are behind by two points and there are three minutes left in the game. The Huskers are playing defense. The stadium is alive with the chants of the fans. The opposing team approaches the line of scrimmage and the quarterback calls out the play. He goes back for a pass but is sacked by a Nebraska lineman. The Huskers take over at their own 40-yard line. The crowd is yelling insanely and the band continuously plays "There Is No Place Like Nebraska." The offense wastes no time pushing their way down the field. The Huskers call a time out to decide the next play.

The set in the living room switches to a commercial. "Ahhhh, I hate it 13 when they do that!" The girl is pacing around the room. The grandmother sits holding a bowl of popcorn, "Would you kindly sit down. You're making me more nervous than the game." She can't believe how caught up she has become. The girl laughs and takes a seat. She grabs a handful of popcorn and waits for the game to resume.

Wild cheers and music fill the stadium. With 30 seconds on the clock 14 the Huskers will attempt a field goal. The ball is on a 35-yard line. The boy's mind is racing, his heart is pounding, and his palms are sweating. He takes a deep breath, says a prayer, "God bless this kick," and waits for the snap. All goes well; he kicks the ball and watches in what seems slow motion as the ball sails beautifully between the goal posts. The stadium explodes with excitement. The fans give each other hugs and high-fives as if they were on the field themselves. His teammates and TV crews bombard the boy. He jumps and cheers and can almost not believe this dream come true.

In Imperial the whole town is alive with cheers and congratulations. 15 The bartender takes out his trumpet and plays the Huskers fight song. The girl and grandmother shout aloud and hug each other. The grandmother says she is proud of that boy and she can't wait to tell him. The girl replies, "I knew he could do it the whole time." Inside she thinks of how much fun the next game is going to be.

## Questions About the Reading

1. Why was the girl in a hurry to get home from the grocery store?
2. Why are there "fewer cars than usual on the streets" of the town on this Saturday?
3. Why is the girl living with her grandmother? What is her grandmother's attitude towards the football game? Does her attitude change?
4. What happened to the boy when he played football in high school?

## Questions About the Writer's Strategies

1. What is the thesis of the essay? Is it stated or implied?
2. The writer shifts the point of view between the thoughts and actions of the girl and those of the boy. Why do you think she does this? Do you think this shift is necessary to the story?
3. What details does the writer use to help the reader understand the excitement and sounds of the football game?

## Writing Assignments

1. Write a narrative essay about a sports event in which you competed.
2. Write a narrative essay about an important school sports event you attended with some friends.
3. *Working Together* Divide your group into two groups. Have each group watch an important football, baseball, or basketball game on television. Then write a narrative essay together using the viewpoints of the opposing teams.

# 3 Description

DESCRIPTION PROVIDES THE reader with a "word picture" of a specific person, the flavor of a special place, or the look of a particular object. To help the reader visualize the object, the writer chooses key details to develop the description: a certain liveliness in a person's eyes, the movement of ocean waves, the design of a favorite chair.

We saw in chapter 2 that writers use descriptive words to add color and vividness to the details they describe. The specific descriptive words the writer chooses depend on the particular **impression,** or image, the writer wants to create. For example, the writer can create the impression of a person who is likable by describing the person's face as "friendly" and "good natured." The writer can create the opposite impression by using such descriptive words as *shifty* or *scowling.* In the following paragraph, the writer develops an effective impression of a chair by the buildup of details and descriptive words that re-create the object for the reader.

Detail: location

Detail: appearance

Detail: appearance

Detail: decoration of chair

The chair was the one piece of furniture I wanted to take with me when I closed up my parents' house for the final time. To look at it, sitting in the same kitchen corner where it had been for fifty years, you'd wonder how it could be my favorite chair. It was nothing but a straight-backed wooden chair, its seat scratched here and there from the soles of a small boy's shoes. The only thing unusual about it was the intricate design carved into its back. But the carving was what made the chair meaningful to me. I had sat in that chair many times as punishment for errors in my ways. I suppose my mother thought it was defiance that led me to sit cross-legged on the seat with my back to her in the kitchen. But it was not defiance. Rather, in that position my eyes and then my fingers could trace the intertwining leaves and flowers of the design carved in the back of the chair. Each time I sat there I seemed to see lines and shapes I hadn't seen before: a heart-shaped leaf, a budding rose, a blade of grass. Perhaps that chair had something to do with my lasting interest in well-made antique furniture. Who knows? I do know that when I drove away on that last day, the chair, carefully wrapped in several old quilts, lay tenderly cradled on the back seat of my car.

Notice that the chair is described only as being a straight-backed wooden chair with a scratched seat and a design carved into its back. However, the writer creates the dominant impression that the chair—in spite of being associated with childhood punishment—remained beautiful to him and probably influenced his lifelong interest in fine woods and antiques. The words *intricate, trace, intertwining, heart-shaped*, and *budding* describe and help the reader picture the design in the back of the chair. And in the last sentence, the phrases *carefully wrapped* and *tenderly cradled* convey indirectly the writer's feelings about the chair. The reader must be given enough detail not only to picture an object but also to understand what touched or moved the writer to single it out.

In descriptive writing you will often find stylistic devices that help convey both the essential qualities of the subject and its significance to the writer. Consider the following paragraph.

> A baseball weighted your hand just so, and fit it. Its red stitches, its good leather and hardness like skin over bone, seemed to call forth a skill both easy and precise. On the catch—the grounder, the fly, the line drive—you could snag a baseball in your mitt, where it stayed, snap, like a mouse locked in its trap, not like some pumpkin of a softball you merely halted, with a terrible sound like a splat. You could curl your fingers around the baseball, and throw it in a straight line. When you hit it with a bat it cracked—and your heart cracked, too, at the sound. It took a grass stain nicely, stayed round, smelled good, and lived lashed in your mitt all winter, hibernating.
>
> Annie Dillard,
> "An American Childhood"

In this paragraph, the writer uses a **figure of speech** called a **simile** to help enhance the description of the baseball. A simile takes items that are considered unlike and then compares them in a way that shows an unexpected similarity. Usually, a simile uses *like* or *as* to establish the connection between the items. For example, three similes in this paragraph are "like skin over bone," "like a mouse locked in its trap," and "not like some pumpkin of a softball."

A figure of speech related to the simile is the **metaphor**, which also compares unlike items but does so without directly stating the connection with *like* or *as*. Metaphors may be used to express an idea that is rather abstract, as in "the *scales* of justice." But they can be used for other effects, too, and they may only be **implied** by the use of a certain verb—"The swimmer *waddled* across the sand."

Read the paragraph that follows. What is the metaphor for the matron and for the electric car? Is there another metaphor?

> In 1900, electric cars were a common sight on city streets. They were high, boxy, and heavy—those early electric cars—and they couldn't get

up much speed. Nor could they be driven very far before the battery had to be recharged. So by the 1930s, the electric car was a curiosity piece that now and then sailed out of a carriage house, usually with a stern-faced matron at the steering tiller. Car and driver were somehow suited to each other: heavily built, elegantly appointed, and quietly majestic. They were quality products. They didn't guzzle fuel, raise their voices above a murmur, or create a public problem as they floated across the streets. But they both disappeared in favor of slim-lined, stripped-down models that drink high-powered fuels, make noise in the streets, and create a public nuisance. Now maybe only a few people would like to see that old-style matron come back. But these days, most of us would like to have a car that didn't use gas, was really quiet, and didn't pollute the environment. That's why our engineers have worked to solve the battery problem: so we can have electric cars again.

**Personification,** another figure of speech, attributes human qualities or abilities to animals or objects. For example, after Red Riding Hood observes that the wolf has big teeth, the wolf answers, "The better to eat you with, my dear!"

Exaggeration, which is called **hyperbole,** is also used. "I could have danced all night" might be possible for a few people, but for most of us, it would be hyperbole.

The organization of a description also contributes to its effectiveness. The writer may arrange the details in **order of importance,** usually moving from the less important to the more important details. The details in the paragraph on page 43 are arranged so that they build to the most significant point—the deeper meaning of the chair to the writer. The writer may choose to arrange the details according to space, called **spatial order.** When a description is organized according to space, the writer takes a physical position in a room or at a scene and then describes what can be seen from that position, using some consistent order such as moving from left to right, from foreground to background, or from top to bottom.

In creating a description, the writer must identify the important characteristics of the object or scene being described and then find the words— nouns and verbs, as well as adjectives and adverbs—that best express these characteristics. In the essay that follows, the student describes the house in which she is living. Notice that she describes the house in **spatial order**—first from the outside and then as she walks through its rooms. Notice, too, that the descriptive details provide the reader with an image of both the house and its owner.

|  |  |
|---|---|
|  | It's really not a striking house, nor is it an old charming   1 |
|  | house. It is, in fact, very plain—just like the houses on each |
| View of the outside of the house | side of it. As I climb up the hilly driveway, its <u>whiteness</u> |
|  | stares blankly back at me, reminding me that I am not the |

| | |
|---|---|
| **Details: preciseness of the landscaping** | owner but just a temporary, unwanted trespasser. There are flowers lining the driveway, which push their faces toward the sun as they lie in their bed perfectly spaced, not too close and not too far apart, perfectly coordinated to reflect all the colors of the spectrum. Through the windows of the house nothing |
| **Thesis statement** | but my reflection can be seen. They are like the house, clean and tinted, allowing no one a look in, keeping life in the house shut off from the rest of the world, uninviting of intrusion, only interested in cleanliness, only leading the people inside to a feeling of loneliness. |

**Entering the house**     Upon entering the house the smell of Pinesol and disin-    2
fectant engulfs my nostrils and shoots directly to my brain,
anesthetizing any emotions that might surface. Like the win-

**Details: cleanliness and coldness of kitchen**
dows, the kitchen floor reflects the cleanliness of the house
with its spotless white surface, scrubbed and shined, casting
off reflections from the bright lights overhead. There is wall-
paper on the walls of the kitchen, but it is void of any pattern
and lends very little color to the whiteness of the room. Only
items of importance for the duties of the kitchen are displayed,
all in their properly appointed places, with the appropriate
covers placed over them to hide them from prying eyes. The
only personality the kitchen portrays is a cold, calculating,
suspicious one, wary of intruders who may cause unneces-
sary filth to enter.

**Moving to dining room**     Around the corner from the kitchen lies the dining room.    3
An elegant, dark, formal table sits in the center of the room,

**Details: formality and whiteness of room**
the surface of which is smooth as glass under my fingertips.
A white centerpiece is carefully placed at the table's center,
with two white candles that have never been lit standing erect
at the centerpiece's ends. The chairs around the table are
hard, providing support for the back but lending the body
no comfort. Above hangs a crystal chandelier—expensive,
elegant, giving the room an artificial brightness. It is made up
of many dangling, teardrop-shaped crystals, all cleaned and
polished, and is the only object in the dining room that speaks
clearly of conspicuous consumption. The drapes covering the
tinted windows are a dark color and keep out the sun of the
day. This room is often cleaned, often walked through, but
never used.

**Entering the living room**     Having walked through the dining room, I enter the living    4
room. Although this is the only room in the house where the

**Details: impersonality of living room**
family can all converge to spend time together, it is not a
cheerful place. The walls are white, like the rest of the house,
with the same drapery as the dining room, and the couch and
loveseat are velvet, stiff, uncomfortable, and well maintained.
A television set is placed in the corner but lies blank with dis-
use. The air of coldness here seems to hold tension though at
the same time it gives the impression of ossification.

    I have heard it said that a person's home is a reflection of    5
that person, a sentiment that, with few exceptions, is true of

this home. <u>Cleanliness</u> is a priority of the owner, and social-
izing with people in this house is considered a nuisance that
only causes more work because of the dirt that people carry
in with them. The walls are kept white because it looks clean
and repainting is made easy. And the smell of disinfectant
pleases the owner, as it proves to the few who do enter that

**Thesis related and conclusion**
the house is clean. This house, the place I am calling home for
this period of my life, offers me no comfort but does provide
shelter and quiet. And with the <u>dark stillness</u> in its rooms, I
can think, read, and plan my escape.

Carol Adams (student),
"An Intruder in the House"

In the introduction to chapter 2, you learned about the difference between writing **objectively** and **subjectively**. Notice, in the previous
essay, that although the writer's style is objective, her choice of specific
descriptive details and words supports her subjective, negative opinion
of the house and its owner.

When brainstorming for a description, it may help to begin by listing
all the features of the subject that come to mind and all the details that
seem related to those features.

Descriptive details often are combined with other modes of development. The following paragraphs, for example, are from a narrative essay
about a young man's visit to the Mexican town that he had left soon after
he was born. Notice his descriptions of the people and the Spanish architecture of the town.

**Description: Spanish architecture**
On my arrival at Morelia airport, I was greeted by the          1
most attractive architecture I had ever seen. All the buildings
had a very strong Spanish influence. Was it possible I had
taken the wrong plane and landed somewhere in Spain?

**People and their clothing**
No, indeed; it was Morelia, and what a town! Its people          2
were very plain and small-townlike. I was amused by some
very oddly dressed people who wore white cotton clothing.
On their heads the men wore straw hats, and the women
wore large Spanish scarves called mantillas. I asked a ticket
agent about the oddly dressed people. He explained that they
were the native people, known as Tarascos. They were the
founders of the land, and even today they are very traditional
in their beliefs and ways.

**Architectural features**
I took a taxi to El Hotel Virrey de Mendoza, located in the     3
middle of the town square. The hotel was made of hewn
stone that was cut and shaped into the most captivating
three-story building I had ever seen. It was built in the traditional Spanish style, with a central open patio completely
surrounded by the building. My room had a spacious view of
the town square and its cathedral. The cathedral was built in
the seventeenth century in a baroque style that was popular

in Europe. Beside the cathedral was the municipal palace and
other government buildings, all in Colonial Spanish style.
The feeling I had from the view was that I was back in the
days when Spanish viceroys ruled the land, and the Catholic
priests taught religion to the native inhabitants.

Arturo E. Ramirez (student),
"Back to Where the Seed Was Planted"

Descriptive words and phrases are essential to effective writing. They
can make an object concrete for the reader by describing how it looks,
sounds, tastes, smells, or feels. Such sensory details can create a distinct
impression or **image** of that which is described and thus help the reader
visualize the writer's ideas. You will find specific descriptive words and
details in all the paragraphs and essays that follow. As you read, notice
that experienced writers select revealing details because, as with the incidents in narrative writing, these details produce the most effective description. In your own writing, select—as the writers of the reading selections
do—the most essential qualities of whatever you describe.

# A Perfect Dog

*John Grogan*

*In this paragraph from* Marley and Me, *John Grogan describes Shaun, a dog he had when he was young—a dog that is very different from his dog Marley.*

### Words to Know

**effortlessly**   without difficulty, easily
**hazard**   danger, risk

### Getting Started

Have you ever had a dog or cat that was especially hard to train?

I brought him home in a cardboard box and named him Shaun. He was one of those dogs that give dogs a good name. He effortlessly mastered every command I taught him and was naturally well behaved. I could drop a crust on the floor and he would not touch it until I gave the okay. He came when I called him and stayed when I told him to. We could let him out alone at night, knowing he would be back after making his rounds. Not that we often did, but we could leave him alone in the house for hours, confident he wouldn't have an accident or disturb a thing. He raced cars without chasing them and walked beside me without a leash. He could dive to the bottom of our lake and emerge with rocks so big they sometimes got stuck in his jaws. He loved nothing more than riding in the car and would sit quietly in the backseat beside me on family road trips, content to spend hours gazing out the window at the passing world. Perhaps best of all, I trained him to pull me through the neighborhood dog-sled-style as I sat on my bicycle, making me the hands-down envy of my friends. Never once did he lead me into hazard.

## Questions About the Reading

1. What would Shaun do if his master dropped a "crust on the floor"?
2. What are the behaviors that the writer tells us gave his dog Shaun "a good name"?

3. What did the writer train Shaun to do that made the writer "the envy" of his friends?
4. How did Shaun behave when he was riding in the car?

## Questions About the Writer's Strategies

1. What is the main idea of the paragraph?
2. What is the point of view (person, time, tone) of the paragraph?
3. What is the order the writer uses in the paragraph?
4. Is the paragraph objective or subjective?

## Writing Assignments

1. Write a descriptive paragraph about a dog, cat, hamster, or other pet you have had.
2. Write a descriptive paragraph about a special friend, a relative, or an elementary school teacher you had.

# The Hiroshima Museum

**Barbara Kingsolver**

> *In this selection from her book* High Tide in Tucson, *Barbara Kingsolver describes her visit to the Peace Memorial Museum in Hiroshima and the items displayed there that speak silently of the impact of an atomic bomb.*

## Words to Know

**artifacts**   objects of historical importance
**histrionic**   emotional, theatrical, dramatic
**hypocenter**   surface beneath the center of a nuclear explosion
**ideological**   reflective of an idea, belief, or culture
**saki**   wine made from rice

## Getting Started

How do you feel when you look at paintings and exhibits in a museum?

---

S ince that day, I've had the chance to visit another bomb museum of a different kind: the one that stands in Hiroshima. A serene building set in a garden, it is strangely quiet inside, with hushed viewers and hushed exhibits. Neither ideological nor histrionic, the displays stand entirely without editorial comment. They are simply artifacts, labeled: china saki cups melted together in a stack. A brass Buddha with his hands relaxed into molten pools and a hole where his face used to be. Dozens of melted watches, all stopped at exactly eight-fifteen. A white eyelet petticoat with great, brown-rimmed holes burned in the left side, stained with black rain, worn by a schoolgirl named Oshita-chan. She was half a mile from the hypocenter of the nuclear blast, wearing also a blue short-sleeved blouse, which was incinerated except for its collar, and a blue metal pin with a small white heart, which melted. Oshita-chan lived for approximately twelve hours after the bomb.

---

## Questions About the Reading

1. Why do you think the displays in the museum "stand entirely without editorial comment"?
2. What do the exhibits tell you about the effect of an atomic bomb?

3. Why do you think the museum visitors are "hushed"?

4. What is the significance of all the watches being "stopped at exactly eight-fifteen"?

## Questions About the Writer's Strategies

1. What is the main idea of the paragraph? Is it stated or implied? State the main idea in your own words.
2. What order does the writer use to describe the artifacts in the museum? Why do you think she chose that order?
3. Is the paragraph objective or subjective or both? Support your answer with examples.
4. What descriptive details does the writer give about Oshita-chan and her clothing? Do the details provide an image of what happened to Oshita-chan?

## Writing Assignments

1. Write a narrative paragraph in which you describe your feelings during a visit to a museum.
2. Write a narrative paragraph in which you describe a visit to a city you had never been to before.
3. Visit an elder-care center, a church other than your own, or a day-care center for preschoolers, and write a narrative paragraph describing the place.

# The Ravine

## Quincy Stott (student)

*In this paragraph, Quincy Stott describes a place where he, his brother, and their cousins played and tells us why it was a special place for them.*

### Words to Know

**billowing**   surging, rising

**crevasse**   deep crack or hole

**verdant**   immature, young

**vibrant**   quivering, moving

### Getting Started

Did you and your friends have a favorite place to play when you were young?

---

**P**ast the small concrete patio behind our house was a typical yard that suffered from crab grass and a chain-link fence. Behind the fence was a dirt alley that would fill with billowing dust when cars or trucks drove by too quickly. But beyond that was green—the vibrant, verdant green of trees and tall pasture grass that created a stark contrast to the dull, brown exterior of our neighborhood. Tall, soaring branches erupted out of the small, canal-shaped cavity in the otherwise dreary landscape behind our backyard. A small, murky stream quietly trickled down the u-shaped crevasse and separated our house from farmland. This place, which my brother and I affectionately called the "Ravine," was the staple environment for most of our free time from spring to summer, and then autumn. Sometimes we would even escape the narrow confines of our house in the winter to play in the magnificent outdoors just a few feet away. In the spring, the trees of the Ravine sprouted leaves. They were small and underdeveloped— merely buds on the branches. During the summer months, they changed into lush green leaves and rustled quietly in hot and muggy summer breezes. In autumn, the leaves turned yellow and orange, slowly fell, and carpeted the crackly, dead underbrush with their lively color. This was the place where my brother, our cousins, and I had some of our best times as children. The Ravine was a fantastic place to play when we were young because we grew closer as family and matured as individuals.

---

## Questions About the Reading

1. Where is the Ravine located?
2. What separated the writer's house from farmland? What did the writer and his brother call this place?
3. When did the writer and his brother play in this place? What was the place like in the different seasons of the year?
4. Why was the Ravine a fantastic place to play?

## Questions About the Writer's Strategies

1. What is the main idea of the paragraph? Is it stated or implied? If stated, identify the sentence or sentences that state the idea. If implied, state the main idea in your own words.
2. What is the point of view (person, time, tone) of the paragraph?
3. What are the descriptive details the writer uses to describe the yard, the alley, and the stream that separated his house from farmland?
4. What are the descriptive details the writer uses to contrast the area past the dirt alley with his neighborhood?

## Writing Assignments

1. Write a paragraph in which you describe an outdoor place where you and your friends played when you were young.
2. Write a paragraph describing a place that is special to you.

# The Wreck

*Richard Mack*

> *This is a true story, which Richard Mack experienced when he was a student in the 1960s. He now has a Ph.D. and operates a horse-boarding and arena business in Oregon.*

### Words to Know

**basalt scree**   dark, volcanic rock accumulation
**firmament**   sky

### Getting Started

Have you ever seen an accident happen or been one of the first people to come across an accident?

---

The pickup lay at the bottom of a rocky ravine halfway between Jordan Valley, Oregon, and McDermott, Nevada. It went off the highway doing about sixty miles an hour on frozen, fog-slick Highway 95. The deputy and I scrambled down from the shoulder of the road, making our way through loose sand and boulders. It was the first real dead person I had ever seen. The pickup had rolled and flipped its way down seventy-five yards of sharp basalt scree and scattered junipers. The driver had been ejected out of the back window, and the last bounce of the truck had crushed the cab against his upper torso. He now lay in the cold November pre-dawn. I hadn't expected this person to look so peaceful. His eyes are closed and the breeze that is drifting up from the bottom of the canyon lifts a lock of hair on his forehead and then releases it . . . lift, release, lift, release. He ended with one arm free of the pickup and his index finger pointing toward the starry firmament. I hope that is where he is headed.

---

## Questions About the Reading

1. What were the road conditions on Highway 95 the night of the wreck?
2. How fast was the vehicle going when it went off the highway?
3. What kind of vehicle had been wrecked? Where was it?
4. Were there people hurt in the wreck? If so, who were they?

## Questions About the Writer's Strategies

1. What is the main idea of the paragraph? Is it stated or implied? If stated, identify the sentences in which it is stated; if implied, state the main idea in your own words.
2. What are the details that the writer uses to describe the scene of the accident?
3. What are the details the writer uses to describe the condition of the driver of the truck?
4. What is the symbolism of the driver's pointing "his index finger . . . toward the starry firmament"? How does the writer feel about that?

## Writing Assignments

1. Write a paragraph in which you describe a bicycle, car, or train accident you have seen.
2. Watch a NASCAR race on television and describe a near-miss among the cars.
3. Watch a professional hockey game and write a paragraph describing it.

# Overindulgence

*Heidi Hall (student)*

*In the following paragraph, Heidi Hall, a student at George Fox College, uses descriptive language to make her Aunt Helen's chicken and dumplings seem larger than life. Through language alone, the reader can almost taste what she describes—and feel the aftereffects of too much of a good thing.*

### Words to Know

**celestial**   heavenly
**primordial**   having to do with the beginning of time
**resolve**   determination
**sentry**   guard; a soldier standing guard

### Getting Started

What would make you want to overindulge in a favorite food?

---

One of my weaknesses is my Aunt Helen's famous chicken and dumplings. If anything could break my resolve to only have one helping, it'd be this celestial dish: Chicken pieces lightly seasoned with herbs and cooked till fork-tender—dumplings floating in the flavorful broth like sentry icebergs in a thick, primordial sea. Never could I stop at just one helping; too many delicious tastes scream, "More! More! This next bite will be even better!" Alas, too often I have staggered from her gracious table a few too many bites past "comfortable," Alka-Seltzer in hand, waistband begging for relief, and my resolve all the firmer to "NEXT time only have one serving."

---

## Questions About the Reading

1. What are some of the sensory details the writer uses to bring her aunt's chicken and dumplings to life? Do you think the dish Hall describes sounds appetizing? Why or why not?
2. What do you learn about the writer from reading this paragraph?
3. Think about the images Hall uses in this paragraph. Is there anything other than the appearance, taste, and smell of the chicken and dumplings that makes her enjoy them so much?

4. Is there anything that can never be "too much of a good thing"—for instance, a hobby, work, or creative endeavor? If you think there is, why do you think that? If you don't think there is, describe some of the possible negative effects of even the most productive activities.

## Questions About the Writer's Strategies

1. Does the writer state the main idea of the paragraph? If so, in which sentence does she state it?
2. The writer uses unusual vocabulary in the second sentence. Why do you think Hall chose to use the words *sentry* and *primordial?*
3. What is the tone of this paragraph? Identify words and expressions that support your answer.
4. Why do you think the writer quotes the food talking to her and then her talking to herself?

## Writing Assignments

1. Write a paragraph in which you describe your own favorite—or least favorite—food. Try to use as many unusual but appropriate descriptive words as possible to make the reader imagine vividly what you describe.
2. Write a paragraph describing a family tradition other than a meal. Describe as vividly as possible some of the things that you find comforting about this tradition.

# Hush, Timmy—
# This Is Like a Church

**Kurt Anderson**

*In this essay, Kurt Anderson, a writer for* Time *magazine, describes the Viet Nam Veterans Memorial in Washington, DC, and the behavior of the people who visit it.*

## Words to Know

**catharsis**   relief, purification
**contemplative**   thoughtful
**liturgical**   public worship
**mandarins**   officials, authorities
**rambunctious**   boisterous, noisy, unruly
**sanctum**   holy place
**stigmatized**   branded, disgraced
**vertex**   highest point

## Getting Started

Is there a place that makes you feel sad or happy?

The veteran and his wife had already stared hard at four particular  1
names. Now the couple walked slowly down the incline in front of the
wall, looking at rows of hundreds, thousands more, amazed at the roster
of the dead. "All the names," she said quietly, sniffling in the early-spring
chill. "It's unreal, how many names." He said nothing. "You have to see
it to believe it," she said.

Just so. In person, close up, the Viet Nam Veterans Memorial—two  2
skinny black granite triangles wedged onto a mount of Washington sod—
is some kind of sanctum, beautiful and terrible. "We didn't plan that,"
says John Wheeler, chairman of the veterans' group that raised the money
and built it. "I had a picture of seven-year-olds throwing a Frisbee around
on the grass in front. But it's treated as a spiritual place." When Wheeler's
colleague Jan Scruggs decided there ought to be a monument, he had
only vague notions of what it might be like. "You don't set out and *build*
a national shrine," Scruggs says. "It *becomes* one."

Washington is thick with monuments, several of them quite affecting.  3
But as the Viet Nam War was singular and strange, the dark, dreamy,

redemptive memorial to its American veterans is like no other. "It's more solemn," says National Park Service Ranger Sarah Page, who has also worked at the memorials honoring Lincoln, Washington and Jefferson. "People give it more respect." Lately it has been the most visited monument in the capital: 2.3 million saw it in 1984, about 45,000 a week, but it is currently drawing 100,000 a week. Where does it get its power—to console, and also to make people sob?

The men who set up the Viet Nam Veterans Memorial Fund wanted    4
something that would include the name of every American killed in Viet Nam, and would be contemplative and apolitical. They conducted an open design competition that drew 1,421 entries, all submitted anonymously. The winner, Maya Ying Lin, was a Chinese-American undergraduate at Yale: to memorialize men killed in a war in Asia, an Asian female studying at an old antiwar hotbed.

Opposition to Lin's design was intense. The opponents wanted some-    5
thing gleaming and grand. To them, the low-slung black wall would send the same old defeatist, elitist messages that had lost the war in the '60s and then stigmatized the veterans in the '70s. "Creating the memorial triggered a lot of old angers and rage among vets about the war," recalls Wheeler, a captain in Viet Nam and now a Yale-trained government lawyer. "It got white hot."

In the end, Lin's sublime and stirring wall was built, 58,022 names in-    6
scribed. As a compromise with opponents, however, a more conventional figurative sculpture was added to the site last fall (at a cost of $400,000). It does not spoil the memorial, as the art mandarins had warned. The three U.S. soldiers, cast in bronze, stand a bit larger than life, carry automatic weapons and wear fatigues, but the pose is not John Wayne-heroic: these American boys are spectral and wary, even slightly bewildered as they gaze southeast toward the wall. While he was planning the figures, sculptor Frederick Hart spent time watching vets at the memorial. Hart now grants that "no modernist monument of its kind has been as successful as that wall. The sculpture and the wall interact beautifully. Everybody won." Nor does Lin, his erstwhile artistic antagonist, still feel that Hart's statue is so awfully trite. "It captures the mood," says Lin. "Their faces have a lost look." Out at the memorial last week, one veteran looked at the new addition and nodded: "That's us."

But it is the wall that vets approach as if it were a force field. It is at the    7
wall that families of the dead cry and leave flowers and mementos and messages, much as Jews leave notes for God in the cracks of Jerusalem's Western Wall. Around the statue, people talk louder and breathe easier, snap vacation photos unselfconsciously, eat Eskimo Pies and Fritos. But near the wall, a young Boston father tells his rambunctious son, "Hush, Timmy—this is like a church." The visitors' processionals do seem to have

a ritual, even liturgical quality. Going slowly down toward the vertex, looking at the names, they chat less and less, then fall silent where the names of the first men killed (July 1959) and the last (May 1975) appear. The talk begins again, softly, as they follow the path up out of the little valley of the shadow of death.

For veterans, the memorial was a touchstone from the beginning, and    8 the 1982 dedication ceremony a delayed national embrace. "The actual act of being at the memorial is healing for the guy or woman who went to Viet Nam," says Wheeler, who visits at least monthly. "It has to do with the felt presence of comrades." He pauses. "I always look at Tommy Hayes' name. Tommy's up on panel 50 east, line 29." Hayes, Wheeler's West Point pal, was killed 17 years ago this month. "I know guys," Wheeler says, "who are still waiting to go, whose wives have told me, 'He hasn't been able to do it yet.'" For those who go, catharsis is common. As Lin says of the names, chronologically ordered, "Veterans can look at the wall, find a name, and in a sense put themselves back in time." The war has left some residual pathologies that the memorial cannot leach away. One veteran killed himself on the amphitheatrical green near the wall. A second, ex-Marine Randolph Taylor, tried and failed in January. "I regret what I did," he said. "I feel like I desecrated a holy place."

The memorial has become a totem, so much so that its tiniest imperfec-   9 tions make news. Last fall somebody noticed a few minute cracks at the seams between several of the granite panels. The cause of the hairlines is still unknown, and the builders are a little worried.

Probably no one is more determined than Wheeler to see the memo-   10 rial's face made perfect, for he savors the startlingly faithful reflections the walls give off: he loves seeing the crowds of visitors looking simultaneously at the names and themselves. "Look!" he said the other day, gesturing at panel 4 east. "You see that plane taking off? You see the blue sky? No one expected that."

## Questions About the Reading

1. About how many people a week visited the Viet Nam Veterans Memorial in 1984?

2. How many people a week were visiting the memorial at the time the essay was written (1985)?

3. What did the men who set up the Viet Nam Veterans Memorial Fund want the memorial to include?

4. Who won the contest for the design of the memorial? Why was her design controversial?

5. How many names were inscribed on the wall?
6. What differences are there between people's behavior at the wall and their behavior at the sculpture?

## Questions About the Writer's Strategies

1. What is the main idea (thesis) of the essay?
2. Is the main idea directly stated or implied?
3. What is the point of view (person, time, tone) of the essay?
4. What is the impression of the memorial that the writer creates?
5. Is the essay objective, subjective, or both?

## Writing Assignments

1. Write a descriptive essay about a place you visited that made you feel particularly sad.
2. Write a descriptive essay about a place you visited that made you feel particularly happy.
3. Use the Internet to research the following historical monuments: the Statue of Liberty in New York City; the Lincoln Memorial in Washington, DC; and Mount Rushmore in Keystone, South Dakota. Write an essay describing each monument, who or what it represents, and when and by whom it was built or created. Include a list of the web addresses you use.

    To find helpful web sites, use a search engine—such as Google (**http://www.google.com**), or Yahoo! (**http://www.yahoo.com**), and type in keywords, such as "Statue of Liberty" or "national monuments."

# A Letter from the Desert

## Lt. Nicole A. Elwell and Jeff Elwell

*A letter from a young U.S. Army lieutenant gives us a true-to-life description of Iraq and its people.*

### Words to Know

**beater**  dilapidated, rusty car
**convoy**  protective escort for troops
**droves**  crowds, groups of people
**emerged**  came out, appeared
**equivalent**  equal
**humbled**  felt smaller
**impoverished**  poor, needy
**regime**  ruler, controlling authority
**sheepish**  guilty, embarrassed
**squelched**  put down, stopped

### Getting Started

Is there an impoverished neighborhood in the city or area in which you live?

T his is an excerpt from a letter from my 24-year-old daughter, a U.S. 1
Army first lieutenant somewhere near Baghdad. She is a 1997 graduate
of Westlake High School. She's bright, beautiful and highly educated—
college classroom educated, that is.

She has just taken the mid-term exam in "Iraq Reality 101." She e-mailed 2
her thoughts and insights to family members. This is the real deal, not a
pasteurized CNN–report. It is from a young soldier on the front lines, in
an environment far removed from our society, which has no concept of
how the Iraqis are living.

I'd say she passed the exam and received a lot more than just a letter 3
grade. She is no longer my little girl; she is my equal.

A few days ago my unit was getting ready to move again. We move 4
often, but most times it is during hours of darkness for obvious reasons.
This particular time we moved during daylight hours, and it was the first
time I really saw Iraq.

Our convoy rolled out onto one of the few hard-surface roads in the 5 country. As we traveled down the pavement, droves of locals lined the road as though they were getting ready to watch a parade. The children ran towards us as fast as their little legs could carry them, not wanting to miss one truck as it went by.

The houses that the locals emerged from were nothing more than 6 earth and mud huts. Some had bricks cemented together with mud, and some had a mixture of mud and palm leaves from the few palm trees along the Euphrates river. These dwellings were far more impoverished than anything I have ever seen in America.

None had running water, electricity or indoor plumbing; most had fires 7 behind the house for cooking. Most, if not all, families have farm animals. These animals physically live with the people, generally in the front yard or on the side of the hut. They do not have pens, and many children find pleasure in playing with them.

Few people have cars. Most of the people I saw used a donkey and 8 buggy or cart to move goods from place to place. The cars I did see were equivalent to an American beater—complete with busted windows and rusted-out quarter panels.

Many times the cars were jammed with people, like the clown car at the 9 circus. I wondered how the car could run at all. As the convoy passed, the people vigorously waved and smiled. Some gave us the "thumbs up" sign to convey their support, which is surprising considering that the "thumbs up" sign in the Arab culture is equivalent to giving someone the finger. (It is amazing to see how quickly the people adapt to our ways and our customs.)

I happily waved back. The men are like the children. They wave and clap 10 and say "thank you." They even like to catcall at the female soldiers. Most of these calls are quickly squelched when they see the M4 I carry, locked and loaded. Their forward demeanor quickly changes to a sheepish grin.

The women are far different. It is evident that they are not allowed to 11 speak. . . . When you pass them on the road, they are usually working in the fields or tending to the livestock. If they are on the shoulder of the road, they are carrying heavy loads. They will rarely make eye contact with you if they are in the presence of a male. If they do make eye contact, it is only for a second, and then they look away. They rarely smile because they aren't allowed, and there seems to be little in their lives to smile about.

They hide behind doors (if their dwellings have them), but you can see 12 they are curious about us. Overall, the people are friendly and are just as interested in us as we are in awe of them.

The children upset me the most. They are dirty and skinny, but they 13 have the most incredible smiles. Their clothes look like hand-me-downs. I didn't see one child with what appeared to be new clothes.

There was one incident that will stay with me forever. We were driving, 14 and the children were standing on the side of the road. There was a little boy up ahead of us about 150 meters. He appeared to be blowing kisses.

I commented to my driver how adorable the little boy was, but as I got 15 closer I realized he wasn't blowing kisses. He was begging for water. His motion that I mistook for blowing kisses was the sign for food and water. By the time I realized this, I didn't have time to toss the remaining water I had in my water bottle out the window. I suddenly felt so guilty. I felt guilty because I couldn't stop, and I hadn't understood his need in time.

A few hours before, a fellow officer and I were talking about my desire 16 to go to the beach on vacation and eat at the Outback every night for a week. It seemed greedy and selfish compared to the simple desire of that one little boy. . . . I will never forget him, and I am humbled by his struggle and his courage.

As I passed more children, returning their waves and smiles, I realized 17 that this is the only life they know. This is the extent of their prosperity, their education, their life, unless someone helps them to change it.

The current regime keeps them in poverty. Seeing their faces makes 18 the time away from friends and loved ones worth it. Knowing that in some way the few months to a year that I spend here will help change their lives. I might have an indirect hand in helping children learn to read or to fearlessly express their own opinions.

I even might help the women in this country gain some equality. With 19 Saddam gone, the possibilities are endless.

Knowing this makes not taking a shower every day, sleeping on the 20 ground out in the open or on top of my vehicle, eating MREs and dealing with the constant movement seem unimportant.

Seeing Iraq has changed my outlook on life. I wish that I could share 21 it with you all firsthand—so that you too may experience the people and appreciate the gift we have in being Americans. . . . I will always remember that little boy each and every time I want to complain about my life . . . each time I gripe about the bills for my electricity, water, food and clothing. We are truly the lucky ones.

---

## Questions About the Reading

1. What were the houses and living conditions that the writer saw as the convoy moved along the road?
2. How did the Iraqi people act toward the U.S. Army soldiers?
3. How did the people react when they saw the lieutenant's M4 gun?
4. How did the Iraqi women act as the convoy passed them?

5. What did the little boy want, and how did the lieutenant feel about not understanding what he wanted?
6. What does the lieutenant hope will result from her tour of duty in Iraq?

## Questions About the Writer's Strategies

1. What is the thesis of the essay? Is it stated or implied? If stated, identify the sentences.
2. Is the essay objective, subjective, or both? If both, identify at least two objective and two subjective sentences.
3. What are some of the details the writer uses to describe the way the Iraqi people treat the soldiers?
4. What are the similes in paragraphs 9, 10, and 13?
5. What order does the writer use? Why do you think she chose that order?

## Writing Assignments

1. Write an essay describing the most impoverished neighborhood in your city or the area in which you live.
2. Write an essay describing the people and children of your neighborhood.
3. Write an essay describing the houses and buildings in a rural area.

# Regular Customer

## Gloria Garrison (student)

*The customer who comes into the coffee shop every morning is not only there every day but also orders the same things and behaves the same way every day.*

### Words to Know

**abduction**   unlawful taking of a person by force, kidnapping
**FBI**   Federal Bureau of Investigation
**periodically**   from time to time, on a regular basis
**tattered**   ragged, worn

### Getting Started

Do you follow the same routine every day in getting ready for school, or do you know a person whom you would call a "creature of habit"?

---

7:00 A.M. and Miss P. enters the coffee shop to order her usual blend, 1 heated in the microwave for 45 seconds. She places her cardboard box on the counter. "Dear, could you watch this for me?" Miss P. asks with a sweet, sane smile. "I am being followed again this morning." The FBI has been following her for the past thirty years; she knows government secrets, you see. I nod my head as I pour her coffee. Like yesterday and the day before, she proceeds to gather a napkin, stir straw, three sugars, and two creamers; places them on her table and comes back for her package. She would like a glass of water for her friend who is joining her this morning; and waves to an empty chair.

Regular customers flow in and out, casting sidelong glances at Miss P. 2 conversing with her friend about FBI aliens and her abduction to Barbados. Customers order and exit; New Orleans' life streams on outside. "The coffee is so good today, I will have to have another cup," Miss P. chirps. "Remember, 45 seconds. It really brings out the flavor. Oh, could I have a little more ice for my friend?"

Miss P., standing at the corner, tall and thin, keeps glancing over her 3 shoulder toward her box. "Help me keep an eye on that would you, dear?" She starts gathering her items again, same order, same amount. Miss P. wears the same blue outfit everyday: blue pants, blue shirt, very clean, very neat. The only thing that she changes are her gloves. Today she is wearing tattered silk elbow gloves, one pink, one dingy white. I give Miss P. her coffee; customers enter, a line forms. Miss P., turning to her corner table, stops. She says to me, "You are a very nice girl. I know because I was a nice girl. I went to Mexico when I was young. . . ." She goes on about her near corruption by a young gentleman, though she explains that she preserved her chastity, and warns I should do the same. Customers shift and roll their eyes, all wanting to order their usual. Miss P. returns to her table. I serve the customers—most order to go, busy, busy, hurry, hurry.

Miss P. has a ritual to drink her coffee. During my first week of train-    4
ing, Sally, one of the other waitresses, nudged me, "Take a look at what she does." Miss P. first arranges a napkin around her coffee cup, then takes the three sugars and packs them furiously, her mouth counting off the number. She pours the sugars, then starts to pack her creamer; she uses one and stashes the other, stirs and stirs. Then Miss P. drinks her coffee and stares out the window.

In between her sips, Miss P. periodically checks everything in her box.    5
She sips, and then pushes her coffee aside and flips through every file folder, twice. Assured, she slides the box aside and returns to her coffee. She sips, and then checks her gloves. She holds out her hand, as if admiring an expensive ring, turns her head this way and that way, brushes off her gloves, straightens and pulls the gloves to order. Satisfied, she sips her coffee and starts to fidget with her hair, patting front and back. Her attention turns to the coffee; she wraps her hands around the cup and frowns and stands. I try to look busy. "Excuse me, my coffee has cooled, could you please warm it up?" She smiles anxiously. "Remember, 45 seconds. It makes all the difference." Coffee placed in the microwave, we wait. Miss P. leans forward. "One day," she pauses and puts her hand to her mouth, smiles and continues, "I want to try the flavored coffee, but I just can't." She sighs, "The regular is so good today." She receives her coffee and toddles off to her table, where she sips.

Midmorning. Miss P. starts to straighten her mess, wiping and stack-    6
ing. She gathers her box, pats her hair. "Good day, I'll see you tomorrow. The coffee was delicious today." I watch her blue form disappear into the day outside. The shop is empty now. A car pulls up, another customer who proceeds to order the usual. I fix it the same way for her today as I will tomorrow. The same way I fix coffee for Miss P., only without the 45 seconds. The day will go the same as it did yesterday, the same tomorrow, the same rituals. Same.

7:00 A.M. and Miss P. enters the coffee shop to order her usual house    7
blend, heated in the microwave for 45 seconds. Like yesterday, she places her cardboard box on the counter. "Dear, could you watch this for me?"

Miss P. says with a sweet, sane smile. "I am being followed again this morning." The FBI has been following her for the past thirty years; she knows government secrets, you see.

---

## Questions About the Reading

1. What is the customer's usual order in the coffee shop?
2. Who is the friend the customer says is with her? What does the customer order for her friend?
3. Who does the customer say is following her? Why?
4. What does the customer say happened to her when she was young?

## Questions About the Writer's Strategies

1. What is the thesis of the essay? Is it stated or implied? If stated, identify the sentence or sentences in which it is stated. If implied, state the thesis in your own words.
2. What is the significance of Miss P.'s always wearing the same blue outfit?
3. Why do you think the first five sentences of the essay and the last paragraph are the same?

## Writing Assignments

1. *Working Together*   Go to at least three coffee shops or breakfast places on three different mornings and observe the customers. Write an essay in which you describe the customers and what they order.
2. Go to a grocery store and observe the customers and what they buy. Write an essay in which you describe the customers and their purchases.

# Limbo

### *Rhonda S. Lucas (student)*

*A new experience, a change in our lives, can make us see familiar objects in a new light. And a new location can make an old possession—a piece of furniture, an article of clothing—look strange. Rhonda S. Lucas, a student at East Los Angeles College, discovered both these things one day as she sat in a garage full of packing boxes and old furniture. In this essay, she describes what she saw.*

### Words to Know

**cryptic**   secret, mystifying

**dilapidated**   fallen into a state of disrepair

**elegy**   a mournful poem or song, often lamenting the dead

**futility**   uselessness

**irony**   the use of words to convey the opposite of their literal meaning

**limbo**   an intermediate place or state; a region or condition of oblivion or neglect

**tubular**   having the form of a tube

### Getting Started

If you had to leave your house tomorrow, what would you miss most about it?

---

**M**y parents' divorce was final. The house had been sold and the day   1
had come to move. Thirty years of the family's life were now crammed into the garage. The two-by-fours that ran the length of the walls were the only uniformity among the clutter of boxes, furniture, and memories. All was frozen in limbo between the life just passed and the one to come.

The sunlight pushing its way through the window splattered against a   2
barricade of boxes. Like a fluorescent river, it streamed down the sides and flooded the cracks of the cold, cement floor. I stood in the doorway between the house and garage and wondered if the sunlight would ever again penetrate the memories packed inside those boxes. For an instant, the cardboard boxes appeared as tombstones, monuments to those memories.

The furnace in the corner, with its huge tubular fingers reaching out and   3
disappearing into the wall, was unaware of the futility of trying to warm the empty house. The rhythmical whir of its effort hummed the elegy for the memories boxed in front of me. I closed the door, sat down on the step,

and listened reverently. The feeling of loss transformed the bad memories into not-so-bad, the not-so-bad memories into good, and committed the good ones to my mind. Still, I felt as vacant as the house inside.

A workbench to my right stood disgustingly empty. Not so much as a 4 nail had been left behind. I noticed, for the first time, what a dull, lifeless green it was. Lacking the disarray of tools that used to cover it, now it seemed as out of place as a bathtub in the kitchen. In fact, as I scanned the room, the only things that did seem to belong were the cobwebs in the corners.

A group of boxes had been set aside from the others and stacked in 5 front of the workbench. Scrawled like graffiti on the walls of dilapidated buildings were the words "Salvation Army." Those words caught my eyes as effectively as a flashing neon sign. They reeked of irony. "Salvation— was a bit too late for this family," I mumbled sarcastically to myself.

The houseful of furniture that had once been so carefully chosen to com- 6 plement and blend with the color schemes of the various rooms was indiscriminately crammed together against a single wall. The uncoordinated colors combined in turmoil and lashed out in the greyness of the room.

I suddenly became aware of the coldness of the garage, but I didn't want 7 to go back inside the house, so I made my way through the boxes to the couch. I cleared a space to lie down and curled up, covering myself with my jacket. I hoped my father would return soon with the truck so we could empty the garage and leave the cryptic silence of parting lives behind.

## Questions About the Reading

1. Why is the title of this essay "Limbo"? Between which two stages of life is the writer?
2. How does the writer feel about moving out of the house?
3. Why does the writer view the empty workbench as disgusting (paragraph 4)?
4. Why didn't she want to go back inside the house?
5. What does Lucas mean in the last line by the "cryptic silence" of the house?

## Questions About the Writer's Strategies

1. Although she never says it, the writer is saddened by her parents' divorce and the subsequent need to move. What details does she use to convey this feeling?

2. In what ways is this an extremely subjective essay?
3. Give your impression of the writer's life before her parents' divorce. What methods does she use to suggest this impression?
4. What is the thesis statement in the essay? Which paragraphs are used to develop the thesis statement? Is there a concluding paragraph?
5. What is the purpose of the metaphor in the last sentence of paragraph 2? In which sentence of paragraph 3 is the metaphor repeated?

## Writing Assignments

1. Write an essay describing your favorite room in the house where you live now or the one where you grew up. Try to use examples from your life to give meaning to the objects you describe.
2. Write an essay describing a walk through your neighborhood or another one with which you are familiar. Describe the things that most interest you or that you think you will remember best in the future.

# 4  Examples

AN EXAMPLE IS a specific instance or fact that is used to support an idea or a general statement. As you learned in chapter 1, the topic sentence states the main idea of a paragraph, and the thesis statement states the main idea of an essay. Both must be supported through a mode of development, which the writer selects. Writers frequently use **examples** to explain or illustrate a main idea, as in the following paragraph.

| | |
|---|---|
| Topic sentence | As they had resolved to do, my siblings took any job they could find to survive. In Montreal, Luong went to work at a |
| Example | plastics factory, mixing resins, until he found a job in the city government. In California, Zuong began working at a hotel, |
| Example | while his wife Hao started assembling electronics components in a factory; they became self-sufficient so quickly that they never had to resort to welfare. In Australia, Phu took a |
| Example | job as a cleaning lady until she got a position in the post office. (My nephew Nam went back to school and, after tak- |
| Example | ing a series of jobs, became a real estate agent.) Tuyet, in |
| Example | Paris, also started out as a cleaning lady for an office, and eventually found a position in a government agency. |

Dugong Van Mai Elliott, *The Sacred Willow,*
Oxford University Press, © 1999, p. 465

Some writers announce their strategy by the transitional words *for instance, to illustrate,* or *for example.* Other times, as in the sentences about the jobs the writer's siblings got, the writer expects the reader to notice that these are examples and that they support the topic of the paragraph.

To make a clear case, the writer usually needs to give several examples. The order in which the examples are presented may be **chronological**— that is, in sequence according to time. In other cases, **order of importance** may be more effective, with the most important or convincing example presented last. In still other cases, the writer may use an example at the beginning of the essay to capture the reader's interest and to illustrate the **thesis,** which is stated later. The selection that follows illustrates the use of an introductory example.

The red-and-white pickup bounced along a gravel road in          1
north-central Washington State. It was just past midnight on
a summer Saturday last year. Two boys and two girls, recent
graduates of Tonasket High School, had been "cruising" for
a couple of hours, talking and laughing. At a sharp curve,
the pickup somehow went off the road, rolled down the
steep, rocky mountainside and twisted around a pine tree.

**Example used to introduce essay**
All four occupants—none wearing a seat belt—were tossed
out of the cab.

Driver Joe McDaniel escaped with cuts on his face and          2
arms. Josh Wheeler suffered bruises but was able to cradle
Amy Burdick in his arms until help arrived. She died the
next day. Katy Watson, a former cheerleader who had won a
scholarship to college, was dead at the scene, with massive
chest and back injuries.

**Thesis statement**
Motor-vehicle injury is the greatest threat to the lives of          3
adolescents in America. During the 1980s, over 74,000 teenagers were killed in such accidents, more than died from all
diseases combined. On average, every two or three weeks the
equivalent of a senior class at a typical high school is wiped
out on our streets and highways. The National Safety Council
(NSC) estimates that the financial toll is at least $10 billion an-
nually for medical and insurance costs, property damage and
lost wages resulting from accidents involving teen drivers.

*Reader's Digest,* June 1991

Examples in an essay can both illustrate and **support** the thesis. That is, if a writer makes a claim or a point in the **thesis statement** and then provides evidence in the form of actual situations that illustrate the thesis, it will help convince the reader that the thesis is valid. When you write, you should also search for examples as a way to test your thesis. For example, if you cannot think of a single specific example that supports your main idea, you will need to rethink your main idea. Or if you think of several examples that support your thesis, but also of several that work against it, you might want to revise your thesis and develop an **objective** essay presenting both sides of the issue.

In addition to providing concrete support for the thesis, examples can be used to enliven and clarify writing. In a description, for instance, examples can supply concrete details that add variety and interest. A single example may also be **extended** throughout an essay to illustrate the thesis, as in the following essay about the Kickapoo Indian Medicine Company. Notice, too, that minor examples are also used within the essay, as in paragraphs 2 and 3, to support the topic sentences of some paragraphs.

**Thesis**
By 1880 several hundred medicine shows were traveling in          1
the United States, giving performances varying from simple

<table>
<tr><td>

Major extended
example—from
here to end of
essay

</td><td>

magic acts to elaborate "med-presentations." Among the largest of such operations from 1880 to 1910 was the Kickapoo Indian Medicine Company, "The King of Road Shows." Founded by two veteran troupers, John E. "Doc" Healy and Charles H. "Texas Charlie" Bigelow, the Kickapoo Company maintained a large headquarters building, "The Principal Wigwam," in New Haven, Connecticut, and from there sent out shows, as many as twenty-five at a time, to cities and villages throughout the country.

</td></tr>
</table>

Major extended example—from here to end of essay

magic acts to elaborate "med-presentations." Among the largest of such operations from 1880 to 1910 was the Kickapoo Indian Medicine Company, "The King of Road Shows." Founded by two veteran troupers, John E. "Doc" Healy and Charles H. "Texas Charlie" Bigelow, the Kickapoo Company maintained a large headquarters building, "The Principal Wigwam," in New Haven, Connecticut, and from there sent out shows, as many as twenty-five at a time, to cities and villages throughout the country.

Minor examples of *performers* who were hired

2 Doc Healy hired performers, both Indian and white—dancers, singers, jugglers, fire-eaters, acrobats, comedians, fiddlers—and Texas Charlie managed the medicine business and trained the "Doctors" and "Professors" who gave "Medical Lectures."

Minor examples of *distinctively garbed* troupe members

3 All troupe members were distinctively garbed. The Indians—including Mohawks, Iroquois, Crees, Sioux, and Blackfeet—billed as "all pure-blooded Kickapoos, the most noted of all Indian Medical People," were adorned with colored beads and feathers and loaded down with primitive weapons; they trailed great strings of unidentified hairy objects. Some lecturers wore western-style leather clothes and boots with silver-capped toes, others fancy silk shirts, frock coats, and high silk hats. One of the most colorful Kickapoo figures was smooth-talking Ned T. Oliver—"Nevada Ned, the King of Gold"—who wore an enormous sombrero from the brim of which dangled 100 gold coins, and a fancy suit loaded with buttons made of gold pieces.

4 The Kickapoo shows were presented under canvas at "Kickapoo Camps" during the summer and in opera houses and town halls in winter. On many nights the show was free to all, on others each adult was charged 10¢. The money poured in from medicine sales.

5 The wonder-working Kickapoo concoctions were "compounded according to secret ancient Kickapoo Indian tribal formulas" from "blood root, feverwort, spirit gum, wild poke berries, sassafras, slippery elm, wintergreen, white oak bark, yellow birch bark, dock root, sarsaparilla, and other Natural Products." The medicines were made in the Connecticut factory in vats so huge the "mixers" had to perch on ladders and wield long paddles. The leader of the Kickapoo line was Sagwa, which sold at 50¢ and $1 per bottle—"Sagwa, the wonderful remedy for catarrh, pulmonary consumption, and all ills that afflict the human body. It is made from roots, barks, gums, leaves, oils, and berries gathered by little Kickapoo children from God's great laboratory, the fertile fields and vast forests. Sagwa, Nature's own great secret cure, now available to all mankind!"

6 Long after the Kickapoo Company was dissolved, a woman who had worked in the medicine factory recalled that one of the ingredients of Kickapoo Cough Syrup was

Jamaica rum. Could this "cure" have been the inspiration for the "Kickapoo Joy Juice" Al Capp featured in his popular comic strip?

Peggy Robbins,
"The Kickapoo Indian Medicine Company"

In this essay, the writer's use of concrete examples gives us a clear picture of the Kickapoo medicine show. In addition, the great number and the variety of minor examples give us a good idea of the crazy-quilt nature of medicine shows in general.

When using examples in your own writing, **brainstorm** for possibilities (as described in chapter 1) and select those that illustrate your idea most accurately. In choosing among possibilities, select those that you sense your reader will respond to as convincing and colorful. Several well-chosen examples will hold your reader's interest and add credibility to your main idea.

# Distance Learning

*Mary Lord*

*Computers and the Internet have opened up a new way of learning for people who need or want to add to their knowledge.*

### Words to Know

**buffing**  polishing, adding to
**credentials**  credit, authority

### Getting Started

Does your college offer some courses through distance learning?

T he old correspondence course has stormed into the high-tech age—and it's proving to be a big hit. As many as 4 million Americans are now buffing their professional credentials by padding over to their PCs and plugging into "distance learning." Need to get over your fear of public speaking? Front Range Community College near Denver will teach you the techniques over the Internet. (Note: There's no escaping four live on-campus presentations.) How about accounting? Great Britain's Open University, with nearly 150,000 students worldwide, offers a highly regarded curriculum. The University of Massachusetts at Dartmouth recently started an online course in writing for the World Wide Web.

## Questions About the Reading

1. According to the writer, how many people are now taking courses by distance learning?
2. What is the special requirement for the public speaking course offered by Front Range Community College?
3. What university offers an accounting course by distance learning?
4. What university offers a distance-learning course in writing?

## Questions About the Writer's Strategies

1. What is the main idea of the paragraph? Is it stated or implied? If stated, identify the sentence or sentences in which it is stated. If implied, state the main idea in your own words.

2. What is the order the writer uses in giving examples of distance-learning courses? Why do you think she uses that order?
3. If you were to change the order of the examples, how would you change them? Why?

## Writing Assignments

1. If your college provides courses through distance learning, write a paragraph in which you give examples of such courses that are related to your major.
2. Write a paragraph in which you give examples of the advantages and disadvantages of taking a course through distance learning.

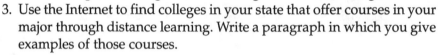

3. Use the Internet to find colleges in your state that offer courses in your major through distance learning. Write a paragraph in which you give examples of those courses.

# The Digital Revolution

*Ellen Cobb Wade*

*In a technological revolution, we have a lot to learn—not the least of which is how to program all those new devices we have. Here, the writer gives us an example of one of them—the digital clock radio—and its programmable options.*

### Words to Know
**activate**   start
**formidable**   fearful, difficult

### Getting Started
What digital devices do you have?

---

The digital revolution caused a lot of . . . confusion. A clock radio, for example, used to have a face and a slender hand that you'd set pointing to the time you wanted to get up. Nowadays, a clock radio is a formidable machine: programmable to the minute, it can wake you and your mate at different times, let one or both of you "snooze," [and] even activate the coffee maker. But just unplug the thing for a tenth of a second, and you'll be back studying the owner's manual as the display automatically blinks out 12:00—as though time were standing still.

---

## Questions About the Reading

1. What can you set a digital clock radio to do?
2. What happens if the digital clock radio is unplugged?

## Questions About the Writer's Strategies

1. What is the main idea of the paragraph? Is it stated or implied? State the main idea (topic) in your own words.
2. What is the point of view of the paragraph?

## Writing Assignments

1. Write a paragraph in which you give examples of one or more of the digital devices you own or would like to own and the capabilities of each one.
2. Write a paragraph in which you give examples of the problems of programming a digital device you own or would like to own.

# Boomtown, U.S.A.

*Jeff Glasser*

*The small town of Bentonville, Arkansas, "booms" after three businesses move into the town.*

## Words to Know

**titan**   person of great size or power

**spurned**   rejected

**Xanadu**   a place in Mongolia described in the poem "Kubla Khan" by Samuel Taylor Coleridge

## Getting Started

Has the town or area in which you live been changed by unemployment, loss of a business, or development of a shopping center?

---

$S$am Walton would not recognize the place. The famously unassuming Wal-Mart founder spurned foreign cars for his red Ford pickup, and he expected his employees to shun a "big showy lifestyle." But today in Mr. Sam's parking lot at Wal-Mart headquarters here, Mercedes Kompressor convertibles shine in the sun alongside BMW M3s. Not far away, Wal-Mart's chief executive and senior vice president live in splendor at Pinnacle, the area's first gated community and its most exclusive country club. Their neighbor, Red Hudson, a retired multimillionaire meat-packer, has built a 17,784-square-foot mansion there—complete with Italian marble and Minnesota stone—for a much-gossiped-about $10 million. Across the new Interstate 540 from Pinnacle, trucking titan J. B. Hunt is trying to erect his own Xanadu, with a dozen deluxe office and condominium towers, a hospital, and, in a first for the region, a skyline. "Everything's a poppin'," says the 74-year-old Hunt as he tools around the site in his tan GMC Sierra truck. "In the next five years, the weeds will be a city."

---

## Questions About the Reading

1. Why would Sam Walton "not recognize the place"?
2. What is Red Hudson's business?
3. What is J. B. Hunt's business? Why is he called a "titan"?

4. What is the "first for the region"?
5. What does J. B. Hunt mean when he says, "In the next five years, the weeds will be a city"?

## Questions About the Writer's Strategies

1. What is the main idea of the paragraph? State it in your own words.
2. What are the examples that support the main idea?
3. What is the metaphor in the paragraph?

## Writing Assignments

1. Write a paragraph giving specific examples of the effect on your town of unemployment or loss of a business.
2. Interview some residents who were displaced by a building project in your town and write a paragraph using examples of how the displacement changed their lives.
3. These are the first two lines of the poem "Kubla Khan."

> In Xanadu did Kubla Khan
> A stately pleasure-dome decree

Write a paragraph explaining the relation of Xanadu to J. B. Hunt's building project.

# Folk Art in the Barrios

*Eric Kroll*

*In this paragraph, Eric Kroll describes the wall paintings in Santa Fe, New Mexico, that depict a bold and colorful Chicano history and that defy stereotypes.*

### Words to Know

**Aztec**   early people of Mexico
**disproportionate**   not in proportion, not actual size
**Father Hidalgo**   Miguel Hidalgo y Costilla (1753–1811), a Catholic priest who launched the revolution to free Mexico from Spanish rule
**Pancho Villa**   Mexican revolutionary leader

### Getting Started

Have you ever looked at a painting of a famous person and thought that it wasn't accurate?

O n ten Santa Fe walls, the history of the Chicanos, both mythical and actual, is depicted in brilliant colors and disproportionate figures. Aztec medicine figures dance and gods protect peasants, all for the glory of the Chicano in the present. On some walls, the chains of bondage are being broken and the Lady of Justice, depicted as an Indian Maiden, watches over both Indians and Chicanos. On others, Pancho Villa and Father Hidalgo lead the Mexican peasants to freedom. But the clenched fist at the end of the grotesquely muscled arms is the most predominant image. It symbolizes unity, determination, ambition, and pride, all traits that Los Artes believe should be a part of Chicano psychology. The figures they paint are bold, upright, strong, and grasping, far from the stereotype of the Mexican-American with drooping moustache and floppy sombrero lying in the shade of a stucco building.

## Questions About the Reading

1. On how many walls in Santa Fe are there paintings of Chicano history?
2. What is the purpose of the paintings?
3. What does the clenched fist in the paintings symbolize?

4. How do the figures in the paintings differ from the stereotype the author describes at the end of the paragraph?

## Questions About the Writer's Strategies

1. What is the main idea (topic) of the paragraph?
2. What examples depict the freedom of Mexican peasants?
3. What is the metaphor for the traits that the artists believe the Chicanos should have?
4. What descriptive words are used for the figures in the paintings?
5. What descriptive words are used for the Mexican-American stereotype?

## Writing Assignments

1. Write a paragraph in which you use examples to describe the behavior of a television personality.
2. Write a paragraph using examples to illustrate the traditions of different ethnic groups in your city.

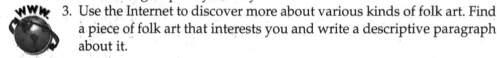

3. Use the Internet to discover more about various kinds of folk art. Find a piece of folk art that interests you and write a descriptive paragraph about it.

# My Suit

*Ricardo Galvez (student)*

*Ricardo Galvez, a student at Los Angeles Harbor College in California, shows us with examples that the way people dress influences the way they are treated by others.*

### Words to Know
**drenching**  soaking, saturating
**merit**  value, worth

### Getting Started
Have you ever felt you were treated better or worse because of the clothes you were wearing?

---

I had once been told that people are treated primarily according to the way they dress. With this in mind, I gathered all of my suits and selected the best one. I wore it to church that Sunday. To my surprise, I found this statement to have some merit. After mass I went to lunch with the singles' group from church. Wearing a tie made my neck feel as if I had been hanging at the end of a rope. I was beginning to perspire quite heavily under the miserably hot sun and drenching humid air. The dress shoes were also uncomfortable and I almost fell as I slipped on a slice of banana near the buffet table. Nevertheless, it was well worth the sacrifice. Usually I had to wait fifteen minutes for a table for two. That day I was tended to immediately, and I even reserved a large table for all of the singles while they found parking spaces outside. More important, I met a sweet, attractive young lady who asked me to accompany her to a dance. The next fourteen months of courtship that followed made me aware of the fact that to feel miserable didn't have to mean that I had to be miserable. Being with her made me forget all discomfort.

---

## Questions About the Reading

1. Did the writer have several suits? If so, which of his suits did the writer select to wear?
2. Whom did the writer go to lunch with after church?

3. How did wearing a tie make the writer feel?
4. Did the writer feel it was worthwhile to be uncomfortable in his suit and shoes? Why?

## Questions About the Writer's Strategies

1. What is the main idea of the paragraph? Does the writer state the main idea directly? If so, in which sentence?
2. What are the examples the writer uses to prove his main idea?
3. What is the order in which the writer tells us about his experience?
4. What is the point of view of the paragraph in person, time, and tone?

## Writing Assignments

1. Write a paragraph in which you use examples to tell about an experience you had that was related to the clothes you were wearing.
2. Assume you have had an interview for a job you want. Write a paragraph in which you give examples of what you wore and how you think your clothes influenced the success or failure of the interview.

# The Social Meaning of T-shirts

*Diana Crane*

*The T-shirt has become popular for expressing the wearer's support for an organization or a cause.*

### Words to Know

**cachet**  approval
**coopted**  used, taken

### Getting Started

What T-shirts are in your closet, and what do they say about you?

$T$ he use of a specific type of clothing—the T-shirt—to communicate  1
other types of information began in the late 1940s, when faces and political slogans appeared on T-shirts and, in the 1960s, with commercial logos
and other designs. Technical developments in the 1950s and 1960s, such
as plastic inks, plastic transfers, and spray paint, led to the use of colored
designs and increased the possibilities of the T-shirt as a means of communication. Approximately one billion T-shirts are purchased annually
in the United States (McGraw 1996).

The T-shirt performs a function formerly associated with the hat, that  2
of identifying an individual's social location instantly. Unlike the hat in the
nineteenth century, which signaled (or concealed) social class status, the
T-shirt speaks to issues related to ideology, difference, and myth: politics,
race, gender, and leisure. The variety of slogans and logos that appear on
T-shirts is enormous. Much of the time, people consent to being coopted
for "unpaid advertising" for global corporations selling clothes, music,
sports, and entertainment in exchange for the social cachet of being associated with certain products (McGraw 1996). Some of the time, people
use T-shirts to indicate their support for social and political causes, groups,
or organizations to which they have made a commitment. Occasionally, the
T-shirt becomes a medium for grass-roots resistance. Bootlegged T-shirts
representing characters on the television show *The Simpsons* appeared in
response to T-shirts marketed by the network that produced the show
(Parisi 1993). The bootlegged T-shirts represented the Simpson family as
African Americans. Bart Simpson was shown as Rastabart, with dreadlocks

and a red, green, and gold headband, as Rasta-dude Bart Marley, and as black Bart, paired with Nelson Mandela. Using clothing behavior as a means of making a statement, the T-shirts appeared to be intended as an affirmation of African Americans as an ethnic group and as a commentary on the narrow range of roles for black characters in the show. Victims of gender-related violence, such as rape, incest, battering, and sexual harassment, have used T-shirts as venues for statements about their experiences that are exhibited in clotheslines in public plazas (Ostrowski 1996). By contrast, some young men use T-shirts to express hostile, aggressive, or obscene sentiments denigrating women or to display pictures of guns and pistols (Cose 1993; *Time* 1992). Teens of both sexes use them as a means of expressing their cynicism about the dominant culture, particularly global advertising (Sepulchre 1994b).

The significance of the T-shirt in Western culture, as a means of social     3 and political expression, is seen by comparing its roles in Western countries with the response to it in a nondemocratic country, the People's Republic of China (Barmé 1993). In 1991, a young Chinese artist created T-shirts bearing humorous statements, some of which could be interpreted as having mild political implications. The T-shirts were enormously successful with the public but were perceived as "a serious political incident" by the Chinese authorities. The artist was arrested and interrogated, and the T-shirts were officially banned. Thousands of them were confiscated and destroyed, although many Chinese continued to wear them.

## Questions About the Reading

1. When did T-shirts begin to be used to communicate information?
2. What developments increased the use of T-shirts to communicate?
3. How does the use of the T-shirt to communicate differ from the use of the hat?
4. What "statement" did the Bart Simpson T-shirt seem to make?
5. What happened to the Chinese artist and the T-shirts he created? Why?

## Questions About the Writer's Strategies

1. What is the thesis of the essay? State it in your own words.
2. What are the specific examples the writer uses to support her thesis?
3. What is each example meant to communicate?

4. Could the second paragraph be made into more than one paragraph? If so, how? What would be the topic sentence of each paragraph?

## Writing Assignments

1. Write an essay using examples of each T-shirt you own that has lettering on it and explain what it "says" about you.
2. *Working Together*   Join with some classmates to write an essay using examples of the T-shirts each of you owns and explain what each T-shirt communicates about the wearer.

# Foreign Flavors, Mainstream Taste

**Debra Aho Williamson**

*Ethnic foods are going mainstream because a taste for them is shared by all of us.*

### Words to Know

**demographically diverse**  statistically different as to race, ethnicity, and other factors

**emporium**  large store, marketplace

**gelatinous**  like gelatin, jellylike

### Getting Started

What ethnic foods are available in your neighborhood grocery store?

---

To understand how the changing tastes of the U.S. consumer are 1 affecting food marketing, pay a visit to the Uwajimaya supermarket in downtown Seattle.

This is no tiny, cluttered store on a side street in Chinatown. A 50,000- 2 square-foot retail emporium a few blocks from Safeco Field, Uwajimaya carries everything you could imagine for Asian cooking. There's an entire aisle of nothing but noodles. A produce section with so many exotic-looking vegetables that the clerks have created handwritten signs describing what they are. There's sushi-grade seafood, several varieties of Chinese black bean sauce and frozen mochi desserts—ice cream balls rolled in a gelatinous coating, sold individually or in six-packs.

On a busy recent afternoon before a Mariners home game, you notice 3 something else unusual. Yes, there are people of Asian descent here, but there also are a striking number of non-Asians. In fact, a full 30% of Uwajimaya's customers are not Asian, and the store has even become a tourist destination.

"Mainstreaming is the name of the game," says Tomoko Moriguchi- 4 Matsuno, Uwajimaya's VP-retail. "It's food. It's not Chinese, Japanese, Korean. People are more interested in food, and they're more open to different things."

That, in a nutshell, is what many in the food business believe is the  5
future of food marketing. As the U.S. has become more demographically
diverse, food and restaurant marketers have expanded their palates to
reach growing Hispanic and Asian populations. But at the same time,
marketers are broadening their offerings to the general market to include
new flavors and stronger tastes.

Even chicken soup stalwart Campbell Soup Co. is getting in the game.  6
Its Stockpot subsidiary, a supplier to restaurants, is planning to launch a
three-item line of Asian-flavor sauces and soup bases, including a Viet-
namese broth called *pho*. So far there's no indication that the red-and-
white label will include pho, but Stockpot acknowledges that Campbell's
foodservice units serve as test kitchens for future grocery products.

"The Away from Home division is a way for Campbell to keep its eye  7
on new flavor trends, so as these trends emerge, there is always an opportunity to incorporate them into retail products," says Kathleen Horner,
Stockpot's president.

Unilever recently introduced a five-item line of Lipton Asian-flavor side  8
dishes, including beef lo mein noodles and sweet and sour noodles. And
General Mills' Pillsbury Co. markets a flavor of Haagen-Dazs ice cream
called Dulce de Leche, a caramel and cream confection inspired by a Latin
American dessert.

There also are growing efforts to market more directly to Hispanics.  9
Gatorade Co.'s new Xtremo sports drink features flavors like mango and
tropical punch. PepsiCo sibling Frito-Lay recently launched a new version
of Doritos aimed at Hispanics in the U.S. And Doctor's Associates' Subway
Restaurants has been steadily ramping up a Hispanic ad campaign from
Havas' MVBMS Hispanic, New York, that launched last year. The campaign now accounts for about 5% to 10% of Subway's overall ad budget,
says Chris Carroll, director of marketing for the Subway Franchisee Advertising Board.

All this activity is coming about because the census is showing a dra-  10
matic rise in the Hispanic and Asian populations in the U.S. In 1990, 9% of
the U.S. population identified themselves as Hispanic and 2.9% as Asian
or Pacific Islander. By 2007, nearly 15% of the U.S. will be of Hispanic
ethnicity and nearly 5% Asian, according to projections from market researcher SRC.

Some marketers, like Kraft Foods, have used the new census data to  11
confirm what they already know. "Fundamentally, the country is changing, and to be where consumers want to be, you've got to change with it,"
says Linda Crowder, director of multicultural marketing. Kraft products
like Mayonesa con Limon (mayo with lemon) and Gelatina par Leche

(Jell-O with milk), both introduced in the past year, aim squarely at U.S. Hispanic tastes.

Hispanic consumers spend nearly 25% more than other consumer groups 12 on food consumed at home, according to researcher Packaged Facts. That's because Latino families tend to be larger and there's more focus on eating a meal at home.

Ethnic groups are "your biggest growth market," says Thomas Tseng, 13 director of marketing for Cultural Access Group, a Los Angeles ethnic market researcher.

While the black population is expected to remain flat, representing 14 about 12% of the population in 2007, according to SRC, it carries great weight. Among all U.S. ethnic groups, Mr. Tseng says African Americans possess the greatest purchasing power at $572 billion. "This consumer group often gets overlooked or is lumped in together with the general market since language is not an issue—most marketers think they reach this group with their general-market strategies, but they don't," he says. "African Americans possess distinct cultural attributes and affinities that translate into distinct food preferences and shopping behaviors. They shop more frequently, spend more money on food consumed at home, and are responsive to advertising aimed at them."

## Questions About the Reading

1. What kind of foods are carried in the Uwajimaya supermarket in Seattle?
2. What is meant by "the future of food marketing"?
3. Which ethnic group is expected to become nearly 15 percent of the United States population by 2007?
4. Which ethnic group spends "more than other consumer groups on food consumed at home"? Why?
5. Which population group has "the greatest purchasing power"? Why? Why is this group often overlooked?

## Questions About the Writer's Strategies

1. What is the thesis of the essay? Is it stated or implied? If stated, identify the sentences.
2. Does the writer use several examples or an extended example to support the thesis?
3. What is the writer's purpose in including the quoted information?

## Writing Assignments

1. *Working Together*   Join with some classmates to write an essay citing examples of the ethnic composition of the streets on which each of you lives.
2. Visit at least three supermarkets or neighborhood grocery stores and write an essay including examples of the various ethnic foods that each store carries.

# Between Two Wars, 1913–1945

*Kathryn VanSpanckeren*

*The writer details the changes that took place in the United States between World War I and World War II and provides examples of writers and novels in which the changes are depicted.*

## Words to Know

**edifice**   large, imposing building

**Freudian psychology**   psychoanalysis; treatment of mental disorders, based on the method developed by Sigmund Freud, an Austrian physician and psychiatrist

**proliferated**   grew by multiplying

**prophetically**   forecast the future

## Getting Started

What changes have taken place in your life since September 11, 2001? What changes do you think will take place in the United States following the end of the war on terrorism?

---

**M**any historians have characterized the period between the two    1
world wars as the United States' traumatic "coming of age," despite the fact that U.S. direct involvement was relatively brief (1917–1918) and its casualties many fewer than those of its European allies and foes. John Dos Passos expressed America's postwar disillusionment in the novel *Three Soldiers* (1921), when he noted that civilization was a "vast edifice of sham, and the war, instead of its crumbling, was its fullest and most ultimate expression." Shocked and permanently changed, Americans returned to their homeland but could never regain their innocence.

Nor could soldiers from rural America easily return to their roots.    2
After experiencing the world, many now yearned for a modern, urban life. New farm machines such as planters, harvesters, and binders had drastically reduced the demand for farm jobs; yet despite their increased productivity, farmers were poor. Crop prices, like urban workers' wages, depended on unrestrained market forces heavily influenced by business interests: Government subsidies for farmers and effective workers' unions had not yet become established. "The chief business of the American people is business," President Calvin Coolidge proclaimed in 1925, and most agreed.

In the postwar "Big Boom," business flourished, and the successful pros-  3
pered beyond their wildest dreams. For the first time, many Americans
enrolled in higher education—in the 1920s college enrollment doubled.
The middle-class prospered; Americans began to enjoy the world's highest national average income in this era, and many people purchased the
ultimate status symbol—an automobile. The typical urban American
home glowed with electric lights and boasted a radio that connected the
house with the outside world, and perhaps a telephone, a camera, a type-
writer, or a sewing machine. Like the businessman protagonist of Sinclair
Lewis's novel *Babbitt* (1922), the average American approved of these
machines because they were modern and because most were American
inventions and American-made.

Americans of the "Roaring Twenties" fell in love with other modern  4
entertainments. Most people went to the movies once a week. Although
Prohibition—a nationwide ban on the production, transport, and sale of
alcohol instituted through the 18th Amendment to the U.S. Constitution—
began in 1919, underground "speakeasies" and nightclubs proliferated,
featuring jazz music, cocktails, and daring modes of dress and dance.
Dancing, moviegoing, automobile touring, and radio were national crazes.
American women, in particular, felt liberated. Many had left farms and
villages for homefront duty in American cities during World War I, and
had become resolutely modern. They cut their hair short ("bobbed"),
wore short "flapper" dresses, and gloried in the right to vote assured by
the 19th Amendment to the Constitution, passed in 1920. They boldly
spoke their mind and took public roles in society.

Western youths were rebelling, angry and disillusioned with the sav-  5
age war, the older generation they held responsible, and difficult postwar
economic conditions that, ironically, allowed Americans with dollars—
like writers F. Scott Fitzgerald, Ernest Hemingway, Gertrude Stein, and
Ezra Pound—to live abroad handsomely on very little money. Intellectual
currents, particularly Freudian psychology and to a lesser extent Marx-
ism (like the earlier Darwinian theory of evolution), implied a "godless"
world view and contributed to the breakdown of traditional values. Americans abroad absorbed these views and brought them back to the United
States where they took root, firing the imagination of young writers and
artists. William Faulkner, for example, a 20th-century American novelist,
employed Freudian elements in all his works, as did virtually all serious
American fiction writers after World War I.

Despite outward gaiety, modernity, and unparalleled material prosper-  6
ity, young Americans of the 1920s were "the lost generation"—so named
by literary portraitist Gertrude Stein. Without a stable, traditional structure
of values, the individual lost a sense of identity. The secure, supportive

family life; the familiar, settled community; the natural and eternal rhythms of nature that guide the planting and harvesting on a farm; the sustaining sense of patriotism; moral values inculcated by religious beliefs and observations—all seemed undermined by World War I and its aftermath.

Numerous novels, notably Hemingway's *The Sun Also Rises* (1926) and  7 Fitzgerald's *This Side of Paradise* (1920), evoke the extravagance and disillusionment of the lost generation. In T. S. Eliot's influential long poem *The Waste Land* (1922), Western civilization is symbolized by a bleak desert in desperate need of rain (spiritual renewal).

The world depression of the 1930s affected most of the population of  8 the United States. Workers lost their jobs, and factories shut down; businesses and banks failed; farmers, unable to harvest, transport, or sell their crops, could not pay their debts and lost their farms. Midwestern droughts turned the "breadbasket" of America into a dust bowl. Many farmers left the Midwest for California in search of jobs, as vividly described in John Steinbeck's *The Grapes of Wrath* (1939). At the peak of the Depression, one-third of all Americans were out of work. Soup kitchens, shanty towns, and armies of hobos—unemployed men illegally riding freight trains—became part of national life. Many saw the Depression as a punishment for sins of excessive materialism and loose living. The dust storms that blackened the midwestern sky, they believed, constituted an Old Testament judgment: the "whirlwind by day and the darkness at noon."

The Depression turned the world upside down. The United States had  9 preached a gospel of business in the 1920s; now, many Americans supported a more active role for government in the New Deal programs of President Franklin D. Roosevelt. Federal money created jobs in public works, conservation, and rural electrification. Artists and intellectuals were paid to create murals and state handbooks. These remedies helped, but only the industrial build-up of World War II renewed prosperity. After Japan attacked the United States at Pearl Harbor on December 7, 1941, disused shipyards and factories came to bustling life mass-producing ships, airplanes, jeeps, and supplies. War production and experimentation led to new technologies, including the nuclear bomb. Witnessing the first experimental nuclear blast, Robert Oppenheimer, leader of an international team of nuclear scientists, prophetically quoted a Hindu poem: "I am become Death, the shatterer of worlds."

---

## Questions About the Reading

1. What does the writer mean by "civilization was a 'vast edifice of sham, and the war, instead of its crumbling, was its fullest and most ultimate expression'"?

2. What was the effect on colleges and American families of the postwar boom in business?
3. What is the 19th Amendment to the Constitution, when was it passed, and whom did it benefit? What is the 18th Amendment to the Constitution, and what was its effect?
4. What changed in people's attitudes toward business and government after the 1930s? What caused the change in attitudes?

## Questions About the Writer's Strategies

1. What is the thesis of the essay? State it in your own words.
2. What is the main idea of each paragraph? Is it stated or implied? If stated, in which sentence or sentences? If implied, state it in your own words.
3. Could any of the paragraphs be combined? If so, which ones? Why?

## Writing Assignments

1. Write an essay using examples to explain the major changes that have taken place in the United States since the end of World War II.

2. Use the Internet to find out more about the Lost Generation. Do some research on Hemingway, Stein, and Fitzgerald, and give examples of their experiences in Paris during the post–World War I years.
3 . Write an essay using examples to explain the significant changes that have taken place in the United States since the September 11, 2001, terror attack.
4. Write an essay using examples to explain how September 11, 2001, affected your life or a relative's or friend's life.

# My Mother Never Worked

### *Bonnie Smith-Yackel*

*Bonnie Smith-Yackel's family survived on a farm during the Great Depression, a time when both the weather and the economy made the hardships of farm life nearly overwhelming. In this personal essay, Smith-Yackel uses the example of her mother's life to illustrate the unfairness in American attitudes toward women and the work they do to keep their families intact.*

### Words to Know

**cholera**  a contagious, often fatal disease, usually restricted to farm animals in this country

**reciprocated**  returned

**sustenance**  nourishment, support for life

**widow's pension**  the Social Security payments made to a widow, based on her deceased husband's eligibility

### Getting Started

What do you think about our government's policy that homemakers are not legally workers?

---

"Social Security Office." (The voice answering the telephone sounds very self-assured.) 1

"I'm calling about . . . I . . . my mother just died . . . I was told to call you and see about a . . . death-benefit check, I think they call it . . ." 2

"I see. Was your mother on Social Security? How old was she?" 3

"Yes . . . she was seventy-eight . . ." 4

"Do you know her number?" 5

"No . . . I, ah . . . don't you have a record?" 6

"Certainly. I'll look it up. Her name?" 7

"Smith. Martha Smith. Or maybe she used Martha Ruth Smith . . . Sometimes she used her maiden name . . . Martha Jerabek Smith." 8

"If you'd care to hold on, I'll check our records—it'll be a few minutes." 9

"Yes . . ." 10

Her love letters—to and from Daddy—were in an old box, tied with ribbons and stiff, rigid-with-age leather thongs: 1918 through 1920; hers written on stationery from the general store she had worked in full-time and managed, single-handed, after her graduation from high school in 1913; and his, at first, on YMCA or Soldiers and Sailors Club stationery 11 dispensed to the fighting men of World War I. He wooed her thoroughly and persistently by mail, and though she reciprocated all his feelings for her, she dreaded marriage . . .

"It's so hard for me to decide when to have my wedding day—that's 12 all I've thought about these last two days. I have told you dozens of times that I won't be afraid of married life, but when it comes down to setting the date and then picturing myself a married woman with half a dozen or more kids to look after, it just makes me sick . . . I am weeping right now—I hope that some day I can look back and say how foolish I was to dread it all."

They married in February, 1921, and began farming. Their first baby, a 13 daughter, was born in January, 1922, when my mother was 26 years old. The second baby, a son, was born in March, 1923. They were renting farms; my father, besides working his own fields, also was a hired man for two other farmers. They had no capital initially, and had to gain it slowly, working from dawn until midnight every day. My town-bred mother learned to set hens and raise chickens, feed pigs, milk cows, plant and harvest a garden, and can every fruit and vegetable she could scrounge. She carried water nearly a quarter of a mile from the well to fill her wash boilers in order to do her laundry on a scrub board. She learned to shuck grain, feed threshers, shuck and husk corn, feed corn pickers. In September, 1925, the third baby came, and in June, 1927, the fourth child—both daughters. In 1930, my parents had enough money to buy their own farm, and that March they moved all their livestock and belongings themselves, 55 miles over rutted, muddy roads.

In the summer of 1930 my mother and her two eldest children reclaimed 14 a 40-acre field from Canadian thistles, by chopping them all out with a hoe. In the other fields, when the oats and flax began to head out, the green and blue of the crops were hidden by the bright yellow of wild mustard. My mother walked the fields day after day, pulling each mustard plant. She raised a new flock of baby chicks—500—and she spaded up, planted, hoed, and harvested a half-acre garden.

During the next spring their hogs caught cholera and died. No cash 15 that fall.

And in the next year the drought hit. My mother and father trudged 16 from the well to the chickens, the well to the calf pasture, the well to the barn, and from the well to the garden. The sun came out hot and bright, endlessly, day after day. The crops shriveled and died. They harvested half the corn, and ground the other half, stalks and all, and fed it to the cattle as fodder. With the price at four cents a bushel for the harvested crop, they couldn't afford to haul it into town. They burned it in the furnace for fuel that winter.

In 1934, in February, when the dust was still so thick in the Minnesota 17 air that my parents couldn't always see from the house to the barn, their fifth child—a fourth daughter—was born. My father hunted rabbits daily, and my mother stewed them, fried them, canned them, and wished out loud that she could taste hamburger once more. In the fall the shotgun brought prairie chickens, ducks, pheasant, and grouse. My mother plucked each bird, carefully reserving the breast feathers for pillows.

In the winter she sewed night after night, endlessly, begging cast-off 18 clothing from relatives, ripping apart coats, dresses, blouses, and trousers to remake them to fit her four daughters and son. Every morning and every evening she milked cows, fed pigs and calves, cared for chickens, picked eggs, cooked meals, washed dishes, scrubbed floors, and tended and loved her children. In the spring she planted a garden once more, dragging pails of water to nourish and sustain the vegetables for the family. In 1936 she lost a baby in her sixth month.

In 1937 her fifth daughter was born. She was 42 years old. In 1939 a 19 second son, and in 1941 her eighth child—and third son.

But the war had come, and prosperity of a sort. The herd of cattle had 20 grown to 30 head; she still milked morning and evening. Her garden was more than a half acre—the rains had come, and by now the Rural Electricity Administration and indoor plumbing. Still she sewed—dresses and jackets for the children, house dresses and aprons for herself, weekly patching of jeans, overalls, and denim shirts. Still she made pillows, using the feathers she had plucked, and quilts every year—intricate patterns as well as patchwork, stitched as well as tied—all necessary bedding for her family. Every scrap of cloth too small to be used in quilts was carefully saved and painstakingly sewed together in strips to make rugs. She still went out in the fields to help with the haying whenever there was a threat of rain.

In 1959 my mother's last child graduated from high school. A year 21 later the cows were sold. She still raised chickens and ducks, plucked feathers, made pillows, baked her own bread, and every year made a new quilt—now for a married child or for a grandchild. And her garden, that huge, undying symbol of sustenance, was as large and cared for as in all the years before. The canning, and now freezing, continued.

In 1969, on a June afternoon, mother and father started out for town 22 so that she could buy sugar to make rhubarb jam for a daughter who lived in Texas. The car crashed into a ditch. She was paralyzed from the waist down.

In 1970 her husband, my father, died. My mother struggled to regain 23 some competence and dignity and order in her life. At the rehabilitation institute, where they gave her physical therapy and trained her to live usefully in a wheelchair, the therapist told me: "She did fifteen pushups today—fifteen! She's almost seventy-five years old! I've never known a woman so strong!"

From her wheelchair she canned pickles, baked bread, ironed clothes, 24 wrote dozens of letters weekly to her friends and her "half dozen or more kids," and made three patchwork housecoats and one quilt. She made balls and balls of carpet rags—enough for five rugs. And kept all her love letters.

"I think I've found your mother's records—Martha Ruth Smith; mar- 25 ried to Ben F. Smith?"

"Yes, that's right." 26

"Well, I see that she was getting a widow's pension . . ." 27

"Yes, that's right." 28

"Well, your mother isn't entitled to our $255 death benefit." 29

"Not entitled! But why?" 30

The voice on the telephone explains patiently: 31

"Well, you see—your mother never worked." 32

## Questions About the Reading

1. Why didn't the writer's mother want to get married?
2. How old was the writer's mother when she had her eighth child? How old was she when she was paralyzed?
3. In her later years, how do you think Mrs. Smith's attitude had changed from the one she expressed in the letter quoted in paragraph 12? What had become of her fears of marriage?
4. Why did Mrs. Smith do the pushups, and why did she continue to work in her final years, when she really didn't have to?
5. Speculate about why Mrs. Smith kept her love letters. Why do you think the writer mentions the fact in paragraph 24?

## Questions About the Writer's Strategies

1. What is the thesis in this essay? Where is it expressed?
2. How well do the writer's examples support her thesis?
3. Aside from the extended example of her mother's life, what other mode of development does the writer use in the essay?
4. Describe the writer's point of view in the essay. How does she use time? Does her tone change during the essay?
5. Why does the writer provide so few details about her father and the family's children?

## Writing Assignments

1. Write an essay giving examples of the obstacles women have to over-come in today's society.
2. Think of an extraordinary person you know, and write an essay using examples to show what makes that person extraordinary and why he or she is important to others.
3. Write an essay using examples, or one extended example, to show what the word *sacrifice* means.

# 5 Classification and Division

SUPPOSE YOU ARE looking over the clothing in your closet, trying to sort out the confusion. You decide to classify your clothing into several categories: good clothes for looking your best on the job; older clothes for weekends and informal occasions; and very old clothes that have some stains and holes (but that you can still use when you wash the car or the dog). You have now classified all your clothes into three orderly categories, according to their various uses. You may even want to expand your classification by adding a fourth category: clothes that are no longer useful and should be thrown away. You may have washed the dog in them once too often.

The purpose of **classification** is to take many of the same type of thing—for example, clothing, school papers, presidents, recipes, or music—and organize this large, unsorted group into categories. You may decide to classify your group of similar things, such as music, into the categories of classical, jazz, and rock and roll. Or you might classify recipes into main dishes, salads, and desserts.

You should determine your categories by a quality or characteristic that the items have in common. In each case, you will have to search for the categories that will help you classify an unsorted group of items.

In the following example, the writer classifies mothers of handicapped children in three categories of attitudes.

| | |
|---|---|
| Topic sentence | Researchers note three frequent attitudes among mothers of handicapped children. The first attitude is reflected by those |
| | mothers who reject their child or are unable to accept the child as a handicapped person. Complex love-hate and acceptance-rejection relationships are found within this group. Rejected |
| Category 1: rejection | children not only have problems in adjusting to themselves and their disabilities, but they also have to contend with disturbed family relationships and emotional insecurity. Unfortunately, such children receive even less encouragement than the normal child and have to absorb more criticism of their behavior. |
| | A second relationship involves mothers who overcompensate in their reactions to their child and the disorder. They |
| Category 2: overcompensation | tend to be unrealistic, rigid, and overprotective. Often, such parents try to compensate by being overzealous and giving |

1

2

continuous instruction and training in the hope of establishing superior ability.

**Category 3: acceptance**

    The third group consists of mothers who accept their    3
children along with their disorders. These mothers have
gained the ability to provide for the special needs of their
handicapped children while continuing to live a normal life
and tending to family and home as well as civic and social
obligations. The child's chances are best with parents who
have accepted both their child and the defects.

Janet W. Lerner,
*Learning Disabilities*, Fifth Edition

A **division** paper requires taking one thing—a man's suit, for example—and dividing it into its component parts or characteristics: jacket, pants, and vest (maybe).

Classification and division are often used together. For example, you might want to *divide* your neighborhood into sections (north, south, east, west). You might then *classify* the sections by how much noise and traffic are present in each—noisy, relatively quiet, and quiet. The purpose of classification and division is to categorize a complex whole into simple, useful categories or subdivisions.

In the following example, the writer classifies three police officer positions and then divides each position by the duties required.

**Classification**

    The presidential crime commission offered a partial solution to overworked police forces: Split up the policeman's job

**Division 1**

three different ways. Under this plan, a "community service officer," often a youth from the ghetto, would perform minor investigative chores, rescue cats, and keep in touch with com-

**Division 2**

bustible young people. A police officer, one step higher, would control traffic, hold back crowds at parades, and investigate

**Division 3**

more serious crimes. A police agent, the best-trained, best-educated man on the ladder, would patrol high-crime areas, respond to delicate racial situations, and take care of tense confrontations.

"The Police Need Help," *Time* (October 4, 1968), p. 27

Whether using classification or division, you should be sure the categories are logical and appropriate, with as little overlap between categories as possible. If you are classifying chocolate desserts, you should not add vanilla custard to your list. You should also make your categories reasonably complete. You would not want to leave out chocolate cake in your classification of chocolate desserts.

If you are groping for a method of classification, you may want to try *several* ways of categorizing the same information. If you are classifying your clothes based on how attractive they look in your closet, you might sort them by color. But if you want to make the best use of the space in your closet, you might sort your clothes by type of garment—jackets, pants, shirts, and so forth. In short, you should choose your method of classifying any group of items based on the idea or point you want to support.

In the following paragraph, the writer uses classification to recommend ways to categorize book owners.

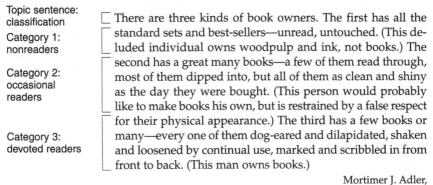

Topic sentence: classification

Category 1: nonreaders

Category 2: occasional readers

Category 3: devoted readers

There are three kinds of book owners. The first has all the standard sets and best-sellers—unread, untouched. (This deluded individual owns woodpulp and ink, not books.) The second has a great many books—a few of them read through, most of them dipped into, but all of them as clean and shiny as the day they were bought. (This person would probably like to make books his own, but is restrained by a false respect for their physical appearance.) The third has a few books or many—every one of them dog-eared and dilapidated, shaken and loosened by continual use, marked and scribbled in from front to back. (This man owns books.)

Mortimer J. Adler,
"How to Mark a Book"

Notice, too, that the transitional words *first, second,* and *third* are used to identify the book owner according to how much each owner reads books. The words *first, second,* and *third* also help move the reader from one point to another. Some other transitional words and phrases that often are used in classification and division are *one, two, three;* and *for one thing, for another thing, finally.* As you write and revise your paragraphs and essays, you will want to think about using transitions to help maintain the **unity** and logical flow, or **coherence,** of your writing.

Like Adler, author of the paragraph on book owners, writers often use topic sentences such as "A safe city street must have three main qualities" (see chapter 1, page 6) or "The treatment prescribed for the disease was aspirin, bed rest, and fluids" to indicate the categories that will follow in the body of a paragraph or essay. Following "A safe city street must have three main qualities," the writer would explain the three specific qualities that make a city street safe. Following "The treatment prescribed for the disease was aspirin, bed rest, and fluids," the writer would probably explain the reasons for prescribing aspirin, bed rest, and fluids.

Usually, too, writers will *follow the same order* in discussing the divisions (or categories) that they used in first introducing them. For instance, suppose the topic is "Four methods can be used to cook fish: broiling, baking, poaching, and frying." Ordinarily the writer would explain (1) broiling, then (2) baking, (3) poaching, and (4) frying. Listing the categories and explaining them in order can make the composition easier for the reader to follow. In the revised student essay that follows, the three students who collaborated in writing it initially classified students as "unconcerned," "ambitious," and "inconsistent." Although they did not follow this order in their first draft, in **revising** the essay, the students changed the order to unconcerned, inconsistent, and ambitious. This order—which followed an undesirable-to-desirable pattern—was then used as the basis for the order of the paragraphs.

| | | |
|---|---|---|
| Thesis statement: classification | Students come in all ages, races, and genders. You can find the unconcerned, inconsistent, and ambitious in any group of students. | 1 |
| Category 1: unconcerned students | First, Ralph, a student in my English class, is an example of a student who has an unconcerned attitude. He has a negative outlook on life, and at times his attitude is downright hostile. He enters the classroom late and disrupts the class by slamming the door or by talking to other students while the teacher is giving a lecture. He does not care at all about the importance of an education. Ralph is more interested in watching sports, enjoying some form of entertainment, or going to parties. | 2 |
| Category 2: inconsistent students | Second, an inconsistent student can be described as a person whose attitude toward education changes or varies. For example, a first grader's grades have gone up and down. She has been in school for only two semesters, but she has shown a big change in her grades. The first semester she received an E (Excellent) in reading and an S (Satisfactory) in math. The second semester she received an N (Not satisfactory) in reading and an E in math. When asked why her reading grade dropped, she said because she no longer liked reading. After her teacher taught her how to have fun doing her math, she no longer concentrated on reading. As a result, she would only take her math homework out of her book bag when it came time to do her homework. | 3 |
| Category 3: ambitious students | Last, there are many ambitious students who are eager to do well in their studies and to achieve degrees. Their priorities have been set, and they have made plans for reaching their goals. Their sole ambition is to excel and succeed. Many students can be classified as ambitious. Valerie, who is pursuing a degree in nursing, is a classic example. She attends class eagerly and regularly, even though she has two children and a home to care for. Recently, she had an illness that caused her to be absent for two weeks and to fall behind in her assignments. She returned and, with her usual ambition, soon caught up with her overdue assignments and achieved Bs or better grades in her courses. | 4 |
| Conclusion: restatement of thesis | In conclusion, the attitudes exemplified above can be found in students of any age, race, or gender. Whether they are attending grade school, high school, or college, students can be found who are unconcerned, inconsistent, or ambitious. | 5 |

As with any piece of writing, a useful practice is to jot down many ideas and make rough lists as part of your **brainstorming** and prewriting. Do not skimp on your planning, and do expect to revise—perhaps several times—to produce a clear, understandable, and effective paragraph or essay.

# Chili

### Charles Kuralt

*There are as many chili recipes as there are chili cooks. Charles Kuralt could have chosen to organize his classification by ingredients or by degree of spiciness, but he instead chooses a classification system that reveals his amused attitude about the subject of chili.*

**Word to Know**
**affectation**   pretension

*Getting Started*
How would you classify your favorite desserts?

---

Some people really like chili, apparently, but nobody can agree how the stuff should be made. C. V. Wood, twice winner at Terlingua, uses flank steak, pork chops, chicken, and green chilis. My friend Hughes Rudd of CBS News, who imported five hundred pounds of chili powder into Russia as a condition of accepting employment as Moscow correspondent, favors coarse-ground beef. Isadore Bleckman, the cameraman I must live with on the road, insists upon one-inch cubes of stew beef and puts garlic in his chili, an Illinois affectation. An Indian of my acquaintance, Mr. Fulton Batisse, who eats chili for breakfast when he can, uses buffalo meat and plays an Indian drum while it's cooking. I ask you.

---

## Questions About the Reading

1. What is the main idea (topic) of the paragraph? Is it directly stated? If so, in which sentences?
2. How does the writer let you know where his cameraman comes from?
3. How does Kuralt feel about the way the Indian cooks chili? Which sentence tells you?

## Questions About the Writer's Strategies

1. Although the writer classifies chili, he does so by combining classification with another **mode.** What is that mode?

2. What is the ingredient that is used consistently by the writer to classify chili?

3. What **order** does the writer use in discussing the different categories of chili?

## Writing Assignments

1. Write a paper in which you *classify* one of the following: people you admire, neighbors, friends, dogs, or cats. Be sure to use a consistent characteristic as the basis for establishing the categories of the classification.

2. Write a paper in which you *divide* and then describe a house according to the functions of its rooms.

3. Think of a food that many people prepare, such as fried chicken, hot dogs, or hamburgers. *Classify* the food according to the different ways cooks prepare it.

# March of Science

*James K. Page Jr.*

*In the paragraph that follows, an unusual subject is classified—the noise of foods when they are eaten.*

**Words to Know**

**alluring**   enticing
**extol**   praise
**spectrum**   range
**vibrations**   rapid back-and-forth movements, sounds from that
   movement

*Getting Started*

How would you classify the sound of women's shoes on a sidewalk?

---

 $\mathbf{Y}$ ou will be relieved to learn that . . . science has now examined yet another habit which Americans indulge to excess: eating—specifically, the delights of eating crunchy, crispy things. . . . Our delight has to do with noise, reports *Chemistry* (Vol. 50, No. 6) a bit breathlessly. Through . . . analysis of the sounds of green peppers, cookies, potato chips and so forth, three categories on the upper end of the noisy-crispy/quiet-not-crispy range can be specified.

- Wet-crisp, as when the living cells of celery or green peppers— filled with fluid and pressure—explode under the force of a tooth. The more pressure, the louder the crunch.
- Dry-crisp, as when the air-filled brittle cells of crackers bend and break, then snap back to position. The vibrations build up into a sound pressure wave.
- Chip-crisp, as when a potato chip is broken by the teeth. Potato chips, only a few cells thick, are noisier (crispier) than you'd expect. Why? Being curved, they are repeatedly broken, which causes many crisp and noisy sounds.

---

## Questions About the Reading

1. Are the words used to describe the noise of foods precise? Support your answer with a statement from the reading.

2. What are the categories of noise that are described by the writer?
3. Why are potato chips noisier than you might expect?

## Questions About the Writer's Strategies

1. What is the **point of view** in the paragraph?
2. What is the **tone** of the paragraph? Support your answer with words or statements from the reading.
3. Does the writer use **examples** to illustrate statements or points made in the paragraph? If so, identify the examples.

## Writing Assignments

1. Write a paper in which you classify the sounds people make when they laugh.
2. Write a paper in which you classify noises in your neighborhood or vocal sounds of various singers.
3. Select a group of fruits and write a paper in which you classify them according to how juicy they are.

# The Mad Dog's Hair: Alcoholism

*Gustave Simons*

*The writer classifies drinkers under three categories and tells us which kind of drinker is the most dangerous.*

**Word to Know**

**recollection**   memory

*Getting Started*

Do you know anyone who is addicted to alcohol, smoking, or dieting? Are you trying to quit smoking or trying to break some other habit?

T here are three categories under which drinkers can be classified: moderate drinkers, who take two cocktails before dinner; heavy drinkers, who take two or three cocktails before lunch, two more cocktails before going home, and another two at home before dinner; and alcoholics, whose intake may begin with a shot or two of bourbon in their morning coffee and continue through the morning, lunch, the afternoon, and evening until they fall into bed with no recollection whatever the next morning as to where they have been or to what they have done during the day before. These are the problems, the dangerous ones; these are the alcoholics, a constant danger not only to themselves, but to their families, their business associates, and possibly to the community where they live.

## Questions About the Reading

1. What are the categories by which the writer classifies drinkers?
2. What are the drinking behaviors of the moderate and heavy drinkers?
3. Who is the most dangerous drinker?
4. How is the alcoholic affected by his drinking?

## Questions About the Writer's Strategies

1. What is the main idea of the paragraph? Is it stated or implied? If stated, state it in your own words.
2. What is the order the writer uses in classifying drinkers?

## Writing Assignments

1. Write a paragraph in which you classify your friends or relatives who smoke.
2. Write a paragraph in which you classify friends or relatives who are dieting.
3. Write a paragraph in which you classify friends or relatives according to their exercise programs.

# Fans

*Paul Gallico*

*Paul Gallico is known for his sports writing and for his books, including*
Mrs. 'Arris Goes to New York *and* The Snow Goose. *In the following
paragraph he classifies sports fans.*

### Words to Know

**aristocratic**  upper-class
**commiseration**  sympathy
**incandescents**  very bright, shining lights
**lurks**  lies in wait

### Getting Started

How would you classify the people who attend a rock concert, a
musical play, a symphony, and an opera performance?

T he fight crowd is a beast that lurks in the darkness behind the fringe
of white light shed over the first six rows by the incandescents atop the
ring, and is not to be trusted with pop bottles or other hardware. The
tennis crowd is always preening and shushing itself. The golf crowd is
the most unwieldy and most sympathetic, and is the only horde given to
mass production of that absurd noise written generally as "tsk tsk tsk
tsk," and made between tongue and teeth with head-waggings to denote
extreme commiseration. The baseball crowd is the most hysterical, the
football crowd the best-natured and the polo crowd the most aristocratic.
Racing crowds are the most restless, wrestling crowds the most tolerant,
and soccer crowds the most easily incitable to riot and disorder. Every
sports crowd takes on the characteristics of the individuals who compose
it. Each has its particular note of hysteria, its own little cruelties, mannerisms, and bad mannerisms, its own code of sportsmanship and its own
method of expressing its emotions.

## Questions About the Reading

1. What are the classifications of sports fans that the writer discusses?
2. Which crowd is the most likely to be disorderly?

3. What determines the characteristics of each sports crowd?
4. What do you think happens to make a golf crowd go "tsk tsk tsk tsk" to show "extreme commiseration"?
5. Which crowd is the most hysterical?

## Questions About the Writer's Strategies

1. What is the main idea (topic) of the paragraph?
2. Which sentence(s) state the topic of the paragraph?
3. Where are the topic sentence(s) located in the paragraph?
4. What is the metaphor the writer uses for the fight crowd?
5. What appears to determine the order in which the writer discusses the different crowds? If you were writing the paragraph, would you use a different order? If so, explain how you might change the order.

## Writing Assignments

1. Write a paragraph in which you classify the crowds at three different musical events.
2. Write a paragraph in which you classify the cars in a parking lot.

# Brain Power

*Lester C. Thurow*

> The writer identifies the inventions that led to our first and second industrial revolutions but maintains that the third, the "information revolution," is not based on information.

### Words to Know

**biotechnology**   application of technology to biology
**denominator**   controlling or common term
**misnomer**   incorrect name or term

### Getting Started

How would you classify the changes that have taken place in your life as a result of the invention of the computer?

---

$\mathbf{F}$uture economic historians looking back will probably see the end of the 20th century as the third industrial revolution. In the first industrial revolution, at the beginning of the 19th century, the steam engine brought 8,000 years of agricultural dominance to an end and created the modern industrial era. At the end of the 19th century, electrification caused the second industrial revolution. Electrical power generation and distribution quickly became a big industry. The telephone could be invented. Electric lights made work or leisure into nighttime as well as daytime activities. People slept less. The third industrial revolution is sometimes called an information revolution, but that is a misnomer since many of the industries involved in the revolution, such as biotechnology and new designer-made materials, are not information industries. Its key distinguishing characteristic and common denominator is not information, but rather a world in which skills and knowledge are the dominant sources of wealth. Bill Gates, now the world's richest man, is the best symbol of this shift.

---

## Questions About the Reading

1. What was the first industrial revolution, and what did it replace as our dominant industry?
2. What inventions led to the first and second industrial revolutions?

3. What is the third revolution called? Why does Thurow say the term is a misnomer?
4. What does Thurow say is the third revolution's characteristic? Why? Who is the best symbol of this revolution?

## Questions About the Writer's Strategies

1. What is the main idea of the paragraph? State it in your own words.
2. What order does the writer use?
3. In addition to classification, what other modes of development does the writer use?
4. If you wanted to divide the paragraph into more than one paragraph, where would you divide it? What would be the main idea and topic sentence of each paragraph?

## Writing Assignments

1. Write a paragraph in which you classify the ways in which the computer has changed or influenced your life.
2. Write a paragraph in which you classify the inventions you use for doing your household tasks and explain how they have changed your way from the way your parents or grandparents did these tasks.

# "Ever Et Raw Meat?"

*Stephen King*

*Stephen King, best known for such horror novels and movies as* Carrie *and* Misery, *classifies readers according to the questions they ask him.*

### Words to Know

**blasphemous**  irreverent, profane

**E. E. Cummings**  American poet known for experimenting with form, punctuation, spelling, and syntax in his poetry

**enumerate**  name one by one

**flagellate**  beat, whip

**kleptomaniac**  a person who has an impulse or compulsion to steal

**laconic**  concise expression; expressed in few words

**modicum**  small amount

**self-abnegation**  self-denial, giving up of one's rights

**Zen**  Buddhist sect

### Getting Started

What questions would you like to ask Stephen King?

---

It seems to me that, in the minds of readers, writers actually exist to 1 serve two purposes, and the more important may not be the writing of books and stories. The primary function of writers, it seems, is to answer readers' questions. These fall into three categories. The third is the one that fascinates me most, but I'll identify the other two first.

## The One-of-a-Kind Question

Each day's mail brings a few of these. Often they reflect the writer's field 2 of interest—history, horror, romance, the American West, outer space, big business. The only thing they have in common is their uniqueness. Novelists are frequently asked where they get their ideas (see category No. 2), but writers must wonder where this relentless curiosity, these really strange questions, come from.

There was, for instance, the young woman who wrote to me from a 3 penal institution in Minnesota. She informed me she was a kleptomaniac. She further informed me that I was her favorite writer, and she had stolen every one of my books she could get her hands on. "But after I stole *Different Seasons* from the library and read it, I felt moved to send it back," she wrote. "Do you think this means you wrote this one the best?" After due consideration, I decided that reform on the part of the reader has nothing to do with artistic merit. I came close to writing back to find out if she had stolen *Misery* yet but decided I ought to just keep my mouth shut.

From Bill V. in North Carolina: "I see you have a beard. Are you morbid of razors?" 4

From Carol K. in Hawaii: "Will you soon write of pimples or some other facial blemish?" 5

From Don G., no address (and a blurry postmark): "Why do you keep up this disgusting mother worship when anyone with any sense knows a MAN has no use to his mother once he is weaned?" 6

From Raymond R. in Mississippi: "Ever et raw meat?" (It's the laconic ones like this that really get me.) 7

I have been asked if I beat my children and/or my wife. I have been asked to parties in places I have never been and hope never to go. I was once asked to give away the bride at a wedding, and one young woman sent me an ounce of pot, with the attached question: "This is where I get my inspiration—where do you get yours?" Actually, mine usually comes in envelopes—the kind through which you can view your name and address printed by a computer—that arrive at the end of every month. 8

My favorite question of this type, from Anchorage, asked simply: "How could you write such a why?" Unsigned. If E. E. Cummings were still alive, I'd try to find out if he'd moved to the Big North. 9

## The Old Standards

These are the questions writers dream of answering when they are collecting rejection slips, and the ones they tire of quickest once they start to publish. In other words, they are the questions that come up without fail in every dull interview the writer has ever given or will ever give. I'll enumerate a few of them: 10

Where do you get your ideas? (I get mine in Utica.) 11

How do you get an agent? (Sell your soul to the Devil.) 12

Do you have to know somebody to get published? (Yes; in fact, it helps to grovel, toady, and be willing to perform twisted acts of sexual depravity at a moment's notice, and in public if necessary.) 13

How do you start a novel? (I usually start by writing the number 1 in the upper right-hand corner of a clean sheet of paper.) 14

How do you write best sellers? (Same way you get an agent.) 15

How do you sell your book to the movies? (Tell them they don't want it.) 16

What time of day do you write? (It doesn't matter; if I don't keep busy 17
enough, the time inevitably comes.)

Do you ever run out of ideas? (Does a bear defecate in the woods?)    18

Who is your favorite writer? (Anyone who writes stories I would have 19
written had I thought of them first.)

There are others, but they're pretty boring, so let us march on.        20

## The Real Weirdies

Here I am, bopping down the street, on my morning walk, when some 21
guy pulls over in his pickup truck or just happens to walk by and says,
"Hi, Steve! Writing any good books lately?" I have an answer for this;
I've developed it over the years out of pure necessity. I say, "I'm taking
some time off." I say that even if I'm working like mad, thundering down
homestretch on a book. The reason why I say this is because no other answer seems to fit. Believe me, I know. In the course of the trial and error
that has finally resulted in "I'm taking some time off," I have discarded
about 500 other answers.

Having an answer for "You writing any good books lately?" is a good 22
thing, but I'd be lying if I said it solves the problem of *what the question
means.* It is this inability on my part to make sense of this odd query,
which reminds me of that Zen riddle—"Why is a mouse when it runs?"—
that leaves me feeling mentally shaken and impotent. You see, it isn't just
*one* question; it is a *bundle* of questions, cunningly wrapped up in one
package. It's like that old favorite, "Are you still beating your wife?"

If I answer in the affirmative, it means I may have written—how many 23
books? two? four?—(all of them good) in the last—how long? Well, how
long is "lately"? It could mean I wrote maybe three good books just last
week, or maybe two *on this very walk up to Bangor International Airport and
back!* On the other hand, if I say no, what does *that* mean? I wrote three
or four *bad* books in the last "lately" (surely "lately" can be no longer
than a month, six weeks at the outside)?

Or here I am, signing books at the Betts' Bookstore or B. Dalton's in the 24
local consumer factory (nicknamed "the mall"). This is something I do
twice a year, and it serves much the same purpose as those little bundles
of twigs religious people in the Middle Ages used to braid into whips
and flagellate themselves with. During the course of this exercise in mad-
ness and self-abnegation, at least a dozen people will approach the little
coffee table where I sit behind a barrier of books and ask brightly, "Don't
you wish you had a rubber stamp?"

I have an answer to this one, too, an answer that has been developed 25
over the years in a trial-and-error method similar to "I'm taking some time
off." The answer to the rubber-stamp questions is: "No, I don't mind."

Never mind if I really do or don't (this time it's my own motivations I 26 want to skip over, you'll notice); the question is, Why does such an illogical query occur to so many people? My signature is actually stamped on the covers of several of my books, but people seem just as eager to get these signed as those that aren't so stamped. Would these questioners stand in line for the privilege of watching me slam a rubber stamp down on the title page of *The Shining* or *Pet Sematary*? I don't think they would.

If you still don't sense something peculiar in these questions, this one 27 might help convince you. I'm sitting in the cafe around the corner from my house, grabbing a little lunch by myself and reading a book (reading at the table is one of the few bad habits acquired in my youth that I have nobly resisted giving up) until a customer or maybe even a waitress sidles up and asks, "How come you're not reading one of your own books?"

This hasn't happened just once, or even occasionally; it happens *a lot.* 28 The computer-generated answer to this question usually gains a chuckle, although it is nothing but the pure, logical and apparent truth. "I know how they all come out," I say. End of exchange. Back to lunch, with only a pause to wonder why people assume you want to read what you wrote, rewrote, read again following the obligatory editorial conference and yet again during the process of correcting the mistakes that a good copy editor always prods, screaming, from their hiding places (I once heard a crime writer suggest that God could have used a copy editor, and while I find the notion slightly blasphemous, I tend to agree).

And then people sometimes ask in that chatty, let's-strike-up-a- 29 conversation way people have, "How long does it take you to write a book?" Perfectly reasonable question—at least until you try to answer it and discover there is no answer. This time the computer-generated answer is a total falsehood, but it at least serves the purpose of advancing the conversation to some more discussable topic. "Usually about nine months," I say, "the same length of time it takes to make a baby." This satisfies everyone but me. I know that nine months is just an average, and probably a completely fictional one at that. It ignores *The Running Man* (published under the name Richard Bachman), which was written in four days during a snowy February vacation when I was teaching high school. It also ignores *It* and my latest, *The Tommyknockers. It* is over 1,000 pages long and took four years to write. *The Tommyknockers* is 400 pages shorter but took five years to write.

Do I mind these questions? Yes . . . and no. Anyone minds questions 30 that have no real answers and thus expose the fellow being questioned to be not a real doctor but a sort of witch doctor. But no one—at least no one with a modicum of simple human kindness—resents questions from people who honestly want answers. And now and then someone will ask

a really interesting question, like, Do you write in the nude? The answer—
not generated by computer—is: I don't think I ever have, but if it works,
I'm willing to try it.

---

## Questions About the Reading

1. According to King, what seems to be the primary function of writers?
2. What do the one-of-a-kind questions have in common?
3. What does the writer mean when he says he gets his inspiration from
   what "comes in envelopes—the kind through which you can view
   your name and address printed by computer—that arrive at the end
   of every month"?
4. What are the writer's definitions of "old standards" and "real weirdies"?
5. What are the four "real weirdies" the writer has been asked?

## Questions About the Writer's Strategies

1. What are the different modes of development that the writer uses in
   the essay?
2. What is the point of view in person and time? Are they consistent
   throughout the essay?
3. What is the tone of the essay? Is it consistent throughout?
4. What organizational pattern and modes of development does the writer
   use in describing "one-of-a-kind questions" and "old standards"?
5. What organizational pattern does the writer use in describing "real
   weirdies"?

## Writing Assignments

1. Choose three or more of the following famous writers represented in
   this text: John Updike, Russell Baker, John Grogan, Barbara Kingsolver,
   Charles Kuralt, Paul Gallico, Stephen King, Anna Quindlen, Thomas L.
   Friedman, Jack London, or Isaac Asimov. Using the Internet or your
   library, choose a book or essay written by each writer and then write
   an essay about the questions you would like to ask each writer about
   his or her book or essay.
2. *Working Together*   Join with some classmates to write an essay about
   the questions you would like to ask Babe Ruth, Michael Jordan, and
   Martina Navratilova.

# Eggs, Twinkies, and Ethnic Stereotypes

*Jeanne Park*

*Jeanne Park, an Asian American, found herself labeled as intelligent while in elementary school. In high school, she learned that her intelligence did not set her apart in the classroom but that outside the classroom her ethnic background did.*

### Words to Know

**condescending**  patronizing
**metamorphose**  change in nature

### Getting Started

At lunchtime, do the students at your school segregate themselves according to their racial or ethnic background?

---

**W**ho am I?                                                                         1

For Asian-American students, the answer is a diligent, hardworking  2
and intelligent young person. But living up to this reputation has secretly
haunted me.

The labeling starts in elementary school. It's not uncommon for a teacher  3
to remark, "You're Asian, you're supposed to do well in math." The under-
lying message is, "You're Asian and you're supposed to be smarter."

Not to say being labeled intelligent isn't flattering, because it is, or not  4
to deny that basking in the limelight of being top of my class isn't ego-
boosting, because frankly it is. But at a certain point, the pressure became
crushing. I felt as if doing poorly on my next spelling quiz would stain
the exalted reputation of all Asian students forever.

So I continued to be an academic overachiever, as were my friends. By  5
junior high school I started to believe I was indeed smarter. I became condescending toward non-Asians. I was a bigot; all my friends were Asians.
The thought of intermingling occurred rarely if ever.

My elitist opinion of Asian students changed, however, in high school. As  6
a student at what is considered one of the nation's most competitive science
and math schools, I found that being on top is no longer an easy feat.

I quickly learned that Asian students were not smarter. How could I  7
ever have believed such a thing? All around me are intelligent, ambitious
people who are not only Asian but white, black and Hispanic.

Superiority complexes aside, the problem of social segregation still 8 exists in the schools. With a few exceptions, each race socializes only with its "own kind." Students see one another in the classroom, but outside the classroom there remains distinct segregation.

Racist lingo abounds. An Asian student who socializes only with other 9 Asians is believed to be an Asian Supremacist or, at the very least, arrogant and closed off. Yet an Asian student who socializes only with whites is called a "twinkie," one who is yellow on the outside but white on the inside.

A white teenager who socializes only with whites is thought of as 10 prejudiced, yet one who socializes with Asians is considered an "egg," white on the outside and yellow on the inside.

These culinary classifications go on endlessly, needless to say, leaving 11 many confused, and leaving many more fearful than ever of social experimentation. Because the stereotypes are accepted almost unanimously, they are rarely challenged. Many develop harmful stereotypes of entire races. We label people before we even know them.

Labels learned at a young age later metamorphose into more visible acts 12 of racism. For example, my parents once accused and ultimately fired a Puerto Rican cashier, believing she had stolen $200 from the register at their grocery store. They later learned it was a mistake. An Asian shopkeeper nearby once beat a young Hispanic youth who worked there with a baseball bat because he believed the boy to be lazy and dishonest.

We all hold misleading stereotypes of people that limit us as individ- 13 uals in that we cheat ourselves out of the benefits different cultures can contribute. We can grow and learn from each culture whether it be Chinese, Korean or African American.

Just recently some Asian boys in my neighborhood were attacked by a 14 group of young white boys who have christened themselves the Master Race. Rather than being angered by this act, I feel pity for this generation that lives in a state of bigotry.

It may be too late for our parents' generation to accept that each person 15 can only be judged for the characteristics that set him or her apart as an individual. We, however, can do better.

## Questions About the Reading

1. How did it affect the writer to be labeled as *intelligent?*
2. What did the writer learn about other students when she went to the competitive high school?

3. What is an Asian Supremacist? A "twinkie"? An "egg"?
4. According to the writer, how do the culinary classifications influence people's behavior?
5. According to the writer, how should we judge people?

## Questions About the Writer's Strategies

1. Is the essay developed using classification or using division?
2. What mode of development does the writer use in paragraph 4?
3. What is the topic of paragraph 12? What mode of development does the writer use in the paragraph?
4. What are some transitional words the writer uses?
5. What is the thesis of the essay? Is it stated or implied?
6. Is the essay objective, subjective, or both?

## Writing Assignments

1. Write an essay in which you classify the people in your neighborhood according to the cars they drive.
2. Write an essay in which you classify the students in your school according to what they eat for lunch.
3. Write an essay in which you divide a house, a car, or an item of clothing into its parts.

# Secrets of Man's Unspoken Language

*Desmond Morris*

*A distinguished scientist offers a classification of the gestures that we experience in our lives and tells us what they mean.*

## Words to Know

**aborigines**   natives, earliest known inhabitants of a region
**doffed**   removed, took off
**effigies**   likeness or replica of, usually, a person
**maligned**   disliked, spoke negatively of
**relic**   souvenir
**repertoire**   stock, group, or knowledge of
**salutation**   greeting, acknowledgment

## Getting Started

What gestures do you and your friends use to greet or say goodbye to each other?

If a Norwegian, a Korean and a Masai were suddenly marooned together 1 on a desert island, communication would still be possible: they could easily convey their basic moods and intentions to one another without words, because all humanity shares a large repertoire of common visual signals. The true origin of many of these gestures is no longer known. But students of human behavior can trace certain actions that we take for granted today. Most are centuries old and steeped in history.

**The nod.** The vertical head nod, always a yes sign, occurs almost 2 everywhere in the world. Remote tribes, from the Australian aborigines to the natives of Tierra del Fuego, were found to be nodding for yes when first encountered by white men. It has even been recorded in people born deaf and blind. This strongly suggests that affirmative nodding may be an inborn action for the human species—a pattern programmed by our genes. Essentially, it is the beginning of a bow—a way of lowering the body to show submission.

**The head shake.** This, too, is virtually global in range and is always a 3 negative sign. Like many important gestures, it is thought to be a relic from our personal past—from our early infancy when we were nursed at the breast or the bottle. The baby who is not hungry rejects the breast by turning the head sharply to the side. From this beginning, it is argued, has come our adult sign for negation. When a parent warns a child not to do something by wagging a forefinger, he is using the finger in imitation of the shaken head—often adding speed and vigor to the signal.

**Crossing the fingers.** When we say, "Keep your fingers crossed," we  4 are, historically speaking, requesting an act of Christian worship. Crossing oneself—making the sign of the cross by moving the arm downward and then sideways in front of the body—is an ancient protective device of the Christian Church. In earlier times, crossing the second finger tightly over the first was the secret version of this, and was done with the hand carefully hidden from view. But lacking any obvious religious character, the action easily slid into everyday use, even by non-Christians, as a casual wish for good fortune. Although still done secretly to protect oneself from the consequences of lying, as a "good luck" sign it has now come out into the open.

**Thumbing the nose.** The origin of this gesture—one of the most com-  5 mon and widespread insults in the world—is uncertain. It is usually thought to represent the hostile, erect comb of a fighting cock. (Animal signs are a favorite form of insult; the mocking, hands-to-ears flapping action popular among children, for example, mimics the long ears of the much-maligned donkey.) But the "cockscomb" sign has also been explained as a deformed salute, an imitation of grotesque, long-nosed effigies, or the mock firing of a catapult.

**The OK sign.** When an American wants to signal that something is  6 OK, fine, perfect, he raises his hand and makes a circle with his thumb and forefinger. This sign derives from a gesture people all over the world make unconsciously when speaking about some fine point. To say that something is precise or exact, we go through the motions of holding something very small between the tips of our thumb and forefinger, which then automatically form a ring. In America this unconscious movement became a deliberate signal meaning "perfect." But be careful with this one: in other countries the circle sign can mean something quite different. In Japan, it means money (because coins are circular); in France it means "nothing" or "worthless" (the circle meaning zero); in Malta, Sardinia and Greece it is an obscene insult.

**Clasped hands raised above the head.** This traditional posture adopted  7 by boxers and wrestlers after winning a fight is one of the many "triumph displays" that grow out of the surge of feeling following a victory. In nearly all triumphant moments, the victor expresses his sudden increase in status by raising his height in some way. Young children are likely to jump up and down excitedly. Among adults, the display differs from context to context, but there is often a raising of the arms high above the head.

Triumphant arm-raising may be amplified by raising the victorious 8 individual on the shoulders of his supporters, or parading him on top of some kind of vehicle. Without realizing it, the modern sports or political hero who parades through the streets of his hometown in an open car is recreating the ancient Roman Triumph, in which a conquering general entered Rome at the head of his army in a four-horse chariot decorated with laurel, a golden crown held above his head by a slave, and his face reddened with vermilion to simulate the blood of sacrificial victims.

**The salute** began as an act of token submission: removing the hat as 9 part of a formal bow. In earlier centuries the bow was so deep that the doffed hat almost touched the floor. This was abbreviated into the modern military salute in which the hand is brought smartly up to touch the temple. The same gesture survives as a friendly greeting: casually touching the brim of the hat, or the temple, with the fingers.

**Thumbs up, thumbs down.** When a Roman gladiator was defeated in 10 combat in the arena, he might be spared, or killed on the spot by his victor; the spectators could influence the decision by the position of their thumbs. The gesture for death was thrusting the thumb downward— apparently an imitation of thrusting the sword into the victim. It is popularly believed that the life sign was thumbs up, but this appears to be a misinterpretation. The phrase used in ancient writings, *pollice compresso*, literally means "thumbs compressed"; the spectators held out their hands with the thumbs hidden inside their closed fingers, meaning do *not* make the sword thrust.

The modern thumbs-up sign meaning "OK, fine, good," like the V-for- 11 Victory sign made famous by Sir Winston Churchill, was spread across much of the world by the British during World War II. Many Italians refer to it as the "English OK" signal. So a popular gesture which started out as a mistranslation from the literature of ancient Rome is now "returning" to the city from which it never really came.

**Tapping the temple.** Many people understand this as a sign for stu- 12 pidity. To make the meaning more precise, you might instead twist your forefinger against your temple, indicating "a screw loose," or rotate your forefinger close to your temple, signaling that the brain is going round and round, but even these actions would be confusing to some people. In Saudi Arabia, for example, stupidity can be signaled by touching the lower eyelid with the tip of the forefinger. Other local stupidity gestures include tapping the elbow of the raised forearm, flapping the hand up and down in front of half-closed eyes, rotating a raised hand or laying one forefinger flat across the forehead.

**The salutation.** People seem almost incapable of beginning or ending 13 any kind of encounter without some type of salutation. Man appears to have needed such "salutation displays" for many thousands of years.

Early man established a major division of labor, with the male hunters leaving the group at specific times, then returning to home base with the kill. The importance of success or failure on the hunt meant that these were vital moments in the life of the primeval tribe, so elaborate rituals of greeting and farewell were developed.

The main moment of greeting was—and is—when actual body con- 14 tact is made; at full intensity this consists of a total embrace, with much hugging, patting, squeezing, kissing, laughing and even weeping. But before this, comes the moment when friends recognize each other from a distance. Apparently some form of arm action at the moment of first sighting is global for mankind. Clearly, the vertical, up-and-down wave of the hand is a way of patting the friend's body at a distance in antici- pation of the embrace to come.

The handshake, too, is a salutation display. Different cultures have 15 formalized, in different ways, the body contact which comes at the key moment of greeting.

Some emphasize head-to-head contact as in nose-rubbing or stylized 16 mutual cheek-kissing. Westerners use a whole range of body contacts of decreasing strength, right down to the formal handshake. But they are all variations on a basic theme—the body embrace. This is the fundamental human-contact action, the one we all know as babies, infants and grow- ing children, and to which we return whenever the rules permit and we wish to demonstrate feelings of attachment for another individual.

## Questions About the Reading

1. How can people who speak different languages communicate with one another?
2. What are the global signals for "yes" and "no"?
3. What is the historical meaning of crossed fingers?
4. What does the crossed fingers signal usually mean now?
5. Why should you be careful about using the OK sign in other countries?

## Questions About the Writer's Strategies

1. What is the thesis of the essay? State it in your own words.
2. Besides classification, what other modes of development does the writer use?
3. What are the divisions of salutations the writer provides in paragraphs 13 through 16?

4. How would you change paragraphs 13 through 16 to clarify the salutation divisions?

## Writing Assignments

1. *Working Together*   Join with some classmates to write an essay in which you classify any special or unique gestures each person uses.
2. Write an essay in which you classify the gestures that are used by the police before and after a large sports event.

3. Research nonverbal communication on the Internet. Classify some examples of gestures from various countries and describe how they differ from your own interpretation of the same gestures.

# Start Spreading the News: Seven Things You Should Know Before Moving to New York City

*Courtney Reimer*

*If you think you might want to live in New York, Courtney Reimer tells you what you need to know about that city before moving there.*

## Words to Know

**accoutrements**   equipment, trappings

**ostensibly**   apparently, evidently

**permeates**   fills, penetrates

**perspective**   view

**plethora**   abundance

**proximity**   closeness

**quixotic**   impractical, idealistic

**unequivocally**   without question, definitely

## Getting Started

What are the characteristics of the town you live in?

L ike many stereotypes, New York City's are grounded for the most 1 part in truth: it is dirty, smelly, loud, expensive, a hassle. And those are just the top five. Plus, thanks to a mayor who says he desires to clear our environment of secondhand smoke, loud nightclubs, and ringing cell phones (but immediately upon entering office slashed a finally operational recycling program), it's only getting worse. Yet the city is crowded with eight million people who, at least ostensibly, want to live here. It's the most populous city in the union and, to judge by the steady stream of fresh-faced wannabe New Yorkers arriving here every day at least, it's only going to get more crowded. Optimists choose to look the other way and follow the advice of all the Pollyannas who've made this place some kind of promised land. Thanks to them, New York City has become known as the place to make it.

Then again, who am I to talk? I too made a run for the Big City, a head 2 full of quixotic dreams fueling my flight. Abetted by Hollywood and countless pop songs (yes, Sinatra), I jumped the oh-so-secure ship of Seattle, shedding the accoutrements of early adulthood (a fuel-efficient sedan; a residence with a parking space; a job with a private office bigger than most New York apartments) and headed East.

Now, with a few years' perspective on the whole thing, I can finally 3 admit it: New York is definitely dirty, smelly, loud, expensive, and a huge hassle. Had I known a few other things prior to moving here, though, I might have been able to duck the blows New York has since dealt me. At least I might have been ready to punch back.

1. **The little things are much bigger in New York.** And I'm not just talk- 4 ing laundry, with which I had a bit of an unfair advantage in Seattle. (Mom was just a fifteen-minute drive away, a drive I took weekly.) But yes, clean garments can be a challenge here. I have rarely found a New York City apartment building that contains a laundry room, and owning an in-apartment washer and dryer is a pipe dream you'd best disabuse yourself of before coming to town.

Then there's getting from your home to your place of work and back 5 again each day. Sure, once you find your groove, the New York commute can be accomplished in your sleep. But take one look at the snake-like snarl of subway lines on any New York map and tell me you're not a little bit daunted. And don't even think about making a phone call en route, since you will be doing most of your commuting on the subway. (Trust me—six million people daily can't be wrong.) Until they find a way to get a cellular signal underground, subways will remain chatter free—which is nice if you want to read, daydream, or nap. But if you've been owing your mom a phone call for two weeks, it can be more than a little frustrating.

And finally: shoes. Your feet are going to hurt here. You may never 6 have considered yourself a "sensible shoe" type, but pain can be a strong motivator. Before you know it, you will be trotting around Manhattan in a pair of Rockports. Trust me on this, too.

2. **Feeding yourself is all too easy here, yet all too difficult.** Whereas in 7 your old hometown eating out was a luxury, a special occasion, in Gotham the opposite becomes true—and all as the result of a lack of acceptable grocery options. Not only are the corner stores known as bodegas tiny, dirty, and poorly stocked; these sorry substitutes for supermarkets keep wildly inconsistent hours. Really, they should amend "The City That Never Sleeps" with the asterisk disclaimer: "except grocery stores." As a result, it's next to impossible to obtain the ingredients needed for a supposedly simple home-cooked meal.

So. Before you pack your things for a move to the Big Apple (ironic 8 that the city should be nicknamed for produce, but I digress), take a long, last look at that clean, well-lighted, stocked-to-the-ceiling-with-multiple-selections-of-whatever-your-tummy-desires, open 24-7 grocery store. You're going to miss it more than you know.

3. **"Love the One You're With" could be a New Yorker's theme song.** 9 Considering the sheer number of people who live here, New York is probably one of the harder places on the planet to make and maintain fulfilling relationships, both platonic and otherwise. In New York, the plethora of options—and the many neighborhoods one could feasibly lay one's head at the end of the night—actually limits the number of acquaintance-ships available. In short, it's the old rule of being paralyzed by too many choices. Because of the excessive planning, commuting, and plain old waiting that a New York social life requires, you have to really, really want to hang out with someone here in order to do it.

On the other hand, that same vastness can foster all kinds of unsavory 10 one-night-stand behavior. That new, ahem, friend you drunkenly brought home last night? The one whose name you can't for the life of you remember? Not to worry. The chances of running into him or her again are slim to zero.

4. **Chicago is the Windy City, Seattle is rainy, Alaska is downright cold.** 11 **So what?** It's nothing compared to the meteorological beating we New Yorkers take on a regular basis. It's dumbfounding to me that eight million people continue to subject themselves to months on end of subfreezing temperatures, followed by endless weeks of heat and humidity so extreme that it actually feels like you're living in a giant bowl of soup. At least in most other cities you can hop into your personal climate-controlled vehicle and protect yourself from the elements—even propel yourself away from them, should you so desire. In New York, the subway stations are neither heated nor air-conditioned. I seriously wouldn't be surprised to learn that people routinely freeze to death while waiting for the N or R train in the winter or expire from the heat on the A train platform in the summer. Sure, you could hail a cab—assuming there's one around when you need it—but that would tap your drink budget. Speaking of which . . .

5. **I'm not as think as you drunk I am.** The food, the theater, the jobs, the 12 music. While all of that's up for debate, one thing that unequivocally is not better in New York, at least for us imbibers, is the drinks. In a word, they are weak. Maybe bartenders in other cities have spoiled me with their generosity, but unless you specifically order a double here, don't expect the person behind the bar to pour liberally. A near and dear Seattle friend nearly socked the bartender the first time she ordered a Jack Daniels and Coke that was, well, heavier on the "and Coke" than she was used to. I'm

guessing the pervading logic among New York bartenders is that if they pour a less-strong drink, they'll make more tips from the more drinks bought to compensate for their miserly ways. Sorry Charlie. At six dollars a pop (on the low end) and twelve dollars a pop (at the high end), we want to be able at least to taste the alcohol in our drinks. Otherwise, why not just stay home and drink your own damn liquor? It's probably not such a good idea to be drunkenly stumbling around the big, bad city of New York, anyway.

6. **New Yorkers aren't the masters of wit and wisdom you may have** 13 **thought.** Perhaps I've seen one too many Woody Allen movies, but one of the many stereotypes about Manhattan I brought with me from Seattle is that people are smarter here. Perhaps you too had the impression that every New Yorker is an OED-toting, Ivy League-educated, world-traveled smarty-pants with ten bulging bookshelves. Clearly I had not accounted for the proximity of New Jersey.

Holy moly, are there a lot of idiots in this joint. Or is it just the number 14 of people who sound dumb when they talk? (No, I'm not going to "cawl.") No wonder longtime New York residents such as Madonna have adopted British accents—years of immersion in the local way of speaking would make anyone run for the nearest diction consultant. For that matter, my nonscientific survey shows that for every nine subway riders reading the Rupert Murdoch–owned tabloid, just one is reading *The New York Times.* Oh wait, I forgot, it is more important to know what hotel heiress was spotted with Jimmy Fallon than how many bodies are piling up in the Middle East and why.

7. **It's actually not rude, it's efficient. Really!** New Yorkers are much eas- 15 ier to be around than a lot of my former neighbors in Seattle. Face it: the person behind the counter at the deli where you buy your coffee doesn't care how your day is, and you don't care how hers is. Sound rude? No, what's rude is wasting a person's time with chitchat. Believe me, the people in line behind you right now are nodding in agreement.

Surprisingly, the people here are much more approachable than the resi- 16 dents of most cities. A sort of "we're in this together" mentality permeates New York, and thus it's not deemed brash to strike up a casual conversation with the person next to you on the subway platform about, I don't know . . . what the hell is taking the train so goddamn long. Were you to do the same thing in many other cities, you'd be met with silence and an attitude. And not simply because there's no subway in most of those cities.

Having said all this—and I've only scratched the surface—New York is 17 the best thing that ever happened to me. All of the above notwithstanding, the city has been good to me. Like a very loving but strict parent,

New York builds character. It's also a perfect de facto finishing school for those of us who've been spoiled by the everybody's-a-star circumstances many years in one's hometown can breed.

The other day, sitting in a pizza place, I looked up and saw a poster, 18 dated 1977, with a quote that resonates particularly well with what I've been trying to convey over the past several pages:

"You have to be crazy to live in New York, but you'd be nuts to live 19 anywhere else."

## Questions About the Reading

1. What are the seven things the writer thinks you should know before moving to New York City?
2. Where did the writer live before she moved to New York?
3. How does the writer describe the weather in New York?
4. Why is it "next to impossible" in New York to get the ingredients to cook a meal at home?

## Questions About the Writer's Strategies

1. What is the thesis of the essay? State it in your own words.
2. What is the point of view (person, time, tone) of the essay?
3. What is the simile the writer uses to describe the map of the New York subway lines?

## Writing Assignments

1. Write a classification/division essay in which you classify the advantages and disadvantages of your hometown.
2. *Working Together*   Join with some classmates to write a classification/ division essay about your college.

# 6 Comparison and Contrast

To COMPARE IS to show how items are alike. To **contrast** is to show how items are different. Thus comparison and contrast involve pointing out the similarities or differences between two (or more) items. Birdwatchers, for instance, may compare bird A with bird B according to their common color but contrast them according to their difference in size.

In the preceding chapter, you learned about the **modes of development** called **classification** and **division.** The comparison and contrast modes are related to those modes. In deciding what to compare or contrast, you will want to make sure that the items share points in common. Thus the items are usually the same kind or **class** of thing, and in comparing or contrasting them, you essentially establish at least two categories, showing the differences or similarities between them. For instance, you can compare two passenger cars—a Ford and a Chevrolet—with more precision than you can a Ford and a helicopter. Fords are compared with Chevrolets because they have many features in common—features that you can pinpoint. Similarly, you can usually compare two paintings more precisely than you can a novel and a painting.

Once you have selected the closely related items, you will want to explain as clearly as possible the ways in which the items are alike or different. In any one piece of writing, you may want to use comparison only—or contrast only. Or you may decide to use both in the same essay. These three possibilities are illustrated in the following paragraphs. Notice, in each case, how the writer compares or contrasts *specific* points.

## Comparison

A Buick and a Cadillac, both built by General Motors, are alike in many ways. A Buick, which measures over 200 inches in length and weighs over 3,000 pounds, is large and holds the road well. A Cadillac is similar in length and weight. Like a Buick, a Cadillac gets relatively low gas mileage compared with smaller economy cars made by the same manufacturer. The Buick provides an unusually comfortable ride, especially on cross-country trips on the highway, as does a Cadillac. And both cars enjoy a certain status as a luxury automobile.

## Contrast

> The twins are as different as two people can be. Sally, who is always hoping someone will have a party, has black hair, brown eyes, and an outgoing personality. She wants to be an actress or a popular singer. Susan, more serious and studious, has blonde hair, blue eyes, and a somewhat shy manner. Since she has done well in all her classes in graphic arts and math, she plans to become an architect or an engineer.

## Mixed Comparison and Contrast

> Most Americans would say it is not really possible to establish an ideal society. But time after time, a small dedicated group of people will drop out of the mainstream of American society to try, once more, to live according to the group's concept of an ideal society. Most of these groups have believed in holding their property in common. Most have used the word *family* to refer to all members of the group. Many of these groups, however, have differed widely in their attitudes toward sex and marriage.

Notice that all three of these paragraphs supply information but do not try to claim that one of the compared items is better or worse than the other. Notice, too, the **objective** tone of these paragraphs. However, writers also use comparison and contrast to support their opinions about subjects or to show how a certain thing or idea is superior to others in the same class. The writer of the paragraph about twins, for instance, could have used her information to support an opinion, as in the following revised paragraph.

Opinion

Opinion

> The twins are as different as two people can be. Sally, who has black hair, brown eyes, and an outgoing, flighty personality, is always hoping someone will have a party. She fritters away her time and money shopping for the latest clothes, and she dreams of being an actress or a popular singer. But until she settles down and applies her energy to something useful, she will probably not be successful at anything. Susan, more serious and studious, has blonde hair, blue eyes, and a somewhat shy manner. Since she works hard and makes good use of her time, she has done well in all her classes in graphic arts and math. She plans to become an architect or an engineer and will no doubt be a good one.

As you plan a comparison-and-contrast composition, it is very useful to **brainstorm** for items of comparison. That is, as described in chapter 1, think about the subjects of your composition and briefly jot down whatever comes to mind about them. You can then use your list in deciding on the content of your paragraph.

## Organization

You should organize your comparison (or contrast) by whichever method suits your material best. One simple method is to explain a characteristic of item A, perhaps its cost, and then immediately compare it with the same characteristic of item B—and then go on to compare the two items point by point. For example, in contrasting two chocolate cakes, you may first want to say cake A is more expensive to prepare than cake B. Second, you may say that cake A, which requires more steps and ingredients, takes more time to make than cake B. Third, cake A is richer—almost too rich—and sweeter than cake B. You may conclude by saying that you recommend cake B. In this manner, you move back and forth, mentioning the specific differences between cake A and cake B in an orderly manner.

When the writer compares (or contrasts) two objects item by item, it is called the **alternating** or **point-by-point method.** The following diagram shows how this method works in the paragraph comparing Buicks and Cadillacs.

### Alternating (or point-by-point) method
Topic sentence: "A Buick and a Cadillac . . . are alike in many ways."

If the writer prefers a second type of organization, the **block method,** he or she explains all the characteristics of the first item together in a block and then explains all the characteristics of the second item in the same order in a corresponding block. The paragraphs contrasting the twins Sally and Susan (page 136) are organized in this block method.

### Block method

Topic sentence: "The twins are as different as two people can be."

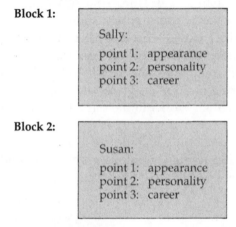

Block 1:

Sally:

point 1: appearance
point 2: personality
point 3: career

Block 2:

Susan:

point 1: appearance
point 2: personality
point 3: career

A third method, the **mixed method,** is useful when the writer wants to both compare and contrast in the same paragraph. All the similarities of the two items may first be explained and then all the differences. (Or, if the writer chooses, the differences may be explained first and then the similarities.) The following diagram shows this third method of organization, which was used in the paragraph on ideal societies (page 136).

### Mixed comparison-and-contrast method

Topic sentence: "people . . . drop out of the mainstream of American society . . . to live according to the group's concept of an ideal society."

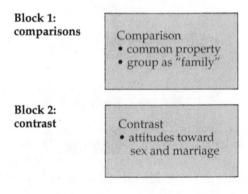

Block 1:
comparisons

Comparison
• common property
• group as "family"

Block 2:
contrast

Contrast
• attitudes toward
  sex and marriage

You will want to use these same three methods—alternating, block, and mixed—in writing longer essays. In the following essay, the writer uses the alternating method of organization to contrast types of people.

There are only two types of people in the world, Type A and Type Z. It isn't hard to tell which type you are. How long before the plane leaves do you arrive at the airport?

**Point 1: catching a plane**

Early plane-catchers, Type A, pack their bags at least a day in advance, and they pack neatly. If they're booked on a flight that leaves at four in the afternoon, they get up at 5:30 that morning. If they haven't left the house by noon, they're worried about missing the plane.

Late plane-catchers, Type Z, pack hastily at the last minute and arrive at the airport too late to buy a newspaper.

**Point 2: reading a book**

What do you do with a new book? Type A reads more carefully and finishes every book, even though it isn't any good.

Type Z skims through a lot of books and is more apt to write in the margins with a pencil.

**Point 3: eating breakfast**

Type A eats a good breakfast; Type Z grabs a cup of coffee.

**Point 4: turning off lights**

Type As turn off the lights when leaving a room and lock the doors when leaving a house. They go back to make sure they've locked it, and they worry later about whether they left the iron on or not. They didn't.

Type Zs leave the lights burning and if they lock the door at all when they leave the house, they're apt to have forgotten their keys.

**Point 5: seeing the dentist**

Type A sees the dentist twice a year, has an annual physical checkup and thinks he may have something.

Type Z has been meaning to see a doctor.

**Point 6: using toothpaste**

Type A squeezes a tube of toothpaste from the bottom, rolls it very carefully as he uses it and puts the top back on every time.

Type Z squeezes the tube from the middle, and he's lost the cap under the radiator.

**Point 7: other characteristics**

Type Zs are more apt to have some Type A characteristics than Type As are apt to have any Type Z characteristics.

**Point 8: marriage**

Type As always marry Type Zs.
Type Zs always marry Type As.

Andy Rooney,
"Types"

The comparison and contrast mode of development gives Rooney a framework for making use of **irony.** Irony is a device used by writers to imply something different or the opposite from what is actually stated. Here, Rooney uses irony for its humorous effect, with the ultimate irony being that Type As and Type Zs always marry their opposites.

Comparison and contrast, like classification and division, is a useful mode of development for writing on the academic subjects you will study in college courses. You will encounter it in textbooks, with comparison indicated by such transitional words as *similarly* and *by comparison* and contrast by *however, on the other hand,* and *on the contrary.* If you become comfortable with this mode, it will come in handy in your writing for other courses. Be alert, for example, to essay assignments and exam questions that begin "Compare and contrast . . ."

In the readings that follow, you will find the alternating, block, and mixed methods of comparison-and-contrast development. You will also see the variety of ideas that writers express through comparison and contrast.

# Happy Returns

*Sarah Bernard*

*Do you return gifts that you have received but don't like, or do you keep them for fear you will offend the giver? Here Sarah Bernard compares opinions about whether it is ethical to return a gift.*

## Words to Know

**Chuck Schumer**   United States senator from New York
**faction**   group of people with common interests or belief
*faux*-**fawning**   false flattery or attitude
**ideological**   idea, opinion
**psychological**   mental

## Getting Started

What is the best gift that you ever received? What is the worst?

---

**B**ut is returning ethical? This is a question that splits giftees into ideological camps. One group holds that, no matter how awful the gift, you should never, ever take it back. You can tell my husband belongs to this faction just by looking at him: His shirts are wrinkled because he wedges them into a closet packed with years of accumulated gift disasters—some of which, I admit, I've given him. (Among my "favorites": a slopey-shouldered Sherlock Holmes–style overcoat and a professional-grade shoe-shine kit.) These people face twin psychological hurdles. They find the very act of approaching the counter, unwanted gift in hand, shameful. (Which is just what stores want, of course—even Chuck Schumer has found time to campaign against repeat-returner blacklists.) And they think that returning the gift is an insult. The other group (of which I am a member) believes in—even encourages—returns. It's our conviction that the point is to get something the recipient likes, so we make it clear adjustments won't offend. In fact, a *faux*-fawning response to gifts you secretly loathe makes a mockery of the giver. How does he learn your taste if you keep sending the wrong message?

---

## Questions About the Reading

1. Why do some people believe a gift should never be taken back?
2. What does the writer's husband think about returning gifts?
3. What are the examples that the writer uses to illustrate her husband's opinion about returning gifts?
4. What is the writer's opinion about returning gifts? Do you think she would be offended if friends returned gifts she had given them?

## Questions About the Writer's Strategies

1. What is the main idea of the paragraph? State it in your own words.
2. What is the tone of the paragraph?
3. Is the point of view (person) consistent throughout the paragraph? If not, are any changes justified?
4. What technique does the writer use in the final sentence of the paragraph?

## Writing Assignments

1. What is the best or a very special birthday gift you have received? Write a paragraph is which you compare, contrast, or compare and contrast that gift with others and explain why you consider it the best or most special one.
2. Write a paragraph in which you compare, contrast, or compare and contrast the way your family members or friends have responded to gifts you have given them.

# Good Girl, Bad Girl

*Anna Quindlen*

> *Understanding why two people become friends is sometimes difficult. In this paragraph, essayist Anna Quindlen provides a candid assessment of an unbalanced friendship from her days at a boarding school for girls.*

### Words to Know

**dialectical**   having to do with two opposite or contradictory forces

**naïve**   innocent

**refectory**   cafeteria, dining hall

### Getting Started

What is it that attracts two friends to each other?

---

She was my best friend, and hard as it may have been to figure by the looks of us, she was the good girl, I the bad. I suppose everyone has at least one friendship like this in their lives. We were dialectical, she the thesis, I the antithesis. She was direct, trustworthy, kind, and naïve; I was manipulative, selfish, and clever. She laughed at all my jokes, took part in all my schemes, told everyone that I was the smartest and the funniest and the best. Like a B movie of boarding school life, we stole peanut butter from the refectory, short-sheeted beds, called drugstores and asked them if they had Prince Albert in a can. Whenever I hear a mother say, "If so-and-so told you to jump off the Brooklyn Bridge, would you do it?" I think of her. On my order, she would have jumped.

---

## Questions About the Reading

1. How do you imagine the author and her friend looked? Reread the first sentence before you describe the two girls.
2. What does the writer mean when she says that her exploits were "like a B movie of boarding school life"?
3. Does the writer believe she and her friend had a healthy relationship? Why or why not?

## Questions About the Writer's Strategies

1. Is the writer's mode of development comparison, contrast, or a combination of the two?
2. What other mode of development does the writer use?
3. What words does the writer use to describe herself? What words does she use to describe how her friend thought of her?
4. What simile does the author use to describe the friendship?

## Writing Assignments

1. Write a narrative paragraph that compares your personality with that of one of your closest friends.
2. Write a paragraph in which you compare and contrast a childhood friendship with a current friendship.
3. In a paragraph, compare and contrast a relationship between friends with one between brothers and sisters. Use examples from your own experience to illustrate similarities and differences.

# Dogs and Cats

*Konrad Lorenz*

> *Konrad Lorenz tells us what our dogs and cats have in common and how they differ.*
>
> ### Words to Know
>
> **carnivores**   meat-eating animals
> **domesticated**   tamed
> **servitude**   in service or bondage to another person
> **sphere**   range
> **uncompromising**   firm, unchanging
>
> ### Getting Started
>
> What pets do you have or have you had in the past?

O nly two animals have entered the human household otherwise than as prisoners and become domesticated by other means than those of enforced servitude: the dog and the cat. Two things they have in common, namely, that both belong to the order of carnivores and both serve man in their capacity of hunters. In all other characteristics, above all in the manner of their association with man, they are as different as the night from the day. There is no domestic animal that has so radically altered its whole way of living, indeed its whole sphere of interests, that has become domestic in so true a sense as the dog; and there is no animal that, in the course of its centuries-old association with man, has altered so little as the cat. There is some truth in the assertion that the cat, with the exception of a few luxury breeds, such as Angoras, Persians and Siamese, is no domestic animal but a completely wild being. Maintaining its full independence it has taken up its abode in the houses and outhouses of man, for the simple reason that there are more mice there than elsewhere. The whole charm of the dog lies in the depth of the friendship and the strength of the spiritual ties with which he has bound himself to man, but the appeal of the cat lies in the very fact that she has formed no close bond with him, that she has the uncompromising independence of a tiger or a leopard while she is hunting in his stables and barns, that she still remains mysterious and remote when she is rubbing herself gently against the legs of her mistress or purring contentedly in front of the fire.

## Questions About the Reading

1. What do a dog and a cat have in common?
2. How do a dog and a cat differ?
3. Why does a cat want to live in houses and outhouses?
4. How do a dog and a cat differ in their association with their owners?

## Questions About the Writer's Strategies

1. What method of comparison and contrast does the writer use?
2. Could the paragraph be made into more than one paragraph? If so, how?
3. What is the main idea of the paragraph? Is it stated or implied? If stated, identify the sentences. If implied, state it in your own words.

## Writing Assignments

1. Write a paragraph in which you compare and contrast the behavior of your pets or those of your friends. Identify the method or methods you used.
2. Visit a zoo and watch two different animals. Write a paragraph in which you explain the behaviors they have in common and those in which they differ. Identify the method or methods you used.
3. Explore animal diversity on the Internet. Choose some examples and compare and contrast two of your favorites.

# Yin and Yang

*Mary Paumier Jones*

*The yin-yang symbol comes from ancient Chinese cosmology. It represents both the dark and the light, or shaded and sunlit, sides of a mountain. The "yin" represents the female or shaded aspects of the symbol such as the earth, darkness, and passivity. The "yang" represents the male aspects of the symbol, such as light, sun, and activity. In this paragraph from her essay "The Opposite of Saffron," Mary Paumier Jones explains that the yin and yang movements in T'ai Chi, a Chinese form of exercise, form a perfect balance. (Adapted from http://www2.cybernex.net/~jefkirsh/ symbol.html.)*

### Words to Know

**inscrutably**   obscurely, mysteriously

**intercourse**   communication

**simultaneous**   at the same time

### Getting Started

How are walking and running alike? How are they different?

---

In T'ai Chi class Dr. Young talked about yin and yang. In the beginning square form, each movement is followed by a pause: the movement is yin, the pause yang. To my Western ears this smacks of sexism; the masculine principle acting, the feminine doing nothing. But I eventually begin to learn the pause is not nothing. Given its proper weight, gravity, and time, the pause does its work, its stretch, its subtle modification of the quality of the move before and the one to come. Later in the round form, the movement is continuous. Yin and yang, though still opposite, are inscrutably simultaneous, engaged in an ancient abstract intercourse.

---

## Questions About the Reading

1. What is yin and what is yang in the beginning square form of T'ai Chi?
2. Why does the writer think the notion of yin and yang "smacks of sexism"?
3. What is the purpose of the pause?
4. How does the round form of T'ai Chi differ from the square?

## Questions About the Writer's Strategies

1. What is the main idea of the paragraph? Is it stated or implied?
2. What is the point of view (person, time, tone) of the paragraph?
3. Is the point of view consistent throughout the paragraph? If not, where and in what way does it change?
4. If the point of view in the paragraph changes, is the change acceptable? Why or why not?

## Writing Assignments

1. Write an essay about two sports you have played, explaining how the sports are alike and how they are different.
2. Write an essay about two subjects you have studied in school and explain how they are alike and how they are different.

# Neat People vs. Sloppy People

*Suzanne Britt*

> *In this essay from her book* Show and Tell, *Suzanne Britt explains the differences between neat and sloppy people, claiming—surprisingly— that neat people are lazier and meaner than sloppy people.*

### Words to Know

**cavalier**   easygoing, offhand
**meticulously**   excessively
**métier**   occupation
**rectitude**   character, principles

### Getting Started

How would you characterize neat people and sloppy people?

---

**I**'ve finally figured out the difference between neat people and sloppy 1 people. The distinction is, as always, moral. Neat people are lazier and meaner than sloppy people.

Sloppy people, you see, are not really sloppy. Their sloppiness is merely 2 the unfortunate consequence of their extreme moral rectitude. Sloppy people carry in their mind's eye a heavenly vision, a precise plan, that is so stupendous, so perfect, it can't be achieved in this world or the next.

Sloppy people live in Never-Never Land. Someday is their métier. 3 Someday they are planning to alphabetize all their books and set up home catalogs. Someday they will go through their wardrobes and mark certain items for tentative mending and certain items for passing on to relatives of similar shape and size. Someday sloppy people will make family scrap-books into which they will put newspaper clippings, postcards, locks of hair, and the dried corsage from their senior prom. Someday they will file everything on the surface on their desk, including the cash receipts from coffee purchases at the snack shop. Someday they will sit down and read all the back issues of *The New Yorker*.

For all these noble reasons and more, sloppy people never get neat. 4 They aim too high and wide. They save everything, planning someday to file, order, and straighten out the world. But while these ambitious plans take clearer and clearer shape in their heads, the books spill from the shelves onto the floor, the clothes pile up in the hamper and closet, the family mementos accumulate in every drawer, the surface of the desk is buried under mounds of paper, and the unread magazines threaten to reach the ceiling.

Sloppy people can't bear to part with anything. They give loving atten-  5
tion to every detail. When sloppy people say they're going to tackle the surface of the desk, they really mean it. Not a paper will go unturned; not a rubber band will go unboxed. Four hours or two weeks into the excavation, the desk looks exactly the same, primarily because the sloppy person is meticulously creating new piles of papers with new headings and scrupulously stopping to read all the old book catalogs before he throws them away. A neat person would just bulldoze the desk.

Neat people are bums and clods at heart. They have cavalier attitudes  6
toward possessions, including family heirlooms. Everything is just another dust-catcher to them. If anything collects dust, it's got to go and that's that. Neat people will toy with the idea of throwing the children out of the house just to cut down on the clutter.

Neat people don't care about process. They like results. What they want  7
to do is get the whole thing over with so they can sit down and watch the rasslin' on TV. Neat people operate on two unvarying principles: Never handle any item twice, and throw everything away.

The only thing messy in a neat person's house is the trash can. The  8
minute something comes to a neat person's hand, he will look at it, try to decide if it has immediate use and, finding none, throw it in the trash.

Neat people are especially vicious with mail. They never go through  9
their mail unless they are standing directly over a trash can. If the trash can is beside the mailbox, even better. All ads, catalogs, pleas for charitable contributions, church bulletins and money-saving coupons go straight into the trash can without being opened. All letters from home, postcards from Europe, bills and paychecks are opened, immediately responded to, then dropped in the trash can. Neat people keep their receipts only for tax purposes. That's it. No sentimental salvaging of birthday cards or the last letter a dying relative ever wrote. Into the trash it goes.

Neat people place neatness above everything, even economics. They  10
are incredibly wasteful. Neat people throw away several toys every time they walk through the den. I knew a neat person once who threw away a perfectly good dish drainer because it had mold on it. The drainer was too much trouble to wash. And neat people sell their furniture when they move. They will sell a La-Z-Boy recliner while you are reclining in it.

Neat people are no good to borrow from. Neat people buy everything  11
in expensive little single portions. They get their flour and sugar in two-pound bags. They wouldn't consider clipping a coupon, saving a leftover, reusing plastic non-dairy whipped cream containers or rinsing off tin foil and draping it over the unmoldy dish drainer. You can never borrow a

neat person's newspaper to see what's playing at the movies. Neat people have the paper all wadded up and in the trash by 7:05 A.M.

Neat people cut a clean swath through the organic as well as the inor- 12 ganic world. People, animals, and things are all one to them. They are so insensitive. After they've finished with the pantry, the medicine cabinet, and the attic, they will throw out the red geranium (too many leaves), sell the dog (too many fleas), and send the children off to boarding school (too many scuff marks on the hardwood floors).

## Questions About the Reading

1. What is the reason, according to the writer, that people are sloppy?
2. What do sloppy people intend to do with everything they keep?
3. Why do sloppy people never get neat?
4. Why are people neat?
5. How do neat people handle their mail?

## Questions About the Writer's Strategies

1. What is the comparison/contrast method used by the writer?
2. What is the topic of each paragraph, beginning with the second?
3. Is each topic stated in a sentence? If so, what are the topic sentences?
4. What is the tone of the essay? Is it consistent throughout?

## Writing Assignments

1. Write an essay in which you compare, contrast, or compare and contrast shopping in different grocery stores.
2. **Working Together**  Join with some classmates to compare, contrast, or compare and contrast how people in different neighborhoods keep their yards.

# Conversational Ballgames

### Nancy Masterson Sakamoto

*The difference between Western and Japanese conversation styles is like the difference between tennis or volleyball and bowling, according to Nancy Sakamoto in this essay from her book* Polite Fictions. *She is an American married to a Japanese man and is a professor of American Studies at a Japanese university.*

### Words to Know

**elaboration**   further information, additional details
**indispensable**   necessary, essential
**unconsciously**   unknowingly

### Getting Started

Is there a difference between the way you talk to a friend and the way you talk to a teacher, a stranger, or an older person?

After I was married and had lived in Japan for a while, my Japanese 1 gradually improved to the point where I could take part in simple conversations with my husband and his friends and family. And I began to notice that often, when I joined in, the others would look startled, and the conversational topic would come to a halt. After this happened several times, it became clear to me that I was doing something wrong. But for a long time, I didn't know what it was.

Finally, after listening carefully to many Japanese conversations, I dis- 2 covered what my problem was. Even though I was speaking Japanese, I was handling the conversation in a western way.

Japanese-style conversations develop quite differently from western- 3 style conversations. And the difference isn't only in the languages. I realized that just as I kept trying to hold western-style conversations even when I was speaking Japanese, so my English students kept trying to hold Japanese-style conversations even when they were speaking English. We were unconsciously playing entirely different conversational ballgames.

A western-style conversation between two people is like a game of 4 tennis. If I introduce a topic, a conversational ball, I expect you to hit it back. If you agree with me, I don't expect you simply to agree and do nothing more. I expect you to add something—a reason for agreeing, another example, or an elaboration to carry the idea further. But I don't expect you always to agree. I am just as happy if you question me, or challenge me, or completely disagree with me. Whether you agree or disagree, your response will return the ball to me.

And then it is my turn again. I don't serve a new ball from my original 5
starting line. I hit your ball back again from where it has bounced. I carry
your idea further, or answer your questions or objections, or challenge or
question you. And so the ball goes back and forth, with each of us doing
our best to give it a new twist, an original spin, or a powerful smash.

And the more vigorous the action, the more interesting and exciting 6
the game. Of course, if one of us gets angry, it spoils the conversation,
just as it spoils a tennis game. But getting excited is not at all the same as
getting angry. After all, we are not trying to hit each other. We are trying
to hit the ball. So long as we attack only each other's opinions, and do not
attack each other personally, we don't expect anyone to get hurt. A good
conversation is supposed to be interesting and exciting.

If there are more than two people in the conversation, then it is like 7
doubles in tennis, or like volleyball. There's no waiting in line. Whoever
is nearest and quickest hits the ball, and if you step back, someone else
will hit it. No one stops the game to give you a turn. You're responsible
for taking your own turn.

But whether it's two players or a group, everyone does his best to keep 8
the ball going, and no one person has the ball for very long.

A Japanese-style conversation, however, is not at all like tennis or volley- 9
ball. It's like bowling. You wait for your turn. And you always know
your place in line. It depends on such things as whether you are older or
younger, a close friend or a relative stranger to the previous speaker, in a
senior or junior position, and so on.

When your turn comes, you step up to the starting line with your bowl- 10
ing ball, and carefully bowl it. Everyone else stands back and watches
politely, murmuring encouragement. Everyone waits until the ball has
reached the end of the alley, and watches to see if it knocks down all the
pins, or only some of them, or none of them. There is a pause, while everyone registers your score.

Then, after everyone is sure that you have completely finished your 11
turn, the next person in line steps up to the same starting line, with a different ball. He doesn't return your ball, and he does not begin from where
your ball stopped. There is no back and forth at all. All the balls run parallel. And there is always a suitable pause between turns. There is no rush,
no excitement, no scramble for the ball.

No wonder everyone looked startled when I took part in Japanese con- 12
versations. I paid no attention to whose turn it was, and kept snatching
the ball halfway down the alley and throwing it back at the bowler. Of
course the conversation died. I was playing the wrong game.

This explains why it is almost impossible to get a western-style conver- 13
sation or discussion going with English students in Japan. I used to think
that the problem was their lack of English language ability. But I finally
came to realize that the biggest problem is that they, too, are playing the
wrong game.

Whenever I serve a volleyball, everyone just stands back and watches 14
it fall, with occasional murmurs of encouragement. No one hits it back.
Everyone waits until I call on someone to take a turn. And when that
person speaks, he doesn't hit my ball back. He serves a new ball. Again,
everyone just watches it fall.

So I call on someone else. This person does not refer to what the pre- 15
vious speaker has said. He also serves a new ball. Nobody seems to have
paid any attention to what anyone else has said. Everyone begins again
from the same starting line, and all the balls run parallel. There is never
any back and forth. Everyone is trying to bowl with a volleyball.

And if I try a simpler conversation, with only two of us, then the other 16
person tries to bowl with my tennis ball. No wonder foreign English
teachers in Japan get discouraged.

Now that you know about the difference in the conversational ball- 17
games, you may think that all your troubles are over. But if you have
been trained all your life to play one game, it is no simple matter to switch
to another, even if you know the rules. Knowing the rules is not at all the
same thing as playing the game.

Even now, during a conversation in Japanese I will notice a startled 18
reaction, and belatedly realize that once again I have rudely interrupted
by instinctively trying to hit back the other person's bowling ball. It is no
easier for me to "just listen" during a conversation, than it is for my
Japanese students to "just relax" when speaking with foreigners. Now I
can truly sympathize with how hard they must find it to try to carry on
a western-style conversation.

If I have not yet learned to do conversational bowling in Japanese, at 19
least I have figured out one thing that puzzled me for a long time. After
his first trip to America, my husband complained that Americans asked
him so many questions and made him talk so much at the dinner table
that he never had a chance to eat. When I asked him why he couldn't talk
and eat at the same time, he said that Japanese do not customarily think
that dinner, especially on fairly formal occasions, is a suitable time for extended conversation.

Since westerners think that conversation is an indispensable part of 20
dining, and indeed would consider it impolite not to converse with one's
dinner partner, I found this Japanese custom rather strange. Still, I could
accept it as a cultural difference even though I didn't really understand

it. But when my husband added, in explanation, that Japanese consider it extremely rude to talk with one's mouth full, I got confused. Talking with one's mouth full is certainly not an American custom. We think it very rude, too. Yet we still manage to talk a lot and eat at the same time. How do we do it?

For a long time, I couldn't explain it, and it bothered me. But after I 21 discovered the conversational ballgames, I finally found the answer. Of course! In a western-style conversation, you hit the ball, and while someone else is hitting it back, you take a bite, chew, and swallow. Then you hit the ball again, and then eat some more. The more people there are in the conversation, the more chances you have to eat. But even with only two of you talking, you still have plenty of chances to eat.

Maybe that's why polite conversation at the dinner table has never 22 been a traditional part of Japanese etiquette. Your turn to talk would last so long without interruption that you'd never get a chance to eat.

## Questions About the Reading

1. How did the writer's Japanese husband, family, and friends react to her participation in conversations?
2. What does the writer say was wrong with how she was handling the conversations?
3. How does the writer characterize Western-style conversation? To what does she compare Western-style conversation?
4. How does the writer characterize Japanese-style conversation? To what does she compare Japanese-style conversation?
5. What did the writer's Japanese husband complain about after his first trip to America?

## Questions About the Writer's Strategies

1. What is the thesis of the essay?
2. What method of comparison-and-contrast organization does the writer use?
3. What is the simile the writer uses for a Western-style conversation between two people? What simile does she use for a conversation among several people?
4. What simile does the writer use for a Japanese-style conversation?
5. How do Westerners manage to carry on a conversation while they are eating and not talk with their mouths full?

6. Does the writer use any mode of development in addition to contrast? If so, what is it and in which paragraphs is it found?

## Writing Assignments

1. Write an essay in which you contrast the way you talk to your best friends with the way you talk to neighborhood or school friends. Use dialogue to illustrate the differences.
2. Go to a shopping mall and listen to the people who are walking around or working in the stores. Classify the different people you see and write an essay in which you compare and/or contrast their conversations.

# Indy 500

## *Chris Hanley (student)*

*We are often told that young drivers are reckless and have a high accident rate. In his essay, Chris Hanley tells us a different story.*

### Words to Know

**ER** Emergency Room
**neurotic** nervous disorder
**paranoid** delusional
**senility** old age infirmity

### Getting Started

What are some things—like driving, washing dishes, or cleaning house—that you feel you do better or more efficiently than other members of your family?

---

H aving lived in St. Louis all my life, I have encountered many a strange  1
driver. I have seen the speedy driver, the crazy driver, and the overly cautious driver, but none of these drivers compares to my mother. My mother is a neurotic, paranoid racecar driver stuck behind the wheel of a four-wheel deathtrap. She scares me to death as I am often forced to ride as a passenger in her car when we run family errands here and there around town. It is during these rides that my life flashes before me, usually more than once, that I realize why I am so confident in my abilities to drive, and why I quickly offer to drive wherever we go. To say that our driving styles are opposites would be like hitting the bull's-eye at the local county fair.

My mother is only fifty-two years old, and I am quite sure that senility  2
has not yet set in, but yet someone would assume something is not right. This lady I admire just hasn't a clue; she seems to have no control over her body when she sits behind the wheel of her car. Sometimes it seems as if she just doesn't care who she runs over or scares the heck out of as she bounces down the road, heading to work or off on some odd errand she must run for the family. Let me try to describe for you the typical scenario that would play out on a short trip to the store. As we pull out into traffic from the four-way stop by our house, she swerves at a car two lanes over and rants that he should not be so close; then she proceeds to drive ten miles over the posted speed limit. Coming to a halt at a stoplight involves a process that an Indy pit crew could only appreciate; screeching brakes

and feeling suspended from the seatbelts truly give one the almost-there feeling. No need to attempt to peel myself off the front windshield because John Force in the driver's seat has burnt rubber leaving the light to try and cut off the guy in a Yugo trying to merge into traffic two lights up from us. From the look on the face of the Yugo driver, somehow he doesn't believe the fact my mom has her blinker on and is fully intending on making a turn that only Paul Tracy would attempt on a good day. Sliding sideways into the parking lot of the local Shop 'N Save, nearly taking out the cart attendant and a little old lady with a walker, she races to the front of the first available lane, gunning for the first open parking spot. Screech go the tires once more as we come to a sliding, grinding halt, finally parked at our destination that is only concluded with my thanking God that I am still alive but praying that I may be allowed to drive home.

My mother's driving skills in no way show in the way I drive; my driv-  3
ing ability makes my mother look like a monkey trying to ride a tricycle. My skills are much more refined and smooth; I pride myself on being a very good driver, an above-average driver in my eyes. As I beg and plead with my mother to allow me to drive home, I use my trump card and inform her that I have an English paper due and wouldn't be able to finish if I ended up in the ER. Unwillingly, my mother finally gives up the keys and lets me drive, though watching her buckle up as though she were being launched into orbit via the space shuttle isn't very reassuring, to say the least. I shrug off this little bit of a visual crack my mother has made about my driving because I know that I am the better driver without any thought. Cautiously, as I place the car in reverse and proceed to check all lines of sight and attempt to back out of the parking space, "LOOK OUT" is all I hear, as if I had run over somebody. "What seems to be the problem?" My mom looks at me and says, "You almost hit that car." Urgently looking to see this mysterious car I almost hit, thus almost blemishing my perfect driving record, I look around, and the closest car to us is a hundred feet away at the beginning of the aisle we were in. I look at my mother and almost fall out of my seat. "What?" I ask. "You could have hit that car pulling out of the parking spot that fast," she comments. "Are you serious?" I say. "Yes," she replies. Reversing out of the parking space with no further issues or near heart attacks, I proceed to exit the parking lot and merge into traffic easily and effortlessly; it's amazing what common sense and blinkers can do for someone. As I drive down the road doing the posted speed limit, my mother constantly asks, "Why are you driving so slow?" "Because it's the speed limit," I reply. She looks at me as if I were wearing a clown suit and telling jokes; she's almost laughing at me because I am obeying the law. Driving carefully and confidently made for an uneventful and much safer trip home than the one to the store. To

say that I was a lot calmer when we got home than when we arrived at the store is an understatement of monumental proportions.

My mother tends to think that I drive too cautiously and that I could   4
learn a thing or two from her style of driving. On the other hand, I tend to think that driving cautiously and safely would be an example my mother would be trying to set for her son, but it seems as if I am way off target. Agreeing to disagree about our driving styles is something that is quite obvious when we bicker about each other's driving types. What is apparent is that although we both drive the same roads, we do them as differently as we can get, but as long as we both continue to arrive at our locations in one piece, I can't really complain.

---

## Questions About the Reading

1. What are the different kinds of drivers the writer has seen in St. Louis?
2. Who, according to the writer, would appreciate the way his mother comes to a halt at a stoplight?
3. What is the "visual crack" the writer's mother makes about his driving when she agrees to let him drive home?

4. Who are John Force and Paul Tracy? How are they related to the title of the essay? Use the Internet to find out about them.

## Questions About the Writer's Strategies

1. What is the tone of the essay?
2. What order does the writer use in contrasting his driving with that of his mother?
3. What modes of development does the writer use in addition to compare or contrast?
4. What is the simile the writer uses in the third paragraph?

## Writing Assignments

1. *Working Together*  Join with some classmates to write an essay in which you compare or contrast your school schedules, registration experiences, or study habits.
2. Write an essay in which you compare, contrast, or compare and contrast your driving, lawn mowing, dishwashing, or performance of another household chore with that of a family member, friend, or neighbor.

# Shopping in Pajamas

### *Francine Mercier (student)*

> Francine Mercier is originally from French Canada and now lives in San Francisco. She is a part-time student at the City College of San Francisco and a volunteer docent for a Victorian house-museum. Her interests are history and architecture, and she hopes to combine those interests in her future occupation.

### Word to Know

avatar   image, replica

### Getting Started

What are the similarities and differences between doing research in a library and on a computer?

---

$\mathbf{H}$ave you ever had a dream in which you are at the supermarket or at the mall shopping in your pajamas? When you wake up, you realize that you are still in bed and that if you want to go shopping, you have to get dressed. What a disappointment. But wait! If you decide to shop online instead of going to the store, you can stay in your pajamas, sit in front of your computer with a steaming cup of coffee, and shop from the comfort of your home. Online shopping is far more convenient than in-store shopping, and it has the additional benefit of allowing substantial savings. 1

I had many unpleasant experiences while shopping in-store, but it was this one particular experience that really convinced me of how much more convenient online shopping can be. One sunny Saturday afternoon, I decided to go shopping downtown. Unfortunately, I was not the only one who thought it was the ideal moment for this activity, and as such, the streets were heavily congested. It took me a long time to get to the parking lot, and when I finally got there, it was full. After going around an additional hour in a sea of vehicles, I was able to park. Reaching my destination was only the beginning of my problems. On that day, the stores, like the roads, were crowded. Everywhere I went, swarms of shoppers surrounded me, which limited my ability to look at the merchandise and created long waiting lines at the cashier. I went shopping planning to have a good time, but instead I came back home with a pair of socks, a book, and a lot of tension created by this whole experience. I could have escaped 2 this nightmare by shopping online. Although I would not have been able to enjoy my pair of socks and my book right away, I could have avoided the traffic, the time spent to find a parking space, the crowd, and the long wait at the cashier. When shopping online, you can shop on your own terms. You can shop when you want, compare items from different stores, and purchase what you need in a fraction of the time you would spend if you were shopping in a store. For additional convenience, your merchandise is delivered at your doorstep, which eliminates all the traffic and parking-related problems.

Besides offering convenience, online shopping provides more oppor-   3 tunities to save money on your purchases than in-store shopping. Comparing prices between stores is one of the golden rules for saving money, and shopping online provides a quick and easy way to do it. Web sites like Nextag.com and Bizrate.com compare the prices of one item from several stores at once. You can then choose the best deal. It would be extremely time-consuming, even impossible, to do this type of comparison if you were shopping in-store. To save even more, online shopping makes many purchasing options available. You can buy new or used items or even auction for what you want on eBay. For example, when I compared the price of books at my neighborhood bookstore and online at Amazon.com, I was surprised to find the same item for 15 to 20 percent less. Not only was the price lower for a new item, but I also had the option to purchase a used item, which was even cheaper. Although it is true that sometimes shipping fees can increase the product's price, overall, the ability to compare prices quickly between different stores and the variety of ways to purchase an item frequently result in lower prices.

In the end, having experienced both shopping in-store and online, I   4 definitely prefer the additional convenience and the lower prices offered by online shopping. The convenience and lower prices compensate for the one thing online shopping does not yet offer, which is direct contact with the product. I have to concede that for some items—for example, shoes or clothing—nothing can replace trying an item on to see how it fits. However, this inconvenience might soon become a thing of the past since online stores like Levi Strauss have started to experiment with the use of technology that can scan your body and create a three-dimensional avatar that provides the online store with your dimensions. With this information, the store is then able to point out which item will fit your body and will even enhance your best features.

## Questions About the Reading

1. What is the writer's opinion of shopping online?
2. What were the problems the writer experienced when she went shopping downtown on a Saturday afternoon?
3. What are the specific conveniences the writer finds in shopping online?
4. What is the experimental technology that may eliminate needing to go to the stores to shop for shoes or clothing?

## Questions About the Writer's Strategies

1. What is the organizational method the writer uses?
2. What is the thesis of the essay? Is it stated or implied? State it in your own words.
3. What is the point of view (person, time, tone) of the essay?
4. What modes of development does the writer use in addition to compare and contrast?

## Writing Assignments

1. Write an essay in which you compare and contrast researching a subject in your school library and on your computer.

2. *Working Together*   Join with some classmates to go on a shopping trip for a specific item. Then use the Internet and shop for the same item. Write an essay in which you compare and contrast the experiences you had in the different stores and the prices you found for the item in stores and on the Internet.

# 7 Process

IF YOU WANT to hook up your new computer, you will probably follow the directions, or a **process,** provided by the manufacturer. A process is a method of doing a task or a job, usually in orderly steps, to achieve a desired result. For example, directions and recipes are both detailed explanations of processes. So are all articles and essays that tell how to prepare for a job interview, assemble a stereo system, dress for success, or operate a personal computer. So, too, are essays that describe how someone else used a process to accomplish something or complete a task.

In an essay explaining how to carry out a process, the writer needs to give clear and accurate guidance or directions, making the steps as simple as possible for the reader to follow. To do this, the writer must decide exactly what the reader already knows and what he or she needs to be told. The burden is on the writer to provide complete information to enable the reader to perform the task. If the writer forgets to mention how long the cookies should bake, the cook may be left with burned chocolate-chip cookies and disappointed friends.

The written explanation of such a process must be organized with particular care. Each step or part of the directions should be discussed in the same order as it occurs in the process. The following sample paragraph is a recipe for shrimp—one you might want to try. Notice that the writer begins with the purchase of the shrimp and then proceeds, step by step, through preparing, cooking, and serving the shrimp.

| | |
|---|---|
| Topic sentence | When fresh shrimp can be had, have it. What size? Medium |
| Step 1: choose size | for reasons of economy and common sense. Huge shrimps are magnificently expensive while small ones come in such numbers per pound that shelling them becomes slave labor. |
| Step 2: choose quantity | Buy two pounds of fresh shrimp and shell them. First, with a thumbnail pinch the tail shell hard crosswise (so the tail segments will come out intact), then handle the headless animals |
| Step 3: shell shrimp | like so many pea pods; split them lengthwise, save the contents, and throw the husks away. Sauté the shrimp with three |
| Step 4: cooking directions | crushed garlic cloves in two-thirds of a stick of butter. When the shrimp turn pink, add a 12-ounce can of Italian tomatoes (which taste better than the fresh supermarket kind), two |

163

> bay leaves, a teaspoon of dried oregano, a half-cup of dry
> white wine, and the juice of a lemon. Simmer for ten minutes,
> sprinkle with chopped parsley and serve with rice.
>
> Philip Kopper,<br>"Delicacies de la Mer"

Because this paragraph is telling the reader what to do, the **point of view** is **second person** (you), and it is in the present tense (*come, buy, save, throw,* and so forth). But the word *you* is unstated, which makes the paragraph seem to address the reader even more directly. This **tone** is commonly used in process writing that instructs the reader.

Not all process essays are such clear-cut models of process writing as the previous example. In some cases, a paragraph or essay describing a process may serve a purpose similar to that of a **narrative** or a **description.** That is, whereas strictly process writing is intended primarily to **instruct,** process writing also can be adapted to situations in which the writer mainly wants to **inform** or **describe.** In such cases, a process is often combined with narration and description, as in the following example. Notice that in describing the process—the way the woman packs her suitcases and leaves the house—the writer describes her character. You also know, by the contrast between her habits and those of her husband, that her basic character differs sharply from his. By detailing the process of packing and combining it with other narrative details, the writer tells you indirectly what has previously happened in the woman's life.

**Introduction— narrative**

He slammed the door angrily behind him, and she heard the squeal of the tires as he raced off in the car. For a moment, she felt her usual fear. She knew he shouldn't drive after he'd been drinking heavily.   1

**Step 1: preparation**

But then she turned, went to the linen closet, and took out a clean towel. She spread the towel out on her neatly made bed.   2

**Step 2: finding suitcases**

Next, she got her overnight bag and a larger suitcase from the closet and put them carefully on the towel on her bed.   3

Methodically, she took neatly folded underwear, stockings, and nightgowns from her drawers and packed them in neat rows in the two bags. One set in the overnight bag, and five in the larger suitcase. She laid aside a nightgown with a matching robe to pack last.

**Step 3: packing suitcases**

Next, she lifted dresses and suits, carefully hung on the hangers and buttoned up so they wouldn't wrinkle, from her closet and folded them into the larger suitcase. Two extra blouses and a dress went into the overnight bag. She'd wear the suit she had on.   4

She brought plastic bags from the kitchen and put her shoes into them. One pair went into the overnight bag; two pairs, one for the dresses and one for the suits, went into the   5

larger bag. Then she put her bedroom slippers and the nightgown with the matching robe on top of the other clothes in
the overnight bag. She would take only the overnight bag
into her parents' house, at least at first. No need for them to
know right away that this time was for more than one night.
They'd always said that she wasn't going to change him and
that the marriage wouldn't last.

6

**Step 4: final
check and look
around**

She sighed again, closed the suitcases, carried them out to
her car, and then went back into the house for one last look
around. Almost ready, she took her coat from the hall closet,
folded it carefully over her arm, and took a last look at his
shoes and socks left beside his chair and the newspaper flung
across the couch where it would leave newsprint on the upholstery. She left the shoes and socks but couldn't resist fold-
ing the newspaper and putting it on a table. Finally, she went
out, closed the door silently behind her, got into her car, and
drove quietly and slowly away.

As you started reading this essay, you probably realized right away
that it would be more narrative and descriptive than instructive of a
process. Two signals that alerted you are that the point of view is **third
person** (*she*) and past tense (*took, packed, lifted, laid,* and so on). Think, for
a minute, about writing a clear process explanation using that person and
tense. Experienced writers may use varying **points of view** in process
writing, but for clear point-by-point process explanations, the **second
person** (*you*), the present tense (*take, pour, measure*), and a straightforward
tone are the most common.

Although a process approach can sometimes be useful in writing narratives and descriptions that deal with significant activities or accomplishments, you usually will use process for giving directions, describing how
a mechanical gadget works, or reporting on science experiments. In these
situations you may combine process with other modes like **definition**
(chapter 9), **examples** (chapter 4), and **cause and effect** (chapter 8). Always
remember that three factors are essential to an effective process essay. First,
be sure that the steps or procedures are carefully organized, step by step—
usually in the same order as they should be carried out—so that the reader
can understand and follow your explanation. Second, be sure that you include any information that the reader needs about any special materials or
preliminary steps. And, third, include *all* the specific steps in the process.

# The Supply Chain

**Thomas L. Friedman**

*In this paragraph from his best-selling book* The World Is Flat, *Tom Friedman,* New York Times *prize-winning columnist, explains the computerized supply-chain used by Wal-Mart to keep merchandise flowing seamlessly from thousands of suppliers—whether they are in China or Maine—to four thousand Wal-Mart stores worldwide.*

### Words to Know

**conveyor belt**   mechanized device for moving an item from one
   place to another
**finale**   ending, conclusion

### Getting Started

What advantages are there to you, as a consumer, from the efficiency of Wal-Mart's supply-chain system?

I had never seen what a supply chain looked like in action until I visited Wal-Mart headquarters in Bentonville, Arkansas. My Wal-Mart hosts took me over to the 1.2-million-square-foot distribution center, where we climbed up to a viewing perch and watched the show. On one side of the building, scores of white Wal-Mart trailer trucks were dropping off boxes of merchandise from thousands of different suppliers. Boxes large and small were fed up a conveyor belt at each loading dock. These little conveyor belts fed into a bigger belt, like streams feeding into a powerful river. Twenty-four hours a day, seven days a week, the suppliers' trucks feed the twelve miles of conveyor streams, and the conveyor streams feed into a huge Wal-Mart river of boxed products. But that is just half the show. As the Wal-Mart river flows along, an electric eye reads the bar codes on each box on its way to the other side of the building. There, the river parts again into a hundred streams. Electric arms from each stream reach out and guide the boxes—ordered by particular Wal-Mart stores—off the main river and down its stream, where another conveyor belt sweeps them into a waiting Wal-Mart truck, which will rush these particular products onto the shelves of a particular Wal-Mart store somewhere in the country. There, a consumer will lift one of these products off the shelf, and the cashier will scan it in, and the moment that happens, a signal will be generated. That signal will go out across the Wal-Mart network to the supplier of that product—whether that supplier's factory is in coastal China or coastal Maine. That signal will pop up on the supplier's computer screen and prompt him to make another of that item and ship it via the Wal-Mart supply chain, and the whole cycle will start anew. So no sooner does your arm lift a product off the local Wal-Mart's shelf and onto the check-out counter than another mechanical arm starts making another one somewhere in the world. Call it "the Wal-Mart Symphony" in multiple movements—with no finale. It just plays over and over 24/7/365: delivery, sorting, packing, distribution, buying, manufacturing, reordering, delivery, sorting, packing. . . .

## Questions About the Reading

1. What is the size of Wal-Mart's distribution center?
2. What are the stages or steps in the supply-chain process?
3. When does the supply chain operate? What makes it start over again?
4. What makes the supply chain an example of the world's being flat?

## Questions About the Writer's Strategies

1. What is the main idea of the paragraph?
2. What is the metaphor the writer uses for the supply chain?
3. What is the simile the writer uses for the little conveyor belts?
4. What is the metaphor the writer uses for the continuous nature of the supply chain?

## Writing Assignments

1. Write a paragraph in which you explain the process you follow in getting ready for and getting to school.
2. Visit your local Wal-Mart, supermarket, or clothing store and ask the manager to let you observe the process followed from the receiving to the selling of its merchandise. Then write an extended paragraph explaining the process.

# How to Bathe a Cat

## *The Dog*

*Don't take this process seriously, but if you've ever owned a cat, would you want to try it?*

### Word to Know
**soothe**   calm

### Getting Started
As they say in television ads showing dangerous stunts, "Don't try this at home."

---

1. Thoroughly clean the toilet. 2. Add the required amount of shampoo to the toilet water and have both lids up. 3. Find the cat and soothe him while you carry him towards the bathroom. 4. In one smooth movement, put the cat in the toilet and close both lids. (You may need to stand on the lid so that he cannot escape.) The cat will self-agitate and make ample suds. Never mind the noises that come from your toilet; the cat is actually enjoying this. CAUTION: Do not get any part of your body too close to the edge, as his paws will be reaching out for anything they can find. 5. Flush the toilet three or four times. This provides a "Power Wash" and "Rinse," which I have found to be quite effective. 6. Have someone open the door to the outside and ensure that there are no people between the toilet and the outside door. 7. Stand behind the toilet as far as you can and quickly lift both lids. 8. The now clean cat will rocket out of the toilet and run outside where he will dry himself.

Sincerely,
The Dog

---

## Questions About the Reading

1. Why should you stand on the lid of the toilet when bathing the cat?
2. What is the purpose of flushing the toilet several times?

## Questions About the Writer's Strategies

1. What is the main idea of the paragraph?
2. What is the point of view of the paragraph?

## Writing Assignments

1. Write a humorous paragraph in which you explain the process of washing dishes, mowing the lawn, getting to school, or studying for an exam.
2. Write a paragraph in which you explain the process you would follow in washing a dog.

# Brewing Beer

**Grace Lichtenstein**

*It's a lengthy and exacting process to produce a bottle of Coors beer.*

### Words to Know
**amber**   brownish gold color
**fermentation**   breakdown of molecules in a compound

### Getting Started
What is your favorite dessert? What is the process in making that dessert?

Like other beers, Coors [beer] is produced from barley. Most of the big Midwestern brewers use barley grown in North Dakota and Minnesota. Coors is the single American brewer to use a Moravian strain, grown under company supervision, on farms in Colorado, Idaho, Wyoming and Montana. At the brewery, the barley is turned into malt by being soaked in water—which must be biologically pure and of a known mineral content—for several days, causing it to sprout and producing a chemical change—breaking down starch into sugar. The malt is toasted, a process that halts the sprouting and determines the color and sweetness (the more the roasting, the darker, more bitter the beer). It is ground into flour and brewed, with more pure water, in huge copper-domed kettles until it is the consistency of oatmeal. Rice and refined starch are added to make mash; solids are strained out, leaving an amber liquid malt extract, which is boiled with hops—the dried cones from the hop vine which add to the bitterness, or tang. The hops are strained, yeast is added, turning the sugar to alcohol, and the beer is aged in huge red vats at near-freezing temperatures for almost two months, during which the second fermentation takes place and the liquid becomes carbonated, or bubbly. (Many breweries chemically age their beer to speed up production; Coors people say only naturally aged brew can be called a true "lager.") Next, the beer is filtered through cellulose filters to remove bacteria, and finally is pumped into cans, bottles or kegs for shipping.

## Questions About the Reading

1. What makes the grain used by Coors different from that used by other brewers?
2. What are the products used in making beer?
3. What is special about the water used in producing beer?
4. What are the steps followed in making beer?
5. What makes beer carbonated or bubbly? What is necessary to make a beer called "lager"?

## Questions About the Writer's Strategies

1. What is the writer's purpose in explaining the beer-making process?
2. What is the point of view in the paragraph? Is it consistent?
3. In addition to process, what other modes of development are used by the writer?

## Writing Assignments

1. Write a paragraph in which you explain the process of making your favorite dessert.
2. Write a paragraph in which you explain, in detail, the process of registering for classes in person.
3. Write a paragraph in which you explain, in detail, the process of registering for classes on the Internet.

# The Right Way to Eat an Ice-Cream Cone

## L. Rust Hills

*Rust Hills was fiction editor of* Esquire *and the* Saturday Evening Post *and is now a free-lance writer. In this paragraph, taken from his book* How To Do Things Right, *he explains his technique, which was perfected through years of taking his children to ice-cream cone stands. Having told us the preliminary pitfalls—melted ice cream on car upholstery, choosing a flavor, holding more than one cone—he delivers the ultimate instructions on eating the cone.*

### Words to Know

**forgoing**   deciding against
**jostling**   bumping together
**molecules**   very small particles
**stance**   way of standing

### Getting Started

What is the best or right way to eat spaghetti?

G rasp the cone with the right hand firmly but gently between thumb and at least one but not more than three fingers, two-thirds of the way up the cone. Then dart swiftly away to an open area, away from the jostling crowd at the stand. Now take up the classic ice-cream-cone-eating stance: feet from one to two feet apart, body bent forward from the waist at a twenty-five-degree angle, right elbow well up, right forearm horizontal, at a level with your collarbone and about twelve inches from it. But don't start eating yet! Check first to see what emergency repairs may be necessary. Sometimes a sugar cone will be so crushed or broken or cracked that all one can do is gulp at the thing like a savage, getting what he can of it and letting the rest drop to the ground, and then evacuating the area of catastrophe as quickly as possible. Checking the cone for possible trouble can be done in a second or two, if one knows where to look and does it systematically. A trouble spot some people overlook is the bottom tip of the cone. This may have been broken off. Or the flap of the cone material at the bottom, usually wrapped over itself in that funny spiral construction, may be folded in a way that is imperfect and leaves an opening. No need to say that through this opening—in a matter of perhaps thirty or, at most, ninety seconds—will begin to pour hundreds of thousands of sticky molecules of melted ice cream. You know in this case that you must instantly get the paper napkin in your left hand under and around the bottom of the cone to stem the forthcoming flow, or else be doomed to eat the cone far too rapidly. It is a grim moment. No one wants to eat a cone under that kind of pressure, but neither does anyone want to end up with the bottom of the cone stuck to a messy napkin. There's one other alternative—one that takes both skill and courage: Forgoing any cradling action, grasp the cone more firmly between thumb and forefinger and extend the other fingers so that they are out of the way of the dripping from the bottom, then increase the waist-bend angle from twenty-five to thirty-five degrees, and then eat the cone, *allowing* it to drip out of the bottom onto the ground in front of you! Experienced and thoughtful cone-eaters enjoy facing up to this kind of sudden challenge.

## Questions About the Reading

1. How many ways are there to eat an ice-cream cone?
2. Despite all of the problems with ice-cream cones, does the writer like to eat them?

## Questions About the Writer's Strategies

1. When faced with having to write a clear and easy-to-understand description of a complicated process (how to prepare income-tax returns, do minor home repairs, or operate a computer), writers must use very precise language. Which words or phrases in this paragraph have a technical precision that makes this process clear to the reader?
2. The writer describes a number of problems associated with ice-cream cones. Which words or phrases does he use to help the reader know when he is about to identify these problems?

## Writing Assignments

1. Choose another popular yet sometimes hard-to-eat food, e.g., spaghetti and meatballs, and imagine that you have to write directions for eating this food for someone who is wearing a new white suit and has never eaten this before. Write a paragraph of directions.
2. Choose some simple, everyday activity such as making a peanut-butter sandwich or brushing your teeth and write a paragraph describing the *process* (steps, necessary equipment) involved. Imagine that your reader has never handled jars, sliced bread, or toothbrush and toothpaste.

# The Cook

### *Barbara Lewis (student)*

*Barbara Lewis takes us through the process of preparing dinner at a busy restaurant. She juggles meat, potatoes, and a seemingly endless stream of sauces and other delectables in a two-hour race with the dinner bell. And she does all this after a day of classes at Cuyahoga Community College in Cleveland, Ohio.*

## Words to Know

**au jus**   natural, unthickened juices or gravy
**escargots**   snails
**requisition**   a formal written order
**sauté**   to fry food quickly in a little fat
**scampi**   shrimp

## Getting Started

At what times in your life have you felt like the busiest, most pressured person in the world? What factors contributed to your state of mind?

P reparing food for the sauté line at the restaurant where I work is a hectic two-hour job. I come to work at 3:00 P.M. knowing that everything must be done by 5:00 P.M. The first thing I do is to check the requisition for the day and order my food. Then I have to clean and season five or six prime rib roasts and place them in the slow-cooking oven. After this, I clean and season five trays of white potatoes for baking and put them in the fast oven. Now I have two things cooking, prime ribs and potatoes, at different times and temperatures, and they both have to be watched very closely. In the meantime, I must put three trays of bacon in the oven. The bacon needs very close watching, too, because it burns very easily. Now I have prime ribs, potatoes, and bacon all cooking at the same time— and all needing constant watching. Next, I make popovers, which are unseasoned rolls. These also go into an oven for baking. Now I have prime ribs, baking potatoes, bacon, and popovers cooking at the same time and all of them needing to be closely watched. With my work area set up, I must make clarified butter and garlic butter. The clarified butter is for cooking liver, veal, and fish. The garlic butter is for stuffing escargots. I have to make ground meat stuffing also. Half of the ground meat will be mixed with wild rice and will be used to stuff breasts of chicken. The other half of the ground meat mixture will be used to stuff mushrooms. I have to prepare veal, cut and season scampi, and clean and sauté mushrooms and onions. In the meantime, I check the prime ribs and potatoes, take the bacon and the popovers out of the oven, and put the veal and chicken into the oven. Now I make au jus, which is served over the prime ribs, make the soup for the day, and cook the vegetables and rice. Then I heat the bordelaise sauce, make the special for the day, and last of all, cook food for the employees. This and sometimes more has to be done by five o'clock. Is it any wonder that I say preparing food for the sauté line at the restaurant where I work is a very hectic two-hour job!

## Questions About the Reading

1. Run through the cook's list again. For about how many people do you think she is preparing food?
2. Classify the food the cook is responsible for.
3. Do you think the cook likes her job? Explain your answer.

## Questions About the Writer's Strategies

1. Where is the topic sentence of the paragraph? Does the writer restate the topic sentence anywhere in the paragraph? If so, where? Does the sentence then serve a second purpose? What is that purpose?
2. Do you think *hectic* is an effective word for describing this job?
3. The cook states at the beginning that she has two things to watch carefully. The list of things she watches continues to grow during the paragraph. Identify the sentences where she reemphasizes this point. Does this help support her statement that the job is hectic?
4. What order does the writer use to organize her information in the paragraph?

## Writing Assignments

1. We all have moments when we feel under pressure. Write a process paragraph illustrating one of your busy days.
2. Imagine that the restaurant has decided to hire you as a helper for the cook. Write a process paragraph explaining the steps you would take to assist the cook and how you would blend your activities with hers.

3. Use the Internet to find out how to prepare a favorite egg-based meal. Write about the process involved so that you will end up with a perfect meal.

# A Guide to Proper Hand-Washing Technique

*Jennifer Traig*

*It's true that you should wash your hands to help prevent disease, but how do you keep them clean when you still have to turn off the faucet, dry them, and get out the door? Jennifer Traig tells you how, but it isn't easy.*

### Words to Know

**contemplate**   think about
**hepatitis**   inflammation of the liver

### Getting Started

What process—doing the laundry, mowing the lawn, or shopping—do you especially dislike? Why?

---

**D**id you know that your hands are loaded with bacteria and other 1
contaminants? They're filthy! They spread disease! Oh, it's just awful. And it's not scientifically possible to sterilize your hands. You can, however, get them really, really clean. Here's how!

1. First, you need to get some water going. We want it hot, hot, hot! The 2
   hot-water tap is contaminated, but that's okay, because you're about to wash. Touch it again, just to show how brave you are. Touch it one more time. Three taps wards off bad things. Now we're ready to wash!
2. Next, choose your poison. What kind of soap is for you? Bar soap is 3
   out; other people have probably used it (a possibility too horrible to contemplate), and even if it's unopened, it's made from animal fats, which is revolting. The whole thing just seems so dirty. Liquid soap it is! Choose an antibacterial formula if you're worried about contamination from germs. If you're worried about contamination from death, choose dishwashing liquid. It's so death-free it's safe to use on plates and flatware! But only if it's BRAND-NEW. Even then, you never know. Okay, let's skip the soap altogether. Plain water will be fine.
3. Rub your hands together vigorously and scrub, scrub, scrub. The 4
   Centers for Disease Control recommend you wash your hands for ten seconds, but what do they know? If they're such geniuses, why do people still get hepatitis? A full minute, minimum. How about

this: you keep your hands under that tap until you answer the philosophical question "Is water clean?"

4. I don't know if water is clean. What if water isn't clean? What if water just makes you dirtier?    5

5. You'll wash and wash and wash, but you'll never be safe.    6

6. Okay, try not to think about it. Let's just say water is clean and move on.    7

7. But what if it's not clean?    8

8. We're moving on. This next part is tricky. Your hands are clean—but they're wet. How to get them dry without getting them dirty again? The air-dry technique is best. Sure, it's slow, but it's safe. Simply hold your hands in the air until they're completely dry. Be sure not to touch anything! If you touch something, or if for some reason you think you maybe touched something, go back to Step 1. Yes, let's go back to Step 1 just to be safe.    9

9. Now we're in a hurry. You're going to have to dry your hands with paper napkins. That's fine. Just make sure it's a new package. Did you touch the part of the package that was sealed with glue? Is that glue? Glue is dirty. Wash again, just to be safe, then dry your hands on a napkin that absolutely for sure didn't touch the glue.    10

10. Use a napkin to turn off the tap and another napkin to open the door on the way out. Some people won't even touch the door with a napkin; they'll just wait until somebody comes to open the door for them. But they're crazy!    11

## Questions About the Reading

1. Why does the writer say you need to get your hands "really, really clean"?

2. How many times does the writer start over in the process of washing her hands?

3. What is the writer's opinion of different soaps? What does she mean by saying dishwashing soap is "death-free"?

## Questions About the Writer's Strategies

1. What is the tone of the essay?

2. Is the point of view (person) of the essay consistent? If it changes, is the change justified or necessary? Why or why not?

3. What is the irony in the essay?

## Writing Assignments

1. Write an essay in which you explain making a peanut butter and jelly sandwich, changing the oil in a car, or opening a bank account.
2. Write an essay in which you explain the process of painting a room in your house.

# The Beekeeper

*Sue Hubbell*

*Preparing for a job as a beekeeper is a painstaking process that actually requires, as Sue Hubbell shows us, taking pain.*

### Words to Know

**anaphylactic**   severe reaction with possible collapse or death
**supers**   wooden boxes that contain the bees' honey

### Getting Started

Do you follow a process in getting ready to do your homework?

---

T he time to harvest honey is summer's end, when it is hot. The temper   1
of the bees requires that we wear protective clothing: a full set of overalls, a zippered bee veil and leather gloves. Even a very strong young man works up a sweat wrapped in a bee suit in the heat, hustling 60-pound supers while being harassed by angry bees. It is a hard job, harder even than haying, but jobs are scarce here and I've always been able to hire help.

This year David, the son of a friend of mine, is working for me. He is big   2
and strong and used to labor, but he was nervous about bees. After we had made the job arrangement I set about desensitizing him to bee stings. I put a piece of ice on his arm to numb it and then, holding a bee carefully by its head, I put it on the numbed spot and let it sting him. A bee stinger is barbed and stays in the flesh, pulling loose from the body of the bee as it struggles to free itself. The bulbous poison sac at the top of the stinger continues to pulsate after the bee has left, pumping the venom and forcing the stinger deeper into the flesh.

That first day I wanted David to have only a partial dose of venom,   3
so after a minute I scraped the stinger out. A few people are seriously sensitive to bee venom; each sting they receive can cause a more severe reaction than the one before—reactions ranging from hives, breathing difficulties, accelerated heart beat and choking to anaphylactic shock and death. I didn't think David would be allergic in that way, but I wanted to make sure.

We sat down and had a cup of coffee and I watched him. The spot where   4
the stinger went in grew red and began to swell. That was a normal reaction, and so was the itching that he felt later on.

The next day I coaxed a bee into stinging him again, repeating the pro-  5
cedure, but I left the stinger in place for 10 minutes, until the venom sac
was empty. Again the spot was red, swollen and itchy but had disappeared in 24 hours. By that time David was ready to catch a bee himself
and administer his own sting. He also decided that the ice cube was a
bother and gave it up. I told him to keep to one sting a day until he had
no redness or swelling and then to increase to two stings. He was ready
for them the next day. The greater amount of venom caused redness and
swelling for a few days, but soon his body could tolerate it without reaction and he increased the number of stings once again.

Today he told me he was up to six stings. His arms look as though they  6
have track marks on them, but the fresh stings are having little effect. I'll
keep him at it until he can tolerate 10 a day with no reaction and then
I'll not worry about taking him out to the bee yard.

## Questions About the Reading

1. When is the honey harvested? Why is the honey harvested then?
2. How much do the supers that hold the honey weigh?
3. Why is the beekeeper able to hire help in harvesting the honey?
4. How many stings per day does the beekeeper want her helper to tolerate before taking him to the bee yard?

## Questions About the Writer's Strategies

1. Identify the steps in the desensitizing process.
2. Could the selection as a whole or the sentences within it be classified
   by any other modes of development? If so, which modes and which
   sentences?
3. What is the thesis of the selection? Is it stated? If so, identify it; if not,
   state the thesis in your own words.

## Writing Assignments

1. Write an essay in which you explain the process you follow in getting
   ready for work, doing your laundry, or repairing your car or some
   household item.
2. Write an essay in which you explain the process you follow in preparing to buy groceries and then in buying them.

# Koto

**Edna Yano (student)**

*In her prize-winning essay, Edna Yano of Leeward Community College, located in Pearl City, Hawaii, helps us understand how difficult it is to learn to play the koto, a Japanese thirteen-string zither.*

**Word to Know**

**simultaneously**   at the same time

*Getting Started*

Is there a musical instrument you would like to learn to play?

---

**W**ho would have ever thought that learning how to play the koto for 1 six months would be of any help? I was in Japan a couple of years ago, and while I was there, I had a valuable opportunity to learn to play the koto (thirteen-string Japanese zither). I bought my very own set of ivory nails . . . it cost 5,000 ¥ (equivalent to about 50 U.S. dollars), and I also bought my Tengaku music book filled with various koto songs. When I first opened that book, my eyes were getting dizzy, as it was impossible to read. I tried not to panic.

The first day of instruction, we had a short prayer to help our hearts 2 to focus on learning. We all sat on the Japanese tatami mats, sitting *seiza* (Japanese-style sitting). My legs started to get numb. The koto lay in front of my knees. My wishes to pick these strings have finally started to unfold in front of my very eyes.

Our teacher, Akari Sensei, told us to put on our three ivory nails, one on 3 the thumb, the other on the index finger, and the third one on our middle finger. I was immediately told, "Yano-san, your nails are facing the wrong way." That was embarrassing. I twisted each one to face the right way, which is opposite of my actual nails.

Now we were learning how to read the notes, and believe me, it wasn't 4 the kind of notes you see in piano books. These koto notes were all squiggly Chinese characters with weird-looking symbols next to them. I was learning this thing from zero. Every so often I could sense that Akari Sensei was getting frustrated with trying to teach me. It was hard enough teaching native Japanese people. And here I was, just a Japanese-American from Hawaii trying to learn something already difficult.

I cried alone a couple of times, practicing this stringed instrument in the  5
music room at night. As much as I was frustrated, I felt like I was being a
nuisance to the other people who could do so well. But I wasn't going to
give up now. I spent fifty bucks on these nails. This was the chance that
I had always dreamt of. So every day after the evening prayer session, I
would go up to the gloomy music room to practice by myself for about
an hour. That room is very old, and sometimes these monster palm-sized
spiders would fall from the ceiling and scurry about on the tatami mat.
It scared me to death. But knowing that practice makes perfect, nothing
seemed to scare me after that. There are even legends that this room is
haunted, and you can hear someone playing the *ryuteki* (bamboo flute) in
the middle of the night. Ahh, let 'em come out. They would be so scared
of my awful playing that they wouldn't even show up.

Whenever I had time, I would go up to that room. I soon got used to  6
picking the strings. I was now able to play most of the songs without even
looking at my notes. Now the teacher started to focus attention on how
much improvement I had made over the course of a few weeks.

During the koto session, there were four separate days reserved for  7
actual service days, in which one of the koto students was assigned to be
the *oya* (the koto leader). This was an important task. She had to take the
rhythm of the entire orchestra, which included the gong, and the several
other instruments like the ryuteki, shichiriki, and the sho. That leader
was responsible for starting the song, and ending it on perfect note. I was
completely out of the question. There was no way the teacher would pick
me. I still lacked practice. I mean there were some veterans in this group;
what can I say?

The autumn service passed; then the winter; then came spring. I still  8
kept practicing in that room, even [though] our koto instruction [had]
ended a while ago. The summer ceremony was the final one, and the
grandest of them all. It was an honor if you were chosen to be oya for this
particular occasion. I knew I was out of the question, so I didn't even want
to know who was going to be chosen. As the service day got close, the roles
were posted on a thin sheet of paper on the bulletin board. I scanned it
quickly; then it caught my eye, Koto (oya): Yano-san. I couldn't believe
my eyes. I read it twice, just to make sure. Then a friend passed by and
said, "Hey, you're the next oya. Good luck." Yes, I needed it. I was very
excited, and nervous at the same time. This time, it's gotta be perfect. I
practiced even more since seeing my name posted up there. Playing the
koto was no problem; singing to the music was a challenge.

The day of the ceremony arrived. All musicians had to be dressed in a  9
white kimono, a black *haori* (Japanese coat) and a purple *hakama* (Japanese
skirt). The adrenaline was making me anxious. I wanted to get over with

it swiftly and safely. The *kachi* (wood clappers) clapped once—signaling me to begin the koto and sing simultaneously. I've never felt so focused in my life. That was only part of my task; part two was ending the ceremony with the orchestra as well, and I had to lead everybody. It was a load of stress because I seriously didn't want to mess up on one note.

The ending kachi clap went off, and I gave my koto a last pinch of har- 10 mony on the two strings. It all ended perfectly. It was one of the proudest moments in my life. It may not mean much for other people, but for me— it was a blessed occasion. After the service was over, I gave my thanks to Akari Sensei for her patience; then she immediately recommended that I take this tradition back to Hawaii to teach the people the art of the koto and Tengaku music (ancient Japanese ceremony music). Believe me, if I was able to play that koto, anybody can.

## Questions About the Reading

1. Why was it particularly difficult for the writer to read the music notes?
2. Why do you think the writer was determined to learn to play the koto? Does she tell you?
3. How long did the writer spend learning to play the koto?

## Questions About the Writer's Strategies

1. What is the thesis of the essay? Is it stated or implied? State the thesis in your own words.
2. What is the point of view (person, tone) of the essay?
3. What is the order the writer uses in the essay?
4. What descriptive words and phrases does the writer use to describe the requirements for the oya ceremony?

## Writing Assignments

1. Write an essay in which you explain the process you follow in writing an essay.
2. If you play a musical instrument, write an essay explaining the process of learning to play that instrument. If you do not play an instrument, interview a piano teacher and write an essay explaining the process you would need to follow to learn to play the piano.

# The Art of Making Fimo Beads

**Julie Gifford (student)**

*Julie Gifford, a student at Pennsylvania State University, tells us how to make fimo beads.*

### Words to Know

**cylindrical**   round
**fimo**   a synthetic, claylike material
**perimeter**   outer boundary or edges
**prisms**   solid, equal-sided figures

### Getting Started

What is the process you would follow in planting a garden, fixing a car or bicycle, or sorting your week's laundry?

T he "Generation X" population of today's society has made the wear- 1
ing of beaded necklaces containing fimo beads quite a fashion statement. These necklaces contain small, round, colored plastic beads and other intricate beads made out of different-colored fimo. Fimo is a synthetic material similar to modeling clay and can be used to make thousands of types of beads. These beads can then be incorporated into necklaces. However, to accurately describe the process of making this style of bead, a simple pattern will be used as an example. Specifically, the fimo example described will have a pattern with a small, yellow, circular center surrounded by three small green triangles and three small red triangles. The following process will allow anyone without artistic ability to create a simple, inexpensive fimo bead that can later be used in stylish necklaces.

The first step in the process involves taking a trip to a local craft store, 2
like A. C. Moore, or a department store such as Wal-Mart, to buy the necessary supplies. For the example fimo bead, red, yellow, and green fimo must be purchased. To make a complete necklace, other colored plastic beads would have to be bought along with a spool of beading thread and a silver clasp. Also, a sharp, flat-edged cutting tool (for example, a razor blade) and a thick, large pin will also be necessary tools in the final stages of the bead making process.

Once the supplies are gathered, the bead making process is ready to 3
begin. The fimo color that will make up the center circle in the bead (in

this case, yellow) is the color that is first readied. A piece of fimo with the diameter of a quarter and the width of a pencil is pinched off from the larger slab of fimo. It is then rubbed between both hands in a circular motion until it is warm and no longer cracks when folded in half. Then, from that small, primed piece of fimo, a smaller, nickel-sized piece is pinched and rolled on a flat surface. The fimo is rolled into a cylindrical log that is approximately three inches long. It is important to ensure that the log is not too thin, meaning it does not easily pull apart. Once the log is rolled to the desired thickness (slightly thinner than that of a pencil), place it aside for later use. The same process is followed for the green and red fimo colors, also, except for those colors three logs must be prepared instead of only one.

After the three logs each of green and red fimo are formed, they must  4 be shaped into three-dimensional triangular prisms. This is easily accomplished by placing them on a flat surface (one at a time) and pinching the pointer finger and thumb together (to form a small triangle). The pinched fingers are then pressed down gently on the top and sides of the fimo logs so the logs become prisms. Once this is finished, the prisms are ready to be placed around the circular, yellow center. First place the base of the green prisms around the yellow log, leaving equal amounts of space between all three prisms. When doing this make sure to press hard enough so the green prisms are firmly attached to the yellow center. Then position the base of each of the red prisms between the spaces left between the green prisms. By this point the spaces around the yellow center should be evenly filled. The addition of the red and green prisms form the perimeter of the new log that contains the desired bead pattern.

Next comes one of the final stages in the fimo bead making process.  5 The new log that has been formed from placing the red and green triangles around the yellow center must be rolled using the palm of the hand. This is done until the outside of the log is smooth and only one color. The purpose of this is to lengthen the log and to decrease the size of the beads. The beads can then be cut from the log so that they are approximately one-quarter inch thick. The beads are cut by using a razor blade (or other sharp cutting tool) and positioning it along the top of the log at the desired thickness of bead. Then the log is gently rolled back and forth while slight pressure is applied to the razor blade until it cuts completely through the log. The reason the log is cut in such a manner is to avoid distorting the design that is on the face of the bead. The small piece that is cut from the original log is the fimo bead. The rest of the log is cut in the same way until no more beads can be obtained. Depending on the exact thickness of each bead and the starting length of the log, there should be a net yield of approximately ten to twenty beads.

Finally, rounding out the bead making process, a thick pin must be used  6
to put a hole on each side and throughout the fimo bead. This is done so
the bead can later be strung along beading thread with other plastic beads
to make a necklace. To make a hole in the bead, place the bead with its two
faces positioned between the pointer and thumb. Then you poke the pin
through the middle of one of the sides and gently twist the pin as it goes
in the bead and eventually comes out the other side. This procedure is
completed for the rest of the beads as well. Lastly, all the beads must be
placed on a baking pan and baked until they are hard, approximately ten
to fifteen minutes at 250 degrees. The finished products can then be used
in many creative ways, in combination with small, round plastic beads to
make beautiful, fashionable necklaces.

The art of making fimo beads is really a study in the art of creativity  7
and patience. It is a relaxing hobby that allows an individual's creativity to
take control. Although many people think that the process requires special
artistic talent, that is really only a myth. Anyone who follows the procedure described above or similar procedures in craft books would be able to
make the simplest of fimo styles. After the simple styles are mastered, they
can easily be combined to form more intricate designs. Once this occurs,
a real sense of accomplishment can be felt, and you can proudly say, "I
created that all by myself!"

## Questions About the Reading

1. What are the supplies you need to make fimo beads?
2. After the material is readied, what are the steps in the process of making a fimo bead?
3. How many logs of yellow should be prepared for the example fimo
   bead? How many red and how many green?
4. What is the purpose of rolling the log?
5. How is the hole in the bead made?
6. What is the final step in the process of making a fimo bead?

## Questions About the Writer's Strategies

1. What is the point of view of the essay? Is it consistent? If it changes, is
   there a reason for the change?
2. Does the writer use any modes of development in addition to process?
   If so, what are they?
3. What is the tone of the essay?

4. Why does the writer paragraph the essay as she does? How does the paragraphing relate to the steps in the process?

## Writing Assignments

1. Write an essay in which you explain the process you would follow in planting a garden.
2. Write an essay in which you explain the process you follow in sorting your week's laundry.
3. Write an essay in which you explain the process you follow in repairing some appliance in your house.

# 8 Cause and Effect

IN YOUR LOCAL newspaper you notice a story about a car accident that took place late on a Saturday night. The driver missed a curve, slammed into a tree, and was badly injured. Police investigators reported that the young victim had been drinking heavily with friends and lost control of the car on the way home. This news article is a relatively clear example of a **cause,** heavy consumption of alcohol, and an **effect,** a serious accident.

Sometimes you can recognize immediately that cause and effect is part of a writer's **mode of development** because the writer uses words that signal a cause-and-effect relationship—transitional words like *because, therefore, as a result,* and *consequently.* However, writers will not necessarily indicate cause and effect so directly. Sometimes a cause-and-effect relationship will be clear only from the arrangement of ideas or the narrative sequence of events. Usually, though, the **topic sentence** or **thesis statement** will indicate that the writer is describing a cause-and-effect situation.

A cause-and-effect explanation tells *why* something turns out the way it does. In some cases, a single cause may contribute to one or more effects. In the following paragraph, the writer says that a single cause—the early release of prisoners—led to an increase in crimes.

Cause

> To save money in the early 1980s, Illinois released 21,000 prisoners an average of three months early. James Austin of

Effects

> the National Council on Crime and Delinquency calculates that the early releases produced 23 homicides, 32 rapes, 262 arsons, 681 robberies, 2,472 burglaries, 2,571 assaults and more than 8,000 other crimes. According to Harvard researchers

Effect

> David P. Cavanaugh and Mark A. R. Kleiman, the $60 million the state saved cost Illinois crime victims $304 million, directly or indirectly.

Eugene H. Methvin,
"Pay Now—Or Pay Later"

A writer may also say that several causes contributed to or resulted in a particular effect.

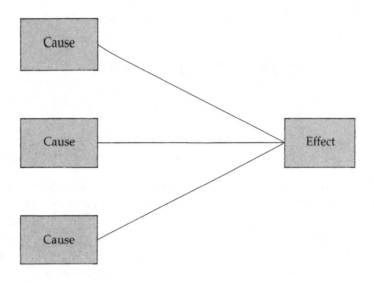

For example, in the following essay, the writer suggests three causes for the disappearance of moonshining—the secret manufacturing of whiskey—as a fine art.

The manufacture of illicit whiskey in the mountains is not    1
dead. Far from it. As long as the operation of a still remains
so financially rewarding, it will never die. There will always
be men ready to take their chances against the law for such an
attractive profit, and willing to take their punishment when
they are caught.

**Effect**

Moonshining as a fine art, however, effectively disap-    2
peared some time ago. There were several reasons. One was

**Cause 1: decline in use of home remedies containing corn whiskey**

the age of aspirin and modern medicine. As home doctoring
lost its stature, the demand for pure corn whiskey as an
essential ingredient of many home remedies vanished along
with those remedies. Increasing affluence was another reason.

**Cause 2: young people finding easier ways to make money**

Young people, rather than follow in their parents' footsteps,
decided that there were easier ways to make money, and they
were right.

**Cause 3: greed causing producers to care more for quantity than quality**

Third, and perhaps most influential of all, was the arrival,    3
even in moonshining, of that peculiarly human disease
known to most of us as greed. One fateful night, some force
whispered in an unsuspecting moonshiner's ear, "Look. Add
this gadget to your still and you'll double your production.
Double your production, and you can double your profits."

Soon the small operators were being forced out of business,    4
and moonshining, like most other manufacturing enterprises,
was quickly taken over by a breed of men bent on making
money—and lots of it. Loss of pride in the product, and loss
of time taken with the product increased in direct proportion
to the desire for production; and thus moonshining as a fine

art was buried in a quiet little ceremony attended only by those mourners who had once been the proud artists, known far and wide across the hills for the excellence of their product. Too old to continue making it themselves, and with no one following behind them, they were reduced to reminiscing about "the good old days when the whiskey that was made was *really* whiskey, and no questions asked."

Suddenly moonshining fell into the same category as faith healing, planting by the signs, and all the other vanishing customs that were a part of a rugged, self-sufficient culture that is now disappearing.

Eliot Wigginton,
"Moonshining as a Fine Art"

In still other cases, one cause may have several effects.

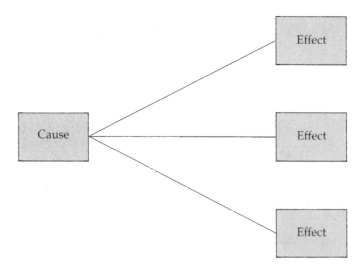

In the following paragraph, the writer explains that the explosion of a nuclear bomb (the cause) has five primary effects. Notice as you read that the writer combines **process** with the cause-and-effect explanation.

Topic

Cause

Effect 1: initial
nuclear radiation

Whereas most conventional bombs produce only one destructive effect—the shock wave—nuclear weapons produce many destructive effects. At the moment of the explosion, when the temperature of the weapon material, instantly gasified, is at the superstellar level, the pressure is millions of times the normal atmospheric pressure. Immediately, radiation, consisting mainly of gamma rays, which are a very high-energy form of electromagnetic radiation, begins to stream outward into the environment. This is called the "initial nuclear radiation," and is the first of the destructive effects of a nuclear explosion. In an air burst of a one-megaton bomb—a bomb with the explosive yield of a million tons of TNT, which is a medium-sized weapon in present-day nuclear arsenals—the initial nuclear radiation can kill unprotected human beings in an area of some six square miles.

**Effect 2: electromagnetic pulse**

Virtually simultaneously with the initial nuclear radiation, in a second destructive effect of the explosion, an electromagnetic pulse is generated by the intense gamma radiation acting on the air. In a high-altitude detonation, the pulse can knock out electrical equipment over a wide area by inducing a powerful surge of voltage through various conductors, such as antennas, overhead power lines, pipes, and railroad tracks. . . . When the fusion and fission reactions have blown themselves out, a fireball takes shape. As it expands, energy

**Effect 3: thermal pulse**

is absorbed in the form of X rays by the surrounding air, and then the air re-radiates a portion of that energy into the environment in the form of the thermal pulse—a wave of blinding light and intense heat—which is the third of the destructive effects of a nuclear explosion. . . . The thermal pulse of a one-megaton bomb lasts for about ten seconds and can cause second-degree burns in exposed human beings at a distance of nine and a half miles, or in an area of more than two hundred and eighty square miles. . . . As

**Effect 4: blast wave**

the fireball expands, it also sends out a blast wave in all directions, and this is the fourth destructive effect of the explosion. The blast wave of an air-burst one-megaton bomb can flatten or severely damage all but the strongest buildings within a radius of four and a half miles. . . . As the fireball burns, it rises, condensing water from the surrounding atmosphere to form the characteristic mushroom cloud. If the bomb has been set off on the ground or close enough to it so that the fireball touches the surface, a so-called ground burst, a crater will be formed, and tons of dust and debris will be fused with the intensely radioactive fission products and sucked up into the

**Effect 5: radioactive fallout**

mushroom cloud. This mixture will return to earth as radioactive fallout, most of it in the form of fine ash, in the fifth destructive effect of the explosion. Depending upon the composition of the surface, from 40 to 70 percent of this fallout—often called the "early" or "local" fallout—descends to earth within about a day of the explosion, in the vicinity of the blast and downwind from it, exposing human beings to radiation disease, an illness that is fatal when exposure is intense.

Jonathan Schell,
*The Fate of the Earth*

You should notice still another characteristic in this sample paragraph: the writer describes both main causes and subordinate causes, and main effects and subordinate effects. One main cause, the explosion of the bomb, causes a series of five initial (main) effects. However, these effects become the causes for still other effects. The initial nuclear radiation (effect 1), for example, is also a cause that results in the death of unprotected human beings in a six-square-mile area (a subordinate effect). The electromagnetic pulse (effect 2) that is generated by the explosion is the cause, in turn, of the knocking out of electrical equipment (a subordinate effect). The thermal pulse (effect 3) causes second-degree burns (a subordinate effect) in exposed humans in a 280-square-mile area. The blast wave (effect 4) causes the destruction of buildings (a subordinate effect), and the radioactive fallout (effect 5) causes radiation disease (a subordinate effect) in humans. As the following chart shows, cause-and-effect relationships can be complicated.

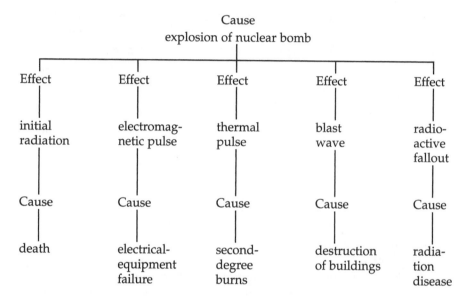

You should keep two factors in mind when you are writing and **revising** a cause-and-effect essay. First, be sure that you have actually thought through the causes and effects very carefully. You should not be satisfied with considering only obvious or simple causes. For example, we tend to oversimplify and cite one cause as the reason for a war—the attack on Pearl Harbor for the United States entering World War II, the firing on Fort Sumter for the start of the Civil War, and so on. For the most part, these tend to be the last of many contributing causes that led to the wars. A thoughtful discussion of such a topic in your writing would include an explanation of some of the contributing, less obvious but perhaps more important, causes.

Second, you should be careful that you do not mistake an event as a cause simply because it preceded a particular effect. For instance, if a child swallows a coin and then comes down with measles, it would be inaccurate and faulty reasoning, a **fallacy**—in this case, a *post hoc* (meaning "after this, therefore because of this") *fallacy*—to assume that swallowing the coin was a cause of the measles. Other common fallacies you should guard against in both your reading and your writing include the following.

- The *hasty generalization,* which is reasoning based on too few examples or insufficient evidence. "The cause of World War II was the Japanese bombing of Pearl Harbor."
- The *non sequitur,* which is claiming an effect that does not necessarily follow from the stated cause. "He believes in the supernatural because he has read the Harry Potter books."

Even though you need to guard against fallacies, you should also be aware that writers do not always state a cause-and-effect relationship directly. Sometimes they **imply** the relationship and leave it to the reader to **infer** the relationship. That is, the writer does not state the relationship, but arranges certain information in such a way that the reader will be able to conclude that the relationship exists, as in the following sentences.

> On the ground next to the parked Jeep, the compass glinted in the moonlight. Deep in the woods, shielded from the moon, the hungry teenager circled in the dark with little idea where he had been or how to get where he wanted to go.

Although the writer does not directly state what happened, it is not hard to infer that the teenager dropped his compass without realizing it, with the effect that he is now lost.

You will need to make inferences when you read cause-and-effect writing as well as other **modes of development.** When you make an inference, be sure that you can pinpoint the information and trace the logic on which your inference is based. When you are writing about cause and effect, be sure to give enough information, directly or indirectly, so that your reader can determine the cause-and-effect relationship.

You use cause-and-effect reasoning every day in solving problems and making decisions. Legislators create laws to address the causes of certain problems. In a similar way, scientists find cures for diseases when they are able to isolate the causes of those diseases. Understanding the relation between causes and effects is extremely important in both day-to-day living and long-range planning. Communicating your understanding in writing is significant evidence of your ability to reason clearly and accurately.

# Giving In

**Michelle Cottle**

*She didn't want to, but Michelle gives in and buys a minivan.*

*Words to Know*

**paraphernalia**   collection of equipment
**sociological**   human, social meaning
**unabashed**   not ashamed, not embarrassed

*Getting Started*

Do you "label" people by the kind of car they drive, clothes they wear, place where they live, or some other notion?

---

**W**e did it. With less than two months to go until our second child is scheduled to arrive, my husband and I swallowed our pride, plundered our savings and joined the much ridiculed ranks of minivan owners. It had to be done. Neither of our old vehicles had what it takes to handle two car seats, two parents, the odd grandparent and the sheer tonnage of baby paraphernalia required for even quick trips to the grocery. Still, it took multiple visits to the dealership before I came to terms with the sociological enormity of what we were about to do. In America, you are what you drive. And as everyone knows, cruising around in a shiny new minivan definitively announces to your fellow road warriors, "I am an unabashed suburban breeder."

---

## Questions About the Reading

1. What is it that the writer and her husband did?
2. What was the cause that made the writer and her husband take the action they did?
3. Why do you think the writer resisted doing what she and her husband eventually did?
4. What does the writer mean by "the sociological enormity" of what they did?

## Questions About the Writer's Strategies

1. What is the point of view in person in the paragraph? Is it consistent? If it changes, is the change justified?
2. What is the symbol in the paragraph? What is it a symbol for, according to the writer?
3. What is the main idea of the paragraph? State it in your own words.

## Writing Assignments

1. Write a paragraph in which you explain the cause or causes of your choice of the car you drive, the jeans you buy, or the school you attend.
2. Suppose that you are going out for dinner and a movie. Write a cause-and-effect paragraph in which you explain your choice of restaurant and movie.

3. Suppose that you need to buy a new (or used) car. Using the Internet, research the market and dealers in your town for the kind of car you want. Then write an extended paragraph in which you explain the cause or causes of your choice of car to buy and of dealer who sells the car. In addition to using cause and effect, include comparison and contrast and examples in your paragraph.

# Why Eat Junk Food?

*Judith Wurtman*

> *Each day, Americans eat 50 million pounds of sugar, 3 million gallons of ice cream, and 5.8 million pounds of chocolate candy. Yet junk foods, as they are commonly known, contain few if any of the nutrients needed to maintain good health. Why, then, do people eat so much junk food? Judith Wurtman suggests two reasons.*

## Words to Know

**confectionaries**   sweets, candies
**depicted**   shown, represented
**euphoria**   a feeling of well-being

## Getting Started

What is your favorite junk food? Do you eat it very often?

---

**W**e crunch and chew our way through vast quantities of snacks and confectionaries and relieve our thirst with multicolored, flavored soft drinks, with and without calories, for two basic reasons. The first is simple: the food tastes good, and we enjoy the sensation of eating it. Second, we associate these foods, often without being aware of it, with the highly pleasurable experiences depicted in the advertisements used to promote their sale. Current television advertisements demonstrate this point: people turn from grumpiness to euphoria after crunching a corn chip. Others water ski into the sunset with their loved ones while drinking a popular soft drink. People entertain on the patio with friends, cook over campfires without mosquitoes, or go to carnivals with granddad munching away at the latest candy or snack food. The people portrayed in these scenarios are all healthy, vigorous, and good looking; one wonders how popular the food they convince us to eat would be if they would crunch or drink away while complaining about low back pain or clogged sinuses.

---

## Questions About the Reading

1. Why do people consume snacks and soft drinks?
2. How do television advertisements portray people eating snack foods?

3. What do you think would happen if television advertisements showed people complaining about poor health while eating snack foods?

## Questions About the Writer's Strategies

1. Is the *topic* of this paragraph stated directly or implied? If it is stated directly, where is it located? If it is implied, state it in your own words.
2. What is the predominant *mode of development* of this paragraph? Are any other modes of development used?
3. Identify the cause-and-effect elements of this essay.

## Writing Assignments

1. Go to the library or the Internet and research some of the long-term effects of eating a steady diet of junk food or food that isn't nutritious. Then write an essay explaining these effects.
2. Have you ever drunk too much coffee or soda that contains caffeine? Write a paragraph explaining the effects of consuming too much caffeine.
3. Aside from eating well, what other steps can you take to ensure good health? Write a paragraph that describes these steps and their effects on your health.

# An Eyewitness Account

*Jack London*

> *Jack London (1876–1916) is best known for such adventure novels as* The Call of the Wild. *In this paragraph from an essay published in May 1906 in* Collier's Weekly, *he describes the effects of the devastating San Francisco earthquake of April 16, 1906.*

> ## Words to Know
>
> **conflagration**  destructive fire
> **imperial**  magnificent, majestic
> **nabobs**  rich men
> **wrought**  caused
>
> ## Getting Started
>
> Have you ever experienced a fire, flood, or other natural disaster?

The earthquake shook down in San Francisco hundreds of thousands of dollars' worth of walls and chimneys. But the conflagration that followed burned up hundreds of millions of dollars' worth of property. There is no estimating within hundreds of millions the actual damage wrought. Not in history has a modern imperial city been so completely destroyed. San Francisco is gone! Nothing remains of it but memories and a fringe of dwelling houses on its outskirts. Its industrial section is wiped out. Its social and residential section is wiped out. The factories and warehouses, the great stores and newspaper buildings, the hotels and the palaces of the nabobs, are all gone. Remains only the fringe of dwelling houses on the outskirts of what was once San Francisco.

## Questions About the Reading

1. According to the writer, how many dollars' worth of property were destroyed by the earthquake?
2. If the earthquake shook down walls and chimneys, what do you think caused the devastating fire that followed?
3. What happened to the San Francisco industrial section?
4. What were the only things that remained of San Francisco after the earthquake?

## Questions About the Writer's Strategies

1. What is the tone of the paragraph?
2. Is the paragraph objective, subjective, or both?
3. Identify the cause-and-effect elements in the paragraph.
4. What modes of development does the writer use in addition to cause and effect?

## Writing Assignments

1. Watch your local news report and write a paragraph in which you suggest the cause and effects of a reported fire, flood, robbery, or accident.
2. Write a paragraph in which you identify some of the effects of the closing of a business that employs many people in your city or town.
3. Write a paragraph in which you explain the possible effects on a business of its product being determined harmful.

# A Momentous Arrest

*Martin Luther King Jr.*

> *Martin Luther King Jr. was catapulted into international fame when, working for the Southern Christian Leadership Conference, he organized blacks in Montgomery, Alabama, to boycott that city's segregated buses in 1955 and 1956. King, preaching nonviolent resistance to segregation, became the most important leader in the civil rights movement that changed American life so radically over the next decade. Here, in a simple, matter-of-fact tone, King tells of the incident that sparked the Montgomery bus boycott.*

### Words to Know

**accommodate**   to make space for, oblige
**complied**   carried out willingly

### Getting Started

Have you ever disobeyed a rule because you thought it was unfair?

---

On December 1, 1955, an attractive Negro seamstress, Mrs. Rosa Parks, boarded the Cleveland Avenue Bus in downtown Montgomery. She was returning home after her regular day's work in the Montgomery Fair—a leading department store. Tired from long hours on her feet, Mrs. Parks sat down in the first seat behind the section reserved for whites. Not long after she took her seat, the bus operator ordered her, along with three other Negro passengers, to move back in order to accommodate boarding white passengers. By this time every seat in the bus was taken. This meant that if Mrs. Parks followed the driver's command she would have to stand while a white male passenger, who had just boarded the bus, would sit. The other three Negro passengers immediately complied with the driver's request. But Mrs. Parks quietly refused. The result was her arrest.

---

## Questions About the Reading

1. Was Mrs. Parks breaking any law or custom in sitting where she did?
2. Why didn't Mrs. Parks move when the bus driver asked her to? Do you think she would have moved if the white passenger had been a woman instead of a man?

3. Was Mrs. Parks thinking about the civil rights movement when she refused to move? Explain your answer.
4. What is it about Mrs. Parks's action that seems so symbolic of the early civil rights movement?

## Questions About the Writer's Strategies

1. Which sentence states the cause in this paragraph? Which one states the effect?
2. Do you think the writer presents the incident objectively or subjectively? Use words and phrases from the paragraph to support your answer.
3. Other than cause and effect, what mode of development dominates in this paragraph?
4. What is the order in which the incidents in the paragraph are arranged?
5. Do you sympathize with Mrs. Parks? Explain your answer, citing examples from the essay that influence your feelings.

## Writing Assignments

1. Think of a situation that made you angry enough to defy authority and risk discipline or even arrest. Perhaps you protested an unfair grade, a school rule, an unjust traffic ticket, or something of more consequence, like contamination of your city's water supply. Using cause and effect as your mode of development, describe in a paragraph what happened. Try to write objectively.
2. The civil rights movement of the 1950s and 1960s brought about many positive changes in our country's attitude towards minorities. There are, however, still steps that can be taken. In a paragraph, suggest one possible change the country can make, and speculate on the effects it could have on the lives of minority citizens.

# On Being Unemployed

*Nelliejean Smith (student)*

> *In the paragraph that follows, we learn of the many effects that unemployment can have on a person's life. The writer makes us see—and feel with her—that unemployment is a traumatic experience. Nelliejean Smith has proven, however, that she can cope with it, for she wrote this paragraph as a student at Cuyahoga Community College.*

### Words to Know

**bureaucracy**   an administrative section of government that is often impersonal and inflexible, red tape

**evoke**   to summon or call forth, to elicit

### Getting Started

In what ways do the effects of unemployment reach deeper than an empty bank account?

---

**B**eing unemployed creates many problems for my family and me. First of all, there are financial problems. We have cut back on the quality of groceries we purchase. We now buy two pounds of hamburger in place of two pounds of sirloin. This hamburger is also divided into quantities sufficient for three meals: one may be creole beef, one chili, and the other spaghetti. There is also less money for clothing. Dresses must be altered and made into blouses; pants make nice skirts after some alteration. I have two more very sticky problems. I've fallen behind in the rental payments for our apartment, and now I am experiencing difficulties trying to pay the back rent. The other sticky problem is my son's tuition payments. There does not seem to be any way that I can send a complete payment to his college. These are not the only problems I face. I also have psychological problems as a result of unemployment. Often I wonder why this has happened to me. Then depression and confusion take over, and I feel drained of all my abilities. The one question that fills my mind most often is the following: Why can't I get employment? This question evokes in me a lack of self-confidence and self-worth. I am haunted by an overall feeling of uselessness. My other problems center on trying to cope with the bureaucracy of the Employment Bureau. Once I get to the Employment Bureau, I stand in line to sign up. I then wait in another line to which I must report. Once I go through all of this, I am sent out for job interviews, only to find that the employer wants someone with more experience. To top every-thing off, I had to wait almost six months to receive my first unemploy-ment check. As you can see, there is often a frustratingly long delay in receiving benefits. My family and I have suffered through many problems because of my unemployment.

## Questions About the Reading

1. What do you think makes the inability to pay rent and her son's tuition particularly "sticky" problems for the writer?
2. What makes the writer feel "drained" of her abilities?
3. What psychological effects do you think the writer's unsuccessful job interviews have on her?

## Questions About the Writer's Strategies

1. What is the main idea of this paragraph? Where is this idea first intro-duced? Where is it repeated?
2. Transitional words and phrases provide a bridge between points in this paragraph. Identify the writer's transitions.
3. The writer uses many examples to illustrate the effects of her unemploy-ment. Identify two effects and two examples for each of these effects.
4. What order does the writer use in discussing the problems?

## Writing Assignments

1. Is the employment bureau the writer describes doing a good job? In a paragraph, describe the effects of the bureau's procedures.

2. *Working Together*  Join with some classmates to discuss the effects unemployment has on the American people as a whole. Do you think it has been affected by the outsourcing of jobs and/or global trade, or has the production of goods such as automobiles within our country offset outsourcing? Using the Internet and your library, read some articles on this topic. Then collaborate with your classmates to write a cause-and-effect essay in which you describe some of the social and economic effects of unemployment.

# Global Warming in Canada

*Liz Sinclair (student)*

> *Global warming threatens the rugged beauty of northern Canada, according to Liz Sinclair, a student at the University of Guelph, and may be causing climate changes in the rest of the Northern Hemisphere.*

### Words to Know

**beneficial**   good, positive
**depletion**   decrease, exhaustion
**detrimental**   bad, negative
**Inuit**   group of people native to the Northwest Territories, Eskimos
**precarious**   uncertain, risky

### Getting Started

What are you doing that contributes to global warming?

---

The land is barren and frozen. The water is unforgiving. The wind is 1 lonely, in pursuit of itself. Isolation reverberates. Welcome to Northern Canada, home to precarious communities and ecosystems in the constant battle throes of survival. Canada's beauty lies in its ruggedness.

But this beauty is in danger. Harsh, inclement conditions are making 2 way for warmer temperatures, and though on the surface this does not seem bad, there are long-term ill effects of this phenomenon.

Warming up the North threatens not only ice, wind and snowstorms, 3 but biodiversity, Inuit livelihood and ecosystems as well. Warming trends in the North may cause cooling in the remaining Northern Hemisphere by disrupting the ocean patterns responsible for warming it.

## What, Precisely, Is the Cause of This Global Warming?

The Earth has a history of strange weather patterns, and some speculate 4 that this warming is part of a long-term natural trend; however, there is a strong scientific belief that greenhouse gases intensify and influence this process. We are quite likely encouraging an unfriendly confrontation with Mother Nature. When looking at this historically, this doesn't bode well for humanity.

Aside from their involvement in global warming, greenhouse gases 5 are responsible for ozone depletion and decreased air quality.

The solution, of course, is not simple. Even Greenpeace activists drive 6 home at night to a warm house with lights, appliances, and probably a television and computer. Most of the power used every day is produced by emission-producing coal-burning plants.

"Regardless of already present damage and other sources of green- 7 house gas emissions, there is a positive impact seen in response to public concern. Many coal-fired power plants across North America are retro-fitting flue gas desulphurisation and selective caltylitic (NOx) reduction units to drastically reduce air impurities," says John Sinclair, engineering manager at a leading international consulting engineering company in Oakville, Ontario.

In the face of global warming, Canada has the power and reason to be 8 an international leader. But we have thus far fallen in step behind our neighbours to the South. International regulations are being manipulated to allow Canadians to continue to be the largest energy consumers per capita, defeating the purpose behind the regulations.

Of those that oppose international protocol (USA, Canada, Japan, 9 Australia), Canada is the only one being harshly affected by global warm-ing and anticipated to encounter unprecedented weather changes in the coming years. Globally, developing countries will see the biggest changes, with devastating outcomes predicted since many already combat drought (and ironically, pollute the least).

Residents of Sachs Harbour (Northwest Territories) are facing problems 10 rooted in Canada's wastefulness. As the ice floes melt, the seals and, in turn, the polar bears are forced to leave. With no seals and no polar bears to hunt, the livelihood of much of the community is at risk. The permafrost is melting, starting 25 per cent further down than in past years. It is melt-ing far enough inland to drain a lake into the sea, killing all the freshwater fish contained there. There's even rain, which is foreign to the northern climate. Understandably, there is much concern regarding the survival of these communities.

## International Discussion

In 1997, in Kyoto, Japan, developed countries agreed to lower greenhouse 11 gas emissions by 5.2 per cent. This agreement became known as the Kyoto Protocol. But talk has since proven cheap, especially Western talk, as Canada's emissions are up 13 per cent, along with rises in many other countries.

Another international meeting was called, this time in the Hague, only 12 two months ago. Two-week-long talks fell apart at the last minute because of demands on ways to cheat regulation. For example, some countries (Canada and the United States included) want a credit system allowing them to buy emission "credits" from underdeveloped countries that pollute less, and they demand to count carbon sinks as reduction measures. (Carbon sinks are trees, plants, and oceans that absorb carbon dioxide.) There are two problems in relying on carbon sinks to regulate greenhouse gases: 1) as temperatures rise, trees and plants absorb less and microorganisms produce more carbon dioxide, and 2) it takes nearly 1,500 trees to consume the daily carbon dioxide emission of one car. We would need a lot of trees to compensate for [the habits of] millions of people.

There are two options to look at for those wanting to clean up our 13 atmosphere. We can clean up our coal-burning industrial process, or we can look at alternative clean power sources. In recent years, clean power has been waiting to claim its place as a major power supply while the coal industry is increasingly filtering its pollutants.

On an individual level, we have incredible influence as consumers and 14 voters. Buy and waste less, vote environmentally, and drive minimally.

"In addition to reducing greenhouse gas emissions, it is necessary to 15 explore potential adaptation strategies, for example, agriculture management," says Lynette Sinclair, a climate change consultant. "The objective of adaptation strategies is to minimise detrimental and maximise beneficial effects of climate change."

## Questions About the Reading

1. What are the causes of global warming that the writer discusses?
2. What are the effects of global warming on the residents of Sachs Harbour?
3. What has been the effect of the Kyoto Protocol? What do Canada and the United States want in relation to the Kyoto Protocol?
4. What are the options the writer suggests for cleaning up the atmosphere? What can consumers and voters do?

## Questions About the Writer's Strategies

1. What is the thesis of the essay? State it in your own words.
2. In addition to cause and effect, what other modes of development does the writer use? Provide specific examples of the other modes.

## Writing Assignments

1. *Working Together* Join with some classmates to write an essay in which you explain how you are contributing to global warming and suggest changes you could make to decrease global warming.

2. Write an essay in which you discuss the cause or causes of any air, water, or other pollution that exists in your neighborhood, town, or school and the effects of that pollution.

3. *Working Together*   Using the Internet and your library, investigate the causes and effects, according to writers and politicians (for example, Al Gore), of global warming in the United States. Then, working together, write an essay in which you suggest changes that could be made to decrease the United States' contribution to global warming. Consider, further, whether the changes you suggest might, in turn, cause unemployment or other social conditions in the United States.

# Racial Stereotypes Go Underground

*Cynthia Merriwether-deVries*

> *We can't dispel our racial misconceptions and stereotypes, according to the writer, unless we are willing to admit we have them and are willing to talk about them.*

## Words to Know

**articulating**   talking or speaking about
**deterrent**   discouragement, prevention
**ingrained**   established, fixed
**intimidated**   made fearful or timid

## Getting Started

Do you have friends who are of a race this is different from yours?

---

Quick: What comes to mind first when you think of an African- 1
American? Can't come up with anything? Or too uncomfortable to admit
what you're thinking?

Everyone is aware of the racial and ethnic preconceptions, miscon- 2
ceptions and stereotypes that exist in American society. Yet many college
students, believe it or not, claim they can't think of a single stereotype
about blacks, Asians, Hispanics and Arabs.

As part of a research project, I interviewed more than 80 students at 3
my predominantly white, middle-class campus about their perceptions
of race and gender. Most had no problem articulating popular stereotypes about men and women: "macho," "aggressive" and "competitive"
for men; "self-conscious" and "sensitive" for women.

But asked to turn their attention to racial stereotypes, many fell silent. 4
More than half claimed they could think of no stereotypes associated
with Asians or Hispanics. A third said they had no preconceptions of
Arabs. About a quarter claimed ignorance of any stereotypes associated
with African-Americans.

What is happening in our country—specifically, on our college 5
campuses—is the result of years of speech codes and "political correctness" that have covered over racial stereotypes and misconceptions but
done little to eliminate them. So instead of honest discourse, we get the
Bambi approach: If you can't say anything nice, don't say anything at all.

But I know racial and ethnic stereotypes still exist: I am an African- 6
American woman from a working-class background at a small, private

liberal arts school, where the most well-meaning students unmask their ingrained stereotypes only when they let their guard down. Some of my students, for example, are surprised to find out I was raised in a two-parent household (married parents, at that).

From an educator's point of view, it's tragic to see college students 7 intimidated into thinking it's taboo to speak certain words or ideas associated with racial and ethnic groups. The thoughts and words are there, but students aren't comfortable expressing them.

As a sociologist and an academic, it's my job to combat misconceptions 8 by putting them on the table where we can talk about their origins, why they're invalid and how to dispel them. The current climate on campus is a deterrent to that goal. So we're left with a social and political climate that suppresses only the expressions—but not the sentiments.

## Questions About the Reading

1. What are the stereotypes that the college students had about men and women?
2. How did the students respond when asked about racial stereotypes? Why?
3. What percentage of the students claimed they had no stereotypes of Asians or Hispanics?
4. What percentage claimed they had no preconceptions of Arabs? What percentage claimed they did not know of any stereotypes associated with African-Americans?

## Questions About the Writer's Strategies

1. What is the thesis of the essay? Is it stated or implied? If stated, identify the sentences. If implied, state the thesis in your own words.
2. What are the cause and the effect in the essay?
3. Besides cause and effect, what other modes of development does the writer use?
4. Is the essay objective or subjective or both? Support your answer with examples from the essay.

## Writing Assignments

1. Write a cause-and-effect essay about the pros and cons of political correctness.
2. *Working Together* Join with some classmates to write a cause-and-effect essay about stereotypes.

# The Thirsty Animal

*Brian Manning*

> In this personal essay, Brian Manning recounts how he developed into a
> problem drinker and describes his life now as an alcoholic who has quit
> drinking. Straightforwardly, he tells of his bittersweet memories of drink-
> ing and of his struggle, successful so far, to keep the thirsty "animal living
> inside" locked in its cage.

### Words to Know

**accouterments**   the items and sensations accompanying a certain
  activity
**Bordeaux**   a type of French wine, usually red
**lolling**   lounging, relaxing

### Getting Started

Can you describe some of the negative effects of alcohol on you or
someone you know?

----

I was very young, but I still vividly remember how my father fascinated 1
my brothers and me at the dinner table by running his finger around the
rim of his wineglass. He sent a wonderful, crystal tone wafting through
the room, and we loved it. When we laughed too raucously, he would stop,
swirl the red liquid in his glass and take a sip.

There was a wine cellar in the basement of the house we moved into 2
when I was eleven. My father put a few cases of Bordeaux down there in
the dark. We played there with other boys in the neighborhood, hid there,
made a secret place. It was musty and cool and private. We wrote things
and stuck them in among the bottles and imagined someone way in the
future baffled by our messages from the past.

Many years later, the very first time I drank, I had far too much. But I 3
found I was suddenly able to tell a girl at my high school that I was mad
about her.

When I drank in college with the men in my class, I was trying to define 4
a self-image I could feel comfortable with. I wanted to be "an Irishman," I
decided, a man who could drink a lot of liquor and hold it. My favorite
play was Eugene O'Neill's *Long Day's Journey into Night,* my model the
drunken Jamie Tyrone.

I got out of college, into the real world, and the drunk on weekends 5
started to slip into the weekdays. Often I didn't know when one drunk

ended and another began. The years were measured in hangovers. It took a long time to accept, and then to let the idea sink in, that I was an alcoholic.

It took even longer to do anything about it. I didn't want to believe it, and I didn't want to deny myself the exciting, brotherly feeling I had whenever I went boozing with my friends. For a long time, in my relationships with women, I could only feel comfortable with a woman who drank as much as I did. So I didn't meet many women and spent my time with men in dark barrooms, trying to be like them and hoping I'd be accepted. 6

It is now two years since I quit drinking, and that, as all alcoholics know who have come to grips with their problem, is not long ago at all. The urge to have "just one" includes a genuine longing for all the accouterments of drink: the popping of a cork, the color of Scotch through a glass, the warmth creeping over my shoulders with the third glass of stout. Those were joys. Ever since I gave them up I remember them as delicious. 7

I go to parties now and start off fine, but I have difficulty dealing with the changing rhythms as the night wears on. Everyone around me seems to be having a better time the more they drink, and I, not they, become awkward. I feel like a kid with a broken chain when everyone else has bicycled around the corner out of sight. I fight against feeling sorry for myself. 8

What were the things I was looking for and needed when I drank? I often find that what I am looking for when I want a drink is not really the alcohol, but the memories and laughter that seemed possible only with a glass in my hand. In a restaurant, I see the bottle of vintage port on the shelf, and imagine lolling in my chair, swirling the liquid around in the glass, inhaling those marvelous fumes. I think of my neighbor, Eileen, the funniest woman I ever got smashed with, and I want to get up on a bar stool next to her to hear again the wonderful stories she told. She could drink any man under the table, she claimed, and I wanted to be one of those men who tried. She always won, but it made me feel I belonged when I staggered out of the bar, her delighted laughter following me. 9

I had found a world to cling to, a way of belonging, and it still attracts me. I pass by the gin mills and pubs now and glance in at the men lined up inside, and I don't see them as suckers or fools. I remember how I felt sitting there after work, or watching a Sunday afternoon ball game, and I long for the smell of the barroom and that ease—toasts and songs, jokes and equality. I have to keep reminding myself of the wasting hangovers, the lost money, the days down the drain. 10

I imagine my problem as an animal living inside me, demanding a drink before it dies of thirst. That's what it says, but it will never die of thirst. The fact an alcoholic faces is that this animal breathes and waits. It is incapable of death and will spring back to lustful, consuming life with even one drop of sustenance. 11

When I was eighteen and my drinking began in earnest, I didn't play  12
in the wine cellar at home anymore; I stole there. I sneaked bottles to my
room, sat in the window and drank alone while my parents were away.
I hated the taste of it, but I kept drinking it, without the kids from the
neighborhood, without any thought that I was feeding the animal. And
one day, I found one of those old notes we had hidden down there years
before. It fell to the ground when I pulled a bottle from its cubbyhole. I
read it with bleary eyes, then put the paper back into the rack. "Beware,"
it said, above a childish skull and crossbones, "all ye who enter here." A
child, wiser than I was that day, had written that note.

I did a lot of stupid, disastrous, sometimes mean things in the years that  13
followed, and remembering them is enough to snap me out of the memories and back to the reality that I quit just in time. I've done something I
had to do, something difficult and necessary, and that gives me satisfac-
tion and the strength to stay on the wagon. I'm very lucky so far. I don't
get mad that I can't drink anymore; I can handle the self-pity that over-
whelmed me in my early days of sobriety. From time to time, I daydream
about summer afternoons and cold beer. I know such dreams will never go
away. The thirsty animal is there, getting a little fainter every day. It will
never die. A lot of my life now is all about keeping it in a very lonely cage.

## Questions About the Reading

1. What went along with drinking for the writer? Why did he need alcohol to get those effects?
2. Why are parties difficult for the writer?
3. Why did the writer stop drinking?
4. When you finished reading the essay, what opinions had you formed
   of the writer's personality and character? Cite specific details from the
   essay to support your opinions.

## Questions About the Writer's Strategies

1. What is the main idea of this essay? In which sentences is it most clearly
   stated?
2. What are the causes in this essay? What are the effects? Do they overlap at all?
3. Other than cause and effect, what modes of development does the writer
   use? Cite paragraphs in which he uses other modes.
4. The "animal" introduced in paragraph 11 is a metaphor. What does it
   stand for? Interpret it in your own words.

5. Identify the simile in paragraph 8. Is it effective in helping you understand how the writer feels?

## Writing Assignments

1. Describe in an essay the effects that alcohol has on you. If you do not drink, describe the effects that you have seen it have on others.
2. Do you know anyone who abuses alcohol or other substances? If not, you have surely come across the lure of drugs in the media or in school awareness programs. On the basis of what you know and what you have learned from reading this essay, write an essay describing the causes and effects of substance abuse.

# More Than Words

### *Victor Flores (student)*

> *Victor Flores is a native of the Northern Mariana Islands who grew up on the picturesque island of Saipan. He attends Leeward Community College and lives in Honolulu, Hawaii. In his essay, he tells us about a mistake he made.*

**Word to Know**

**enticed**  lured, tempted

*Getting Started*

Do you remember a particular experience that taught you the importance of being dependable?

---

I stood there frozen. My feet feeling like they were rooted into the ground, 1 planted too deeply to be moved. My father, in his anger, was yelling at me, and during those minutes that passed, it felt like an eternity. To this day I still remember those words forcing their way into my mind while piercing my heart. My father's bronze, tanned face turned red right before my eyes, like a piece of hot glowing coal. He yelled, "I'm not your friend. I'm your father. Don't treat me like your friends." I was hurt, and I masked my pain over the fear and disappointment.

My father, a hard-working and diligent man who rarely, if ever, stood 2 idle, was furious with me. He was always ready to greet people with a smile. Caring about his appearance, he always neatly combed his thinning hair. He was well dressed and wore comfortable shoes. But on this day it didn't matter. I had exhausted his patience as he waited for me to return home from school. After school that day, with my parents' car, I had driven my friend home. Time had whisked by. When I got home, it was after 5 P.M. It was too late. My father needed me to do something important. At sixteen and with my parents' car, coming home after school wasn't my idea of enjoying the privileges of my free afternoon. Enticed by sitting behind the wheel, it was too easy to get wrapped up in friends and lose track of time.

For as long as I can remember, my parents have always been self- 3 employed. They ran a small retail store, just the two of them for the most part. It was a well-stocked store with fishing supplies, clothing, guitar supplies, sporting goods and comfortable shoes. Every day except Sundays and holidays, going to the post office two and often three times a day was routine. Nearly everything that filled the store's shelves was sent through the post office. Maybe my father had promised a customer that his or her order would be in that afternoon. Or maybe he needed a certain part to repair a fishing reel. Whatever the reason, my father had depended on me to get to the post office, pick up the merchandise and bring it back to the store. Before that day when he yelled at me, I had not realized how important that simple task was and how much they needed me.

## Questions About the Reading

1. What was the "task" that the writer's father expected the writer to do? Was the writer usually responsible for doing this task?
2. What did the writer do that made his father angry?
3. What did the writer learn from disappointing his father?

## Questions About the Writer's Strategies

1. What is the point of view (person, time, tone) of the essay?
2. What modes of development does the writer use in the essay?
3. What is the simile in the first paragraph of the essay?

## Writing Assignments

1. Write an essay in which you tell about a personal experience that taught you an important lesson.
2. Think of an invention or convenience that has had positive effects on your life. Identify the invention or convenience and write an essay explaining its effects on your life.

# 9 Definition

WHEN WRITERS USE words that they think may be unfamiliar to their readers, they usually will define the words. A **definition** is an explanation of the meaning of a word or term.

In its shortest form, the definition may be simply a **synonym**—a familiar word or phrase that has the same meaning as the unfamiliar word. For example, in "she shows more *empathy* for, or true understanding of, older people than her sister," the word understanding is a synonym for *empathy.* Or the writer may choose to use an **antonym**—a word or phrase that has the opposite meaning of the unfamiliar word—as in "she is a compassionate rather than an *inconsiderate* person." Here the word inconsiderate gives the reader the opposite meaning of *compassionate.*

The writer may also choose to use the kind of precise definition found in dictionaries, called a **formal definition.** In a formal definition, the writer first uses a form of **classification,** assigning the word to the **class** of items to which it belongs, and then describing the characteristics that distinguish it from other items of that class. Here is an example of a formal definition.

Word defined:
tiger; class: cat
family         A tiger, a member of the cat family, is native to Asia,
Description of  usually weighs over 350 pounds, and has tawny and black-
characteristics striped fur.

**Connotation,** which refers to the impressions or qualities we associate with a word, and **denotation,** the dictionary definition of a word, are important in writing a definition. Think of the word *pig,* for instance. The dictionary may tell you that a pig is simply a domestic animal with hooves, short legs, bristly hair, and a blunt snout; and a farmer may tell you that a pig is relatively smarter and cleaner than other farm animals. However, the negative connotations of this word are so strong that you are likely to have trouble thinking of a pig without thinking of filth, fat, and greed.

In writing definitions, it is particularly important to choose your words in such a way that their connotations as well as their denotations will give your readers the correct impression of what you are defining. As you are writing and **revising,** remember to search for the single best word for conveying your ideas.

When you search for connotative words and expressions to use in your writing, beware of **clichés.** Clichés are words or phrases—such as "rosy red," "silly goose," "bull in a china shop," "weird," or "outrageous"—which have become so overused that they indicate a lack of imagination and thought on the part of the writer who uses them. Symbols, too, can be clichés. If you are defining *courage*, for example, using Superman as a symbol to enhance your definition is unlikely to impress your readers. You should also be aware that many clichés take the form of **similes:** "as filthy as a pig," for example. Try to make sure your similes are always of your own creation, not ones you have heard before.

Many complex words and abstract ideas—such as *truth* and *justice*—require longer and more detailed explanations, which are called **extended definitions.** In an extended definition, the writer may use one or more of the methods of development—description, examples, classification, and so forth—that you have learned about in the earlier chapters of this book. For example, the writer might use **process, description,** or **narration**—or all three—as the method of development in an extended definition.

| | |
|---|---|
| Topic sentence: formal definition | A glacier is an accumulation of snow and ice that continually flows from a mountain ice field toward sea level. Glaciers are |
| Process | formed when successive snowfalls pile up, creating pressure on the bottom layers. Gradually, the pressure causes the snow on the bottom to undergo a structural change into an extremely dense form of ice called glacier ice, a process that may take several years. Once the ice begins to accumulate, gravity causes the mass to move downhill. Glaciers |
| Extended definition: descriptive narration | usually take the path of least resistance, following stream beds or other natural channels down the mountainside. As they move, they scrape along the surface of the earth, picking up rocks and other sediment on the way. The ice and the debris carve a deep U-shaped valley as they proceed down the mountain. If they advance far enough, they will eventually reach the sea and become tidewater glaciers that break off, or calve, directly into salt water. Southeast |

Alaska is one of only three places in the world where tidewater glaciers exist. (They also are found in Scandinavia and Chile.) Other glaciers, called hanging glaciers, spill out of icy basins high up on valley walls and tumble toward the valley floor.

Sarah Eppenbach,
*Alaska's Southeast*

In the example that follows, the writer combines a formal definition with **classification, examples, comparison** and **contrast.**

Formal definition:
map
Classification:
conventional
picture
Characteristics:
area of land, sea,
or sky

Example: road
maps

Example: simple
maps

Contrast: chart
represents water;
map represents
land

Contrast: chart
for navigation

Example: use of
maps

Example:
features of some
maps

Comparison:
features of early
maps with ones
of modern maps

A map is a conventional picture of an area of land, sea, or sky. Perhaps the maps most widely used are the road maps given away by the oil companies. They show the cultural features such as states, towns, parks, and roads, especially paved roads. They show also natural features, such as rivers and lakes, and sometimes mountains. As simple maps, most automobile drivers have on various occasions used sketches drawn by service station men, or by friends, to show the best automobile route from one town to another.  **1**

The distinction usually made between "maps" and "charts" is that a chart is a representation of an area consisting chiefly of water; a map represents an area that is predominantly land. It is easy to see how this distinction arose in the days when there was no navigation over land, but a truer distinction is that charts are specially designed for use in navigation, whether at sea or in the air.  **2**

Maps have been used since the earliest civilizations, and explorers find that they are used in rather simple civilizations at the present time by people who are accustomed to traveling. For example, Arctic explorers have obtained considerable help from maps of the coast lines showing settlements, drawn by Eskimo people. Occasionally maps show not only the roads, but pictures of other features. One of the earliest such maps dates from about 1400 B.C. It shows not only roads, but also lakes with fish, and a canal with crocodiles and a bridge over the canal. This is somewhat similar to the modern maps of a state which show for each large town some feature of interest or the chief products of that town.  **3**

C. C. Wylie,
*Astronomy, Maps, and Weather*

As you can see, you may use any method of development that is appropriate when you need to extend the definition of a word or term.

Whether you are writing an extended definition or relying primarily on some other mode of development, always remember to define any words or terms you use that may be unfamiliar to your readers—particularly any words they must know to understand your meaning. You should also define words with any special or technical meaning.

# Running with the Cardio-Bots

*Walter Kirn*

> *Stop by any gym or health center and check out Walter Kirn's definition of the people working out on the treadmills, StairMasters, and bicycles!*

**Words to Know**

**oblivious**   unaware
**profoundly**   deeply
**simulated**   imagined, feigned

**Getting Started**

Do you follow a regular exercise program?

---

I walk into the gym, and there they are, the cardio-bots, half human, half machine, eyes fixed on banks of televisions and ears glued to iPods as they scale imaginary mountains or jog down simulated country roads. How driven they seem, how profoundly self-conscious. Digital monitors strapped around their biceps register their blood pressures and heart rates as their tissues absorb L-glutamine-laced protein drinks that taste like the sort of thing computers would drink if computers got thirsty. And though there must be 30 cardio-bots, lifting their sinewy thighs in unison as their StairMasters and treadmills tick off the number of calories they've burned, each one of them seems to exist in his or her own universe, oblivious to the rest.

---

## Questions About the Reading

1. What is the writer's opinion of the "cardio-bots" in the gym?
2. Why does the writer describe the cardio-bots as being "half human, half machine"?

## Questions About the Writer's Strategies

1. What is the main idea of the paragraph? State it in your own words.

2. What modes of development does the writer use in the paragraph to define the cardio-bots?

## Writing Assignments

1. Write a paragraph in which you define one of the following terms: *walking, running,* or *sleeping.*
2. Write a paragraph in which you define the terms *grocery shopping, doing your laundry,* or *cleaning your room* (assuming you ever do!).

# The Ultimate Kitchen Gadget

*Robert Capon*

*Anyone who likes to cook owns a number of kitchen gadgets. What is your favorite: a garlic press, a food processor, or a blender? In the following selection, Robert Capon, an Episcopal priest and lover of cooking, defines the ultimate kitchen gadget.*

### Word to Know

trice   a very short time

### Getting Started

What is your favorite gadget: a cell phone, an iPod, a Walkman, or some other device you carry with you?

I t is the ultimate kitchen gadget. It serves as a juicier for lemons, oranges and grapefruit, and as a combination seed remover and pulp crusher for tomatoes. It functions as a bowl scraper, an egg separator and a remover of unwelcome particles—the stray bit of eggshell, the odd grain of black rice—from mixing bowl or saucepan. It is a thermometer capable of gauging temperatures up to 500 degrees Fahrenheit and, in addition, is a measuring device for dry ingredients in amounts from 1 tablespoon down to 1/8 teaspoon or less, and for whatever liquids may be called for in the cooking of grains and stocks. It can be used as tongs for removing hot cup custards from the oven, as a mixer of water into pastry dough and as a kneader of bread. Best of all, it cleans up in a trice, presents no storage problems, will not chip, rust or tarnish and, if it cannot be said to be unlosable or indestructible, it nevertheless comes with a lifetime guarantee to remain the one household convenience you will have the least desire either to lose or to destroy. It is, of course, the human hand.

## Questions About the Reading

1. Temperatures above about 160 degrees will burn a person's hand. How can the hand be used to gauge temperatures up to 500 degrees?
2. What is the lifetime guarantee of the ultimate kitchen gadget?
3. At what point in the paragraph did you guess what the ultimate kitchen gadget is?

## Questions About the Writer's Strategies

1. What is the predominant mode of development used to define the ultimate kitchen gadget?
2. Why doesn't the writer identify what he is defining until the very last sentence?
3. What is the tone of this paragraph?
4. What connotations does the word *gadget* have? Would you normally associate these connotations with the human hand?
5. What is the **irony** in this paragraph?

## Writing Assignments

1. Write a paragraph in which you define a household appliance (such as a blender, a vacuum cleaner, or a toaster) by giving examples of its uses and the purposes it serves.
2. Write a definition of the human hand from another point of view. Instead of giving examples of what it can do in the kitchen, describe its physical anatomy—what it looks like underneath the skin. Use the Internet to get correct biological and anatomical information.
3. Write a definition of the human body by giving examples of some of the things it can do.

# Nostalgia

### Richard Shelton

*What is the* crepuscular? *Richard Shelton misses it, along with the* bucolic *and* idyllic. *Although he does not define the word, a careful reading tells us what it means.*

### Words to Know

**bucolic**   pastoral, rural, rustic
**carnage**   slaughter, bloodshed
**gentility**   politeness, refinement
**idyllic**   pleasing, simple, picturesque
**mayhem**   mutilation

### Getting Started

Is there something that you remember from your childhood and now miss?

---

**W**hatever happened to the crepuscular? It's never mentioned anymore. Years since I heard any reference to the crepuscular. I wonder if anybody notices it now as we once did, creeping in and out with silent majesty, leaving some of us with lumps in our throats. It would be a relief from the carnage and mayhem. I remember sometimes at that time of day in the autumn when there was a chill in the air and somebody was burning leaves somewhere, I could nearly die of happiness. But I am older now and it's illegal to burn leaves. So I guess nobody notices the crepuscular anymore. Or the bucolic. Nobody ever says, "Let's go spend a bucolic weekend in the country." And nobody calls anything idyllic. Whatever became of idyllic afternoons beside the river? And grand passions? Passions don't seem to be grand anymore, just sort of everyday affairs. I guess it's hard to have a grand passion without idyllic afternoons and crepuscular evenings, and we are just too busy to take the time for such things. And nightingales? I never heard one myself, but I certainly read about them, and they seemed to be almost everywhere at one time. Perhaps they were no longer needed and they died out or somebody shot them. Might be a few left in a zoo somewhere, I wouldn't know about that. But surely gentility has survived. You mean gentility is gone too? Lord! But whatever happened to peace and quiet? Somewhere there still must be some peace and quiet. And whatever happened to kindness . . . ?

## Questions About the Reading

1. According to the writer, how did people feel when they noticed the crepuscular?
2. How did the writer feel when somebody was burning leaves somewhere?
3. What would a bucolic weekend in the country be like?
4. What would an idyllic afternoon be like?

## Questions About the Writer's Strategies

1. What is the main idea of the paragraph? Is it stated or implied?
2. What does *crepuscular* mean? How did you figure out the meaning?
3. What modes of development does the writer use?
4. What is the tone of the paragraph?

## Writing Assignments

1. Write a paragraph in which you define one of the following terms: *democracy, religion, ethics*. Include a formal definition from an online dictionary such as yourDictionary.com (**www.yourdictionary.com**), and use at least two other modes of development. Make a copy of the web page on which you find your definition and attach it to your paragraph.
2. Write a paragraph in which you define one of the following sports: baseball, football, basketball, soccer.
3. Write a paragraph about some holiday celebration that you remember and now miss.

# What Does It Mean to Be Creative?

**S. I. Hayakawa**

*S. I. Hayakawa was a United States senator, the president of San Francisco State College, and an authority on semantics—the study of the development, structure, and changes of language. In this paragraph, he defines the creative person.*

### Word to Know
**examining**   investigating, looking at

### Getting Started
What do you think it means to be creative?

A creative person, first, is not limited in his thinking to "what everyone knows." "Everyone knows" that trees are green. The creative artist is able to see that in certain lights some trees look blue or purple or yellow. The creative person looks at the world with his or her own eyes, not with the eyes of others. The creative individual also knows his or her own feelings better than the average person. Most people don't know the answer to the question, "How are you? How do you feel?" The reason they don't know is that they are so busy feeling what they are supposed to feel, thinking what they are supposed to think, that they never get down to examining their own deepest feelings.

## Questions About the Reading

1. According to the writer, how does the creative person look at the world?
2. What distinguishes the creative individual from the average person?
3. Why do most people not know the answer to "How are you? How do you feel?"

## Questions About the Writer's Strategies

1. What is the writer's definition of a creative person?
2. What are two transitional words the writer uses? Would the definition be clearer by changing one of the transitional words? What transitional words would you use in the definition?

## Writing Assignments

1. Write a paragraph in which you define and give examples of a creative person.
2. Write a paragraph in which you explain how someone in a certain sport might be creative.

# Grandparents

## Nancy Merrell (student)

*In the paragraph that follows, Nancy Merrell provides us with an extended
definition of the word* grandparents *by telling us what they do and how
we feel about them at different times in our lives and theirs. By making
us understand her feelings about grandparents, she makes us aware of our
own attitudes and feelings.*

### Words to Know
**accomplishments**   achievements
**appreciated**   valued

### Getting Started
How would you define an excellent teacher?

Of all family members, grandparents are probably the least appreciated. They are just people who are always around. They make a fuss over the children in the family, brag to their friends about the accomplishments of this child or that child, and show countless pictures of new babies. Grandfathers can fix anything, and grandmothers always have homemade cookies around. When you are small, it's fun to stay with your grandparents because they always let you do things you can't do at home, and of course they buy you things. They are always available to babysit because they don't go out much and actually prefer to see their grandchildren. They are usually good for a small loan now and then that doesn't need to be paid back because they turn it into a gift. You respectfully listen to their advice but don't follow it because they are old and don't understand how things are in this day and age. You thank them politely for what they do for you, and then don't call or visit them until you need something else. And of course you never tell them how dear they are to you because they know how you feel about them anyway. Then all of a sudden, they are no longer there to do the things that only grandparents do, and you find yourself wishing that you had told them what they meant to you as people and not just as grandparents.

## Questions About the Reading

1. What inferences can you draw about the writer's grandparents from the paragraph? Support your answer with statements from the paragraph.
2. What is the function of the last sentence of the paragraph?
3. What are some of the examples that the writer uses to define grandparents? What are some of the examples she uses to explain how we treat grandparents?

## Questions About the Writer's Strategies

1. What is the main mode of development that the writer uses to define grandparents?
2. Does the writer use more than one mode? If so, which one(s)?
3. What is the point of view in the paragraph? Does it change? If so, could the writer have maintained the same point of view throughout the paragraph? If so, explain how this could be done.

## Writing Assignments

1. Write a paragraph in which you define a true friend by giving examples of the person's behavior.
2. Write a paragraph in which you define a person or place by using descriptive details.
3. Write a paragraph in which you define what the word *parent* means to you. Use several modes of development—such as examples, description, or narration. You might want to consider process; in particular, how to be a good parent.

# What Is Poverty?

## Jo Goodwin Parker

*In this powerful essay, Jo Goodwin Parker uses **parallelism** to leave us with an unforgettable definition of* poverty—*one that she hopes will stir us to action.*

### Word to Know

**malnutrition**   insufficient nutrition, lack of food

### Getting Started

What services does your town or city provide for homeless or impoverished people?

---

Y ou ask me what is poverty? Listen to me. Here I am, dirty, smelly, and   1
with no "proper" underwear on and with the stench of my rotting teeth near you. I will tell you. Listen to me. Listen without pity. I cannot use your pity. Listen with understanding. Put yourself in my dirty, worn out, ill-fitting shoes, and hear me.

Poverty is getting up every morning from a dirt- and illness-stained   2
mattress. The sheets have long since been used for diapers. Poverty is living in a smell that never leaves. This is a smell of urine, sour milk, and spoiling food sometimes joined with the strong smell of long-cooked onions. Onions are cheap. If you have smelled this smell, you did not know how it came. It is the smell of the outdoor privy. It is the smell of young children who cannot walk the long dark way in the night. It is the smell of the mattresses where years of "accidents" have happened. It is the smell of the milk which has gone sour because the refrigerator long has not worked, and it costs money to get it fixed. It is the smell of rotting garbage. I could bury it, but where is the shovel? Shovels cost money.

Poverty is being tired. I have always been tired. They told me at the   3
hospital when the last baby came that I had chronic anemia caused from poor diet, a bad case of worms, and that I needed a corrective operation. I listened politely—the poor are always polite. The poor always listen. They don't say that there is no money for iron pills, or better food, or worm medicine. The idea of an operation is frightening and costs so much that, if I had dared, I would have laughed. Who takes care of my children? Recovery from an operation takes a long time. I have three children. When I left them with "Granny" the last time I had a job, I came home to find the

baby covered with fly specks, and a diaper that had not been changed since I left. When the dried diaper came off, bits of my baby's flesh came with it. My other child was playing with a sharp bit of broken glass, and my oldest was playing alone at the edge of a lake. I made twenty-two dollars a week, and a good nursery school costs twenty dollars a week for three children. I quit my job.

Poverty is dirt. You can say in your clean clothes coming from your 4 clean house, "Anybody can be clean." Let me explain about housekeeping with no money. For breakfast I give my children grits with no oleo or cornbread without eggs and oleo. This does not use up many dishes. What dishes there are, I wash in cold water and with no soap. Even the cheapest soap has to be saved for the baby's diapers. Look at my hands, so cracked and red. Once I saved for two months to buy a jar of Vaseline for my hands and the baby's diaper rash. When I had saved enough, I went to buy it and the price had gone up two cents. The baby and I suffered on. I have to decide every day if I can bear to put my cracked sore hands into the cold water and strong soap. But you ask, why not hot water? Fuel costs money. If you have a wood fire it costs money. If you burn electricity, it costs money. Hot water is a luxury. I do not have luxuries. I know you will be surprised when I tell you how young I am. I look so much older. My back has been bent over the wash tubs every day for so long, I cannot remember when I ever did anything else. Every night I wash every stitch my school-age child has on and just hope her clothes will be dry by morning.

Poverty is staying up all night on cold nights to watch the fire knowing 5 one spark on the newspaper covering the walls means your sleeping child dies in flames. In summer poverty is watching gnats and flies devour your baby's tears when he cries. The screens are torn and you pay so little rent you know they will never be fixed. Poverty means insects in your food, in your nose, in your eyes, and crawling over you when you sleep. Poverty is hoping it never rains because diapers won't dry when it rains and soon you are using newspapers. Poverty is seeing your children forever with runny noses. Paper handkerchiefs cost money and all your rags you need for other things. Even more costly are antihistamines. Poverty is cooking without food and cleaning without soap.

Poverty is asking for help. Have you ever had to ask for help, know- 6 ing your children will suffer unless you get it? Think about asking for a loan from a relative, if this is the only way you can imagine asking for help. I will tell you how it feels. You find out where the office is that you are supposed to visit. You circle that block four or five times. Thinking of your children, you go in. Everyone is very busy. Finally, someone comes out and you tell her that you need help. That never is the person you need to see. You go see another person, and after spilling the whole shame of your poverty all over the desk between you, you find that this isn't the right office after all—you must repeat the whole process, and it never is any easier at the next place.

You have asked for help, and after all it has a cost. You are again told 7 to wait. You are told why, but you don't really hear because of the red cloud of shame and the rising cloud of despair.

Poverty is remembering. It is remembering quitting school in junior 8 high because "nice" children had been so cruel about my clothes and my smell. The attendance officer came. My mother told him I was pregnant. I wasn't, but she thought that I could get a job and help out. I had jobs off and on, but never long enough to learn anything. Mostly I remember being married. I was so young then. I am still young. For a time, we had all the things you have. There was a little house in another town, with hot water and everything. Then my husband lost his job. There was unemployment insurance for a while and what few jobs I could get. Soon, all our nice things were repossessed and we moved back here. I was pregnant then. This house didn't look so bad when we first moved in. Every week it gets worse. Nothing is ever fixed. We now had no money. There were a few odd jobs for my husband, but everything went for food then, as it does now. I don't know how we lived through three years and three babies, but we did. I'll tell you something; after the last baby I destroyed my marriage. It had been a good one, but could you keep on bringing children in this dirt? Did you ever think how much it costs for any kind of birth control? I knew my husband was leaving the day he left, but there were no goodbyes between us. I hope he has been able to climb out of this mess somewhere. He never could hope with us to drag him down.

That's when I asked for help. When I got it, you know how much it 9 was? It was, and is, seventy-eight dollars a month for the four of us; that is all I ever can get. Now you know why there is no soap, no needles and thread, no hot water, no aspirin, no worm medicine, no hand cream, no shampoo. None of these things forever and ever and ever. So that you can see clearly, I pay twenty dollars a month rent, and most of the rest goes for food. For grits and cornmeal, and rice and milk and beans. I try my best to use only the minimum electricity. If I use more, there is that much less for food.

Poverty is looking into a black future. Your children won't play with my 10 boys. They will turn to other boys who steal to get what they want. I can already see them behind the bars of their prison instead of behind the bars of my poverty. Or they will turn to the freedom of alcohol or drugs, and find themselves enslaved. And my daughter? At best, there is for her a life like mine.

But you say to me, there are schools. Yes, there are schools. My children 11
have no extra books, no magazines, no extra pencils, or crayons, or paper
and most important of all, they do not have health. They have worms, they
have infections, they have pink-eye all summer. They do not sleep well
on the floor, or with me in my one bed. They do not suffer from hunger,
my seventy-eight dollars keeps us alive, but they do suffer from malnutrition. Oh yes, I do remember what I was taught about health in school.
It doesn't do much good. In some places there is a surplus commodities
program. Not here. The country said it cost too much. There is a school
lunch program. But I have two children who will already be damaged by
the time they get to school.

But, you say to me, there are health clinics. Yes, there are health clinics 12
and they are in the towns. I live out here eight miles from town. I can walk
that far (even if it is sixteen miles both ways), but can my little children?
My neighbor will take me when he goes; but he expects to get paid, *one way
or another.* I bet you know my neighbor. He is that large man who spends
his time at the gas station, the barbershop, and the corner store complaining about the government spending money on the immoral mothers of
illegitimate children.

Poverty is an acid that drips on pride until all pride is worn away. 13
Poverty is a chisel that chips on honor until honor is worn away. Some
of you say that you would do *something* in my situation, and maybe
you would, for the first week or the first month, but for year after year
after year?

Even the poor can dream. A dream of a time when there is money. 14
Money for the right kinds of food, for worm medicine, for iron pills, for
toothbrushes, for hand cream, for a hammer and nails and a bit of screen-
ing, for a shovel, for a bit of paint, for some sheeting, for needles and
thread. Money to pay *in money* for a trip to town. And, oh, money for hot
water and money for soap. A dream of when asking for help does not eat
away the last bit of pride. When the office you visit is as nice as the offices
of other governmental agencies, when there are enough workers to help
you quickly, when workers do not quit in defeat and despair. When you
have to tell your story to only one person, and that person can send you
for other help and you don't have to prove your poverty over and over
and over again.

I have come out of my despair to tell you this. Remember I did not come 15
from another place or another time. Others like me are all around you. Look
at us with an angry heart, anger that will help you help me. Anger that will
let you tell of me. The poor are always silent. Can you be silent too?

## Questions About the Reading

1. What does the writer want the reader to do about poverty?
2. How would you summarize the writer's definition of *poverty*?
3. Why, according to the writer, is she impoverished?
4. Why, according to the writer, is she unable to work?

## Questions About the Writer's Strategies

1. What modes of development does the writer use to define *poverty*?
2. What is the technique the writer uses to add emphasis to her definition of *poverty*?
3. What is the point of view (person, tone) of the essay? Would any other point of view be as effective? Why or why not?

## Writing Assignments

1. *Working Together*   Join with some classmates to find out what services are provided in your city or state for homeless people. Write an essay in which you define the services and the criteria by which a person qualifies for those services.
2. *Working Together*   Join with some classmates to write an essay in which you define what constitutes the "poverty level" according to the federal government and explain what services are available at that level for a single woman with children.
3. Write an essay in which you define the services in which you can or do participate to help impoverished people.

# What Is Intelligence, Anyway?

*Isaac Asimov*

*Many of us think that intelligence is something one is simply born with or that it has to do with doing well in school or getting high scores on IQ tests. But did you ever stop to think about what IQ tests really measure? In the essay that follows, Isaac Asimov asks us to rethink our definition of intelligence.*

### Words to Know

**aptitude**   ability, talent
**arbiter**   someone who has the power to judge
**complacent**   self-satisfied
**intricate**   elaborate
**KP**   kitchen patrol
**oracles**   wise expressions or answers
**raucously**   loudly

### Getting Started

Do you think that tests can ever really measure intelligence?

---

**W**hat is intelligence, anyway? When I was in the army I received a   1
kind of aptitude test that all soldiers took and, against a normal of 100, scored 160. No one at the base had ever seen a figure like that, and for two hours they made a big fuss over me. (It didn't mean anything. The next day I was still a buck private with KP as my highest duty.)

All my life I've been registering scores like that, so that I have the com-   2
placent feeling that I'm highly intelligent, and I expect other people to think so, too. Actually, though, don't such scores simply mean that I am very good at answering the type of academic questions that are considered worthy of answers by the people who make up the intelligence tests—people with intellectual bents similar to mine?

For instance, I had an auto-repair man once, who, on these intelligence   3
tests, could not possibly have scored more than 80, by my estimate. I always took it for granted that I was far more intelligent than he was. Yet, when anything went wrong with my car I hastened to him with it, watched him anxiously as he explored its vitals, and listened to his pronouncements as though they were divine oracles—and he always fixed my car.

Well, then, suppose my auto-repair man devised questions for an in-   4
telligence test. Or suppose a carpenter did, or a farmer, or, indeed, almost
anyone but an academician. By every one of those tests, I'd prove myself
a moron. And I'd *be* a moron, too. In a world where I could not use my
academic training and my verbal talents but had to do something intricate or hard, working with my hands, I would do poorly. My intelligence,
then, is not absolute but is a function of the society I live in and of the fact
that a small subsection of that society has managed to foist itself on the
rest as an arbiter of such matters.

Consider my auto-repair man, again. He had a habit of telling me jokes   5
whenever he saw me. One time he raised his head from under the automobile hood to say: "Doc, a deaf-and-dumb guy went into a hardware
store to ask for some nails. He put two fingers together on the counter
and made hammering motions with the other hand. The clerk brought
him a hammer. He shook his head and pointed to the two fingers he was
hammering. The clerk brought him nails. He picked out the sizes he
wanted, and left. Well, Doc, the next guy who came in was a blind man.
He wanted scissors. How do you suppose he asked for them?"

Indulgently, I lifted my right hand and made scissoring motions with   6
my first two fingers. Whereupon my auto-repair man laughed raucously
and said, "Why, you dumb jerk, he used his *voice* and asked for them."
Then he said, smugly, "I've been trying that on all my customers today."
"Did you catch many?" I asked. "Quite a few," he said, "but I knew for sure
I'd catch *you*." "Why is that?" I asked. "Because you're so goddamned
educated, Doc, I *knew* you couldn't be very smart."

And I have an uneasy feeling he had something there.                     7

---

## Questions About the Reading

1. What does the writer mean when he says, "My intelligence, then, is not
   absolute but is a function of the society I live in . . ." (paragraph 4)?
2. What distinction does the writer make between being educated and
   being smart?
3. Do you think the repairman is smarter than the writer? Why or why
   not?

## Questions About the Writer's Strategies

1. What mode of development does the writer use in paragraphs 5 and 6?
   What is the purpose of these paragraphs?

2. Does the writer actually define *intelligence*? If so, state his definition in your own words. If not, explain why you think he didn't.
3. In paragraph 6, the writer says he made the scissoring motions "indulgently." What does this tell you about his attitude towards the joke? Why is his attitude ironic?
4. Does the essay contain a thesis statement? If so, where is it located? If not, state it in your own words.
5. Is the repairman a symbol? If so, what does he represent?

## Writing Assignments

1. Imagine a society in which intelligence is measured by how well people can work with their hands and fix machinery. Write a definition of *intelligence* for that society.
2. Write an essay defining the term *joke*. Use examples to illustrate your definition.
3. Pick one of the following terms and define it in an essay: *beauty, truth, wisdom,* or *quality.*

# Total Eclipse of the Son

*Tiffany Kary*

> *In Japan, a society long known for valuing and respecting parents and elders, young people are withdrawing from them in a phenomenon known as* hikikomori.

### Words to Know

**agoraphobia**   fear of being in the open or in public places
**bastion**   protector
**controversial**   debatable, arguable
**ramifications**   consequences
**syndrome**   illness, disease

### Getting Started

How would you define *good parenting* and *bad parenting*?

---

A syndrome known as *hikikomori,* in which the outside world is 1 shunned, is wreaking havoc on young people in Japan, a country known for its communal values. And an older generation—the very bastion of those old-fashioned values—may be to blame, according to a controversial new theory.

*Hikikomori* (the term refers to the behavior itself and to those who suffer 2 from it) was first recognized in the early 1990s. One million Japanese, or almost 1 percent of the population, are estimated to suffer from *hikikomori,* defined as a withdrawal from friends and family for months or even years. Some 40 percent of *hikikomori* are below the age of 21, according to a 2001 government report.

Western psychologists compare *hikikomori* with social anxiety and agora- 3 phobia, a fear of open places. The affliction has also been likened to Asperger's syndrome, a mild variant of autism. But these theories carry little weight in Japan, where the disorder is considered culturally unique and is linked to violence.

Yuichi Hattori, MA, a psychologist currently treating 18 patients with 4 the disorder, believes that *hikikomori* is caused by emotionally neglectful parenting. Hattori argues that none of his patients had been sexually or physically abused, yet they all show signs of posttraumatic stress disorder.

As the cultural gap between Japan's youth and elders widens, some 5 young Japanese may view their parents as too stony-faced and reserved.

Hattori speaks of Japanese society's deep-rooted division between *hone* and *tatemae*—one's true feelings and one's actions—to illustrate the frustration his patients express toward aloof parents.

"Patients tell me their mothers have no emotions," says Hattori. "Six  6 patients have called their parents zombies."

Hattori's findings, presented in November to the International society  7 for the Study of Dissociation, are reminiscent of the now-discredited theory of the "refrigerator mother," which attributed autism to a detached style of parenting.

"*Hikikomori* looks more to me like an extreme case of social anxiety,"  8 says David Kupfer, PhD, a psychologist with a private practice in Virginia. Emotionally unresponsive parents are only one of the factors involved in the development of this disorder, says Kupfer, who points out that "in Japan, the pressure to succeed is a unique cultural source of trauma."

For now, Eastern and Western psychologists agree only that *hikikomori*  9 is unique to Japan and has serious ramifications for both generations.

## Questions About the Reading

1. What is *hikikomori?*
2. What percentage of the Japanese population suffer from *hikikomori?*
3. What is the age of 40 percent of the persons who suffer from *hikikomori?*
4. What is the cause of *hikikomori,* according to the psychologist Yuichi Hattori?

## Questions About the Writer's Strategies

1. What is the definition of *hikikomori?*
2. What other modes of development does the writer use? Identify them.
3. Could the essay be classified under any other modes of development? If so, what are they?
4. What is the tone of the essay?

## Writing Assignments

1. Write an essay in which you define *good parenting* and *bad parenting.* Identify the modes of development you use.
2. Write an essay in which you define *good teaching.* Identify the modes of development you use.

# Earning Their Pinstripes

## *Rick Reilly*

*It may look like an easy job and lots of fun, but Rick Reilly shows us that being a batboy for a major league baseball team is a tough, demanding, and low-paying job. (Rick Reilly, "Earning Their Pinstripes," Sports Illustrated, Sept. 23, 2002, p. 92. Reprinted by permission of Sports Illustrated.)*

### Word to Know

**volcanic**   violent, explosive

M. 1

S.P.

### Getting Started

What job would you like to have? Do you know what the requirements of the job are and what it pays?

---

**S**o, kid, you want to be a New York Yankees batboy? Hang out with   1
Derek Jeter? Ride in the parades? Great. But, first, maybe you'd better
take a look at a batboy's typical day.

2 P.M.—Pete Shalhoub, 17, shows up for a 7:15 game and starts setting   2
up the dugout. Sure, most of the players won't be arriving for at least
two hours, but so what? Pete'll be here two hours after the players have
left, too.

You think batboys still only run out and get Johnny Blanchard's bat? Get   3
real. Pete and the six other Yankees batboys—clubhouse boys are valets,
cabbies, maids, deliverymen, shrinks and short-order cooks. And they're
not 12 years old anymore. They're all 16 and older because the average
sixth-grader doesn't do well when he's also working 75-hour weeks.

Some nights Pete has to show up at 3 in the morning to help unload   4
the road-trip truck, do laundry and set up players' lockers. That takes
four hours. Then he goes straight to high school in Jersey City, and then
right back to the Stadium, where he'll work until about 1 A.M., go to bed
at 2 and get up again at 6 the next morning to go to class.

"It's like I tell him," says Joe Lee, another member of the crew. "In this   5
job you've got to sleep twice as fast."

3:45 P.M.—One of Pete's 1,000 jobs is mixing Gatorade for the dugout.   6
That can be dangerous. A few years ago former visiting team batboy Joe
Rocchio made green, not knowing volcanic Cleveland Indians star Albert
Belle drank only red. Belle spit it out, knocked the jug over in the dugout,
and Joe had to clean it up. Glamorous job, no?

240

4 P.M.—When players arrive, batboys start hopping. They're each 7 player's little Jeeves. "Anything they ask for, they pretty much get," says Pete. That includes everything from, "Go get my wife a birthday present" to "Go get my brother-in-law at the airport." From going to a player's home to pack his bags to making dinner reservations. One player asked Lee to go to the ballpark every day during a 12-day road trip and idle his car for a half hour. "Keeps the engine clean," the player said.

Of course, there are rewards. When Jason Giambi was with Oakland, 8 he sent an A's batboy to McDonald's. Giambi got three hits that day, so he kept sending the kid for the rest of the season. When Giambi won the MVP, he tipped him $5,000.

4:30 P.M.—A new kid shows up, the winner of a contest to be a batboy 9 for a day. He's lucky he doesn't get the initiation Craig Postolowski got. To start, Jeter sent him off to look for the key to the batter's box. Then Joe Torre told him to go get the knuckleballs ready. Then Don Zimmer needed the lefthanded fungo bat. Finally, when Bernie Williams asked him to get a bucket of steam from the shower to clean home plate, he realized he'd been had.

5:45 P.M.—It's Pete's day to shag flies in the outfield and run the balls 10 back to the batting practice pitcher. This is a gas. There's other cool stuff too. Some nights the clubhouse is lousy with celebs. You get to be in the team photo. And players have been known to lend batboys their sweet sleds for the prom. Of course, two years ago Manny Alexander of the Boston Red Sox lent his car to a batboy. Problem is, the kid got pulled over and police found steroids in it. Oops. Always check the glove compartment, Kid.

7:05 P.M.—Tonight Pete works balls for the home plate umpire. Another 11 guy works the rightfield line, snagging foul balls, and another works bats in the dugout. (The rest are stuck in the clubhouse.) Problem is, sometimes a kid will be so tired from lack of sleep that he'll be out there nodding off in front of 50,000 people. "I've done it," says Lee. "I'm just glad a line drive didn't wake me up."

10:30 P.M.—Game's over. The real, nasty work starts. "Everybody thinks 12 this is when we go home," says Pete. "But we've still got two hours of work to do." They pick up dirty uniforms, vacuum, straighten lockers, make food runs, empty trash, clean and polish 40 pairs of shoes. And they've got to do it all while dodging flying jocks, socks and towels thrown at their heads by millionaires. *Fwomp!*

12:30 a.m.—O.K., everything's done. Pete's spent, but he'll be in bed 13 before 2 A.M. for once. At least he saw some baseball. The boys who worked the clubhouse have to watch the highlights later.

So there it is, Kid. And remember, don't ask for tickets, autographs or 14 a raise. With the Yankees, you get the minimum, $5.15 an hour, even if you've been on the job 10 years. Hey, don't forget your boss is George Steinbrenner!

So, you want the job? Kid? *Kid?*                                    15

## Questions About the Reading

1. How many batboys do the Yankees have?
2. How old must a batboy be?
3. What are the responsibilities of the batboys?
4. Are there any "rewards" to being a batboy? What are the examples the writer provides?

## Questions About the Writer's Strategies

1. What is the point of view of the essay?
2. Is the essay objective or subjective or both? Support your answer with examples from the essay.
3. What is the order of the essay?
4. What does the last sentence of the essay imply?

## Writing Assignments

1. Write an essay in which you define the requirements of a job you would like to have.
2. *Working Together*   Join with some classmates to select a term or terms related to government and write an essay in which you define the terms. Identify the modes of development you use.

# Argumentation and Persuasion

# 10

ALL EFFECTIVE WRITING involves, to some extent, argumentation or persuasion. As you have learned from the preceding chapters, writers use various kinds of information to develop a **topic** or **thesis.** Such information can be said to "argue" or "persuade" in the sense that it convinces the reader that the writer's idea is true or believable. However, as **modes of development,** argumentation and persuasion have some particular characteristics that you should know about and be able to use in your own writing.

Let's look first at **persuasion** in its most obvious form—the advertisement. You should not use sentence fragments in your writing assignments, as the advertisement below does; and of course, you should continue to structure your writing according to a main (general) idea and to support it according to the various modes of development. But you will want to appeal to the emotions, qualities, or values that a reader is likely to share or find desirable, as advertisers do. One way to appeal to a reader is to use words for their **connotations**—explained in the preceding chapter as the feelings or qualities a reader may associate with a word—rather than for their **denotations,** or dictionary definitions.

In the following example, the advertiser uses the words *clean, smooth, fresh,* and *pure innocence.* We associate such words with highly desirable qualities, and the advertiser intends to persuade us that a particular soap will give our skin these qualities. The word *new* implies that the product has been improved and, therefore, is better or more desirable than its predecessor or a competing product. Notice, too, that the ad appeals to our senses when it describes the soap's lather as *silky* and *soft.*

| | |
|---|---|
| Connotation | Now. Clean skin with the touch of innocence. The joy of it. |
| Connotation | Of having skin so clean, so smooth, so fresh, it has the touch of pure innocence. Today, you can capture that feeling, sim- |
| Connotation | ply by cleansing with the extraordinary new Olay Beauty |
| Connotation | Bar. Its special Olay lather, silky and soft, creams up to clean |
| Connotation | when you work it in. The tinier bubbles work in natural harmony with your skin. They lift out impurities, then rinse |
| Connotation | cleanly away, leaving better skin even before you raise your eyes to the mirror—fresher skin each time, smoother skin at |

Connotation          every touch. Again and again, new Olay Beauty Bar cleanses
                     ⌐ innocence into your skin.

The purpose of persuasion is to make the reader accept the writer's idea. That idea may be an opinion or judgment that the reader might not ordinarily share or have knowledge of. The idea may be controversial—as we shall see later, the idea of an argument must be—but it does not have to be. The idea may even be humorous. Whatever the idea, the writer will use words and information to appeal to the reader's emotions. Such information may be biased in favor of the writer's idea, but it should be honest and accurate. Notice the emotional strength of the writer's examples in the letter that follows.

R. J. Reynolds Tobacco Co.
4th and Main Street
Winston-Salem, NC 27102

Dear Sirs:

When my wife died of lung cancer in 1976, I wanted to write you about her love affair with Camel cigarettes. I concluded, however, that it would be an exercise in futility.    1

I take up the challenge now, because you have publicly announced an advertising campaign to cast doubt on medical reports that cigarettes are a public-health hazard. You call for an open debate. Okay, let's debate.    2

**Example 1: wife**

My wife died a painful death. She was just 56 and had smoked at least a pack of Camels a day for 40 years. Coincidentally, just 30 days before her demise her 47-year-old    3

**Example 2: brother-in-law**

brother died of the same illness. Both experienced unbearable pain. He, too, was a heavy smoker.

But there is more to this horror story. In 1958, my father died suddenly of a cardiovascular ailment. He'd been a two-pack-a-day man for years, and would "walk a mile for a Camel" when younger. Later in life, he could hardly walk at all. But he still puffed away, day and night, before breakfast and with his meals. He endured continual nasal and respiratory problems, and never enjoyed a day free of a hacking cough.    4

**Example 3: father**

A popular pharmacist, he had many doctor friends who urged him to stop smoking. But he was firmly hooked and had been since 1909. Ill with lung disease (emphysema and chronic bronchitis), he had long suffered intensely painful attacks of near-suffocation. In 1955 he was forced to retire and spend his "golden years" either lying on our sofa or propped up in a lounge chair.    5

In late summer of 1957, I took him to a specialist at the University of Maryland Hospital in Baltimore. There he was told there was no cure for his condition. But he could help himself. "How?" he asked. "Stop smoking," was the reply.    6

That is a tall order for anyone who has smoked for almost 50 years. But my father did not want to live the life of an invalid, so he determined to try. That he succeeded—cold turkey—is nothing short of a miracle. But he really had no other choice, except to suffer. 7

Within weeks he was breathing easier, and it was not long before he was walking about and driving his car. He got to enjoy life a bit. I'm convinced that giving up smoking added that near-year to his life. 8

**Example 4: daughter**

Today, I have a daughter—a working mother of two—who has been addicted to cigarettes since peer pressure in high school encouraged her to smoke. She wants desperately to quit. In fact, she has done so several times, only to be lured back by the smoking of others in her workplace. 9

Having presented four powerful extended examples, this writer goes on to a thorough persuasive conclusion. You will see next that he uses rhetorical questions to introduce and structure his conclusion. A **rhetorical question** is a question to which no real answer is expected because only one obvious reply can be made—and that reply will either support or restate the writer's point. Rhetorical questions are fairly common in persuasive writing and in argumentation because they offer a way for writers to emphasize the correctness of their viewpoints.

Okay, R. J. Reynolds, that's my story. What's yours? Are you prepared to tell us that the National Institutes of Health, the Surgeon General and the various voluntary health agencies are all wrong? Are the many scientific studies indicting smoking just so much hogwash? 10

For the sake of debate, let's assume smoking's critics are wrong. Can you deny that cigarette smoking is addictive? Isn't that fact precisely the reason why you sell so many cigarettes? Is it moral to manufacture and sell any product that causes addiction—even if it might otherwise be harmless? As bad as alcohol abuse is, alcohol is addictive to only a relatively small number of consumers. You can't say that about cigarettes. Smoking hooks nearly every consumer. And once hooked it is difficult to stop; for some, it seems impossible. 11

In a free society, people can't be forbidden to smoke. But government does have the obligation to warn the public of the dangers involved. It has the responsibility to hold R. J. Reynolds Tobacco Co. and others accountable for luring impressionable people to smoke, while suggesting that medical findings establishing a relationship between smoking and cancer, cardiovascular diseases and respiratory ailments are inconclusive. 12

It's hard to fight the rich tobacco industry, but just maybe, through education, we non-smokers will eventually win. As a witness to so much tragedy caused by smoking, I feel compelled to hope so. 13

Sincerely,
Gil Crandall

In summary, then, a persuasive paragraph or essay, like the other modes of development, is based on a **main (general) idea** developed by one or more of the modes of development and is characterized by the use of words or information that appeals to the reader's emotions. The information or evidence used in persuasion may be one-sided, but it should be honest and accurate. The topic, or thesis, of persuasion may be controversial, but it does not have to be.

**Argumentation,** on the other hand, must be based on a controversial idea—an idea that people have conflicting views or opinions about. Although argumentation may include some persuasion, its appeal to the reader should be rational and logical, as opposed to emotional, and **objective,** rather than one-sided. A classic or formal argument includes five elements:

- *Statement of the problem*
- *Solution,* the writer's thesis or answer to the problem
- *Evidence,* the information the writer presents to support or prove the thesis
- *Refutation,* the writer's acknowledgment of and response to opposing views
- *Conclusion,* the writer's summation of the evidence and, generally, a restatement of the thesis

Although you may seldom need to write a paragraph-length argument, it is helpful to examine an example of one. Notice in the following example that the writer has explained the problem, stated a solution or answer to the problem—which is the topic of the paragraph—provided evidence in support of the solution, refuted the opposing view, and summarized the position taken on the topic.

|  |  |
|---|---|
| | During the late sixties and early seventies, political and social activism was rampant on college campuses. Student protests—which were sometimes peaceful and other times violent—addressed issues related to civil rights, the environment, war, nuclear arms, and consumer protection and |
| Statement of the problem | rights. In recent years, student protests have been much less frequent and, generally, peaceful, causing some writers and politicians to label present-day students as apathetic. Non- |
| Solution | sense! Today's students are not apathetic. They simply have different concerns from the ones of the sixties and seven- |
| Evidence | ties. They are more concerned about, for instance, employment and the quality of their own lives. They are assessing, confronting even, themselves—their hopes, plans, desires, ambitions, and values. They are fighting quietly for their causes—personal or otherwise—by pursuing training and |

**Refutation**

retraining opportunities and by exercising their voting privileges. To say they are apathetic is to ignore the steadfastness
with which they are pursuing their goals. To say they are
apathetic is to imply that a person is not concerned about an
issue unless that person takes to the streets or possibly en-
gages in violent acts on behalf of that issue. The fact is, the
current college population is older—the average age of community college students nationwide is about twenty-eight—
more experienced, and in some ways wiser. As a consequence, they have perhaps learned that confrontation may
win a battle but lose the war, that in the long run, they must
live and work with those persons who hold opposing views.

**Conclusion**

Thus, while they are indeed quieter than their predecessors,
they continue to be concerned about such important issues
as employment (their own and others), nuclear arms, the
environment, civil rights, and war. We make a mistake if
we write off today's college students as apathetic simply
because we do not see overt evidence of their concern.

In a full-length essay, you can develop your argument more fully and
convincingly than you can in a paragraph. The order in which you present the elements of an argument may differ from the classic organization
represented by the preceding paragraph. For instance, you may want to
state the refutation before presenting the evidence for your argument. And
sometimes one of the elements of your argument may be **implied** rather
than stated, just as the topic sentence of a paragraph or the main idea of an
essay may be implied.

No matter what method is used to develop an argument, however,
always remember that the evidence presented to support the solution
and the conclusion must be valid—true, supported by facts, accurately
expressed, and based on sound reasoning. This is something to watch for
not only in your own writing but also when you are reading arguments
composed by others. When you read or write an argument, analyze not
only the main conclusion but also all the ideas that support it. A conclusion may seem quite sensible based on the evidence the writer supplies,
but if the evidence itself is not true and not presented logically, the conclusion will be viewed as faulty.

In the essay below, the writer follows the classic model in presenting her
argument and supports her opinion with facts that give the reader sound
reasons to accept her conclusion. Notice that she uses several modes of
development, such as **contrast** and **examples.**

**Statement of the problem**

Each year, from late spring to early fall, thousands of high          1
school students and their parents spend a great deal of time
and money driving around the country to visit expensive and
prestigious colleges that the students think they might like to

**Solution**

attend. Each year, thousands of students go through the ritual of applying to and being rejected by these colleges. Instead, they should go to a community college and, after earning their associate degree, transfer to a four-year university to complete their education.

**Evidence**

Most community colleges offer a wide choice of career or technical programs as well as a curriculum paralleling that offered by a university. If the student has already made a career choice, an associate degree prepares the student to enter the workforce or to continue his or her career study in a four-year university. If the student has not decided on a career, a community college is an excellent place to learn more about many different career possibilities and to complete the general education courses required by either a career or university-parallel program.                                                                 2

**Evidence**

Most community colleges also have a more diverse population than that of the student's high school. In a community college the student has the opportunity to meet persons of all ages, abilities, and ethnic and racial backgrounds and to improve his or her knowledge and understanding of others.                     3

**Evidence**

A community college is also much less expensive than most colleges. In addition to the lower cost of tuition and fees, the student can usually live at home and commute to classes, which also saves the high cost of dorm or apartment fees.                                 4

**Refutation**

It is true, of course, that a community college does not offer the prestige of the more famous universities. But if prestige is significant, the student could complete a baccalaureate and graduate work at a better-known school. Also, whether the education the student receives at a community college is equal to that provided by a more prestigious university can be determined only on a case-by-case basis, since much of the success of any education depends on the individual student.         5

**Conclusion**

The fact is, for most students a community college is a sound educational and economic choice. Instead of engaging in the expensive and time-consuming spring-to-fall ritual of college shopping, most students would be as well or better served by taking advantage of the educational opportunity offered by their local community college.                             6

When you read an argument, remember, too, that a writer may present facts selectively. That is, the writer may not give you all the facts relating to an issue or problem. For this reason, it is advisable to read and consider arguments on both sides of the controversy and to carefully analyze the facts when you are trying to form an opinion about an important issue. It will then be up to you when writing an argumentation paper to interpret the facts and conclusions, to decide which ones are most valid, and to choose the ones you will use to support your own thesis.

Be alert, too, for **fallacies** in your reasoning. In addition to the fallacies identified in chapter 8 (pp. 193–194), guard against the following:

- *False analogy.* A false analogy assumes that two things that are alike are alike in all respects. A Honda and a Cadillac are both cars, but they are not alike in all respects.
- *Circular argument.* A circular argument restates an idea in different words: "The airports are too crowded because too many people are traveling."
- *Argument to the man* (argument ad hominem). An argument to the man attacks the person rather than the issue: "He gets poor grades. After all, he's a computer nerd."
- *Bandwagon.* A bandwagon fallacy claims that something is true because the majority believe or act on it: "Everyone thinks she should be elected class president" or "We should go to the concert because everyone else is."
- *Either-or.* An either-or argument assumes that only two things are possible: "The submarine sank because of either poor maintenance or poor personnel training."
- *Begging the question.* Begging the question presents as a fact an idea or premise that is not proven: "If we removed all chat rooms from the Internet, children would not be enticed to meet people who could do them harm."

In summary, although argumentation and persuasion have a common **purpose**—to convince the reader to accept the writer's opinion—they differ principally in the way the writer appeals to the reader. In argumentation, the writer supports the topic or thesis by presenting objective, logical evidence that appeals to the reader's reason. In persuasion, the writer does not necessarily abandon objectivity or logic, but uses words or other information that appeals to the reader's emotions. Also, although the thesis of persuasion *may* be controversial, the thesis of an argument *must* be. In both argumentation and persuasion, the writer makes use of whatever modes of development are effective and appropriate.

In school and beyond, there will be occasions when you will want to use argumentation or persuasion to make a point to your **audience.** Whether you are doing so orally or in writing, being familiar with techniques used in argumentation and persuasion will help you.

# Tax Junk Food? Yes

*Michael F. Jacobson*

*The writer claims that taxing junk food would raise billions that could be used to promote healthy eating and improve our health.*

**Word to Know**

**subsidized**   funded, paid for

*Getting Started*

Would a tax on junk food and sugary drinks discourage you from buying them?

H eart disease, cancer, stroke, and other diet-related conditions (together with too little physical activity) prematurely kill several hundred thousand Americans each year, and treatment of those conditions costs taxpayers more than $100 billion each year. Yet the government spends almost nothing to promote better diet and more exercise, which would prevent disease. A one-cent-per-can tax on sugary soft drinks, though, or small taxes on other disease-promoting foods could raise billions of dollars to

- Put more fresh fruits and vegetables on the plates of school-age kids
- Encourage Americans to switch from high-fat milk to 1 percent or skim
- Fund after-school athletic programs now sometimes subsidized by the shameful practice of selling junk food to schools
- Fund major media campaigns designed to encourage kids to take up physical activity (the Bush administration recently urged zeroing out the only such government program along these lines)

## Questions About the Reading

1. What are the consequences of an unhealthy diet and lack of exercise?
2. What is the cost of treatment of diet-related conditions to taxpayers?
3. What could a tax on junk food and sugary soft drinks be used for?

## Questions About the Writer's Strategies

1. What is the problem the writer is addressing?
2. What is the writer's solution to the problem?
3. What evidence does the writer provide to support his solution to the problem?
4. Does the writer acknowledge any opposing views? If so, what are they?

## Writing Assignments

1. Write a persuasive or argumentative paragraph for or against a tax on junk food. Be sure to define what you mean by the term *junk food*.
2. Write a persuasive or argumentative paragraph for or against a fee for parking your car on your school grounds.

# Frightening—and Fantastic

## Anna Quindlen

*It's a scary world out there, with bad people seemingly everywhere. Every hour the television news makes us aware of that fact. But Anna Quindlen reminds us that we should also let the children know that there are good people out there, too.*

### Words to Know
**Good Samaritan**   someone who helps another person
**Oscar Wilde**   Nineteenth-century British playwright, poet, and novelist

### Getting Started
What precautions do you take if you go out by yourself at night?

---

S o this is a plea for parents to remember to have That Talk with their kids. No, not the one about smoking cigarettes or driving under the influence. That's the one they will certainly get. What they need to hear occasionally is about the pleasures, not just the perils. Even when we talk about September 11, we can tell a tale of human goodness as well as evil, a tale of those who saved strangers as well as those who murdered them. For all the sleazebags who will try to lure a kid into a car, there are many Good Samaritans who are just concerned when they see a 12-year-old trudging along the road in the rain. I suppose we live at a time when we can't afford to let them accept the Samaritan's ride. But we also can't afford to have them think that Samaritans no longer exist. All these lectures, lessons and cautionary tales can't be to preserve a lifetime of looking over one shoulder. As Oscar Wilde wrote, "We are all in the gutter, but some of us are looking at the stars."

---

## Questions About the Reading

1. What is "That Talk" the writer wants parents to have with their kids?
2. What should the kids hear about the September 11 terrorist attacks on the World Trade Center?

3. Why must parents tell their kids about the Good Samaritans?
4. What is the meaning of the Oscar Wilde quotation? Why is it appropriate to the main idea of the paragraph?

## Questions About the Writer's Strategies

1. What is the main idea of the paragraph? State it in your own words.
2. Is the paragraph persuasion or argumentation? Explain your answer.
3. What modes of development does the writer use in the paragraph?

## Writing Assignments

1. Write an argumentative or persuasive paragraph in which you explain the main "cautions" your parents have taught you and why you do or do not follow them.
2. Write an argumentative or persuasive paragraph for or against abolishing some rule or regulation established by your school or your town.

# Drinking—What Age?

## Barrett Seaman

*Sixteen is old enough to drive a car, and eighteen is old enough to vote
and join the army, but you have to be twenty-one to buy an alcoholic
drink. Barrett Seaman says that eighteen-year-old college students may
"go overboard" initially if permitted to drink but that most of them will
soon "put drinking in its proper place."*

### Words to Know

**exploiting**   using, taking advantage of
**savored**   tasted, enjoyed

### Getting Started

Is a person's age a reliable measure for whether he or she will
drink responsibly?

---

**W**hat would happen if the drinking age was rolled back to 18 or 19?
Initially, there would be a surge in binge drinking as young adults savored
their new-found freedom. But over time, I predict, U.S. college students
would settle into the saner approach to alcohol I saw on the one campus
I visited where the legal drinking age is 18: Montreal's McGill University,
which enrolls about 2,000 American undergraduates a year. Many, when
they first arrive, go overboard, exploiting their ability to drink legally.
But by midterms, when McGill's demanding academic standards must
be met, the vast majority have put drinking into its practical place among
their priorities.

---

## Questions About the Reading

1. What would happen initially if the legal age for drinking were lowered to eighteen?
2. How did McGill University students handle being able to drink
   legally at age eighteen? Did their behavior change over time? Why?
3. What does the writer mean by "put drinking into its practical place"?
   What do you think is the "practical place" for drinking?

## Questions About the Writer's Strategies

1. What is the main idea of the paragraph? State it in your own words.
2. What modes of development does the writer use in the paragraph?

## Writing Assignments

1. Write a paragraph in which you argue or persuade your reader that the legal age for driving a car should be lowered or raised or that there should be a maximum age at which a person is allowed to drive.
2. Do you object to some of the courses required for your major? Write an argumentation or persuasion paragraph for the changes you want in the curriculum for your major.

# The Measure of Our Success

*Marian Wright Edelman*

> *"Children—my own and other people's—became the passion of my personal and professional life. For it is they who are God's presence, promise, and hope for humankind."* These are the words of Marian Wright Edelman, the African-American civil rights lawyer and founder of the Children's Defense League. In the following paragraph from her book The Measure of Our Success: A Letter to My Children and Yours, *Edelman urges her readers to face the mounting crisis of our country's impoverished children and families by taking action themselves.*

## Words to Know

**empathy**   understanding
**mentoring**   being a counselor or teacher
**neonatal**   having to do with infants

## Getting Started

What are some things you can do to help build a stronger community for all our children and their children's children?

---

T he place to begin is with ourselves. Care. As you read about or meet some of the children and families in this country who need your help, put yourself in their places as fellow Americans. Imagine you or your spouse being pregnant, and not being able to get enough to eat or see a doctor or know that you have a hospital for delivery. Imagine your child hungry or injured, and you cannot pay for food or find health care. Imagine losing your job and having no income, having your unemployment compensation run out, not being able to pay your note or rent, having no place to sleep with your children, having nothing. Imagine having to stand in a soup line at a church or Salvation Army station after you've worked all your life, or having to sleep in a shelter with strangers and get up and out early each morning, find some place to go with your children, and not know if you can sleep there again that night. If you take the time to imagine this, perhaps you can also take the time to do for them what you would want a fellow citizen to do for you. Volunteer in a homeless shelter or soup kitchen or an afterschool tutoring or mentoring program. Vote. Help to organize your community to speak out for the children who need you. Visit a hospital neonatal intensive care nursery or AIDS and boarder baby ward and spend time rocking and caring for an individual child.

Adopt as a pen pal a lonely child who never gets a letter from anyone. Give a youth a summer job. Teach your child tolerance and empathy by your example.

## Questions About the Reading

1. According to the writer, how can people begin to make a difference in this country? Do you agree or disagree with her argument? Why?
2. What different methods of action does Edelman describe? Pick out some of the examples she uses.
3. What do you think Edelman means by the last sentence? Do you agree or disagree with her statement? Why?
4. Think about all the different suggestions Edelman makes. Which have you tried? Which might you consider trying?

## Questions About the Writer's Strategies

1. Is there a topic sentence in the paragraph? If so, where is it? If not, state the main idea in your own words.
2. Is this a paragraph of argumentation, persuasion, or both? Support your answer with details from the paragraph.
3. Besides persuasion, what other mode of development does the writer use? Support your answer with details from the text.
4. Edelman uses numerous powerful images to support her thesis that we all need to work together to rebuild this country. What are some of the images Edelman uses when she asks us to imagine trading places with our less fortunate fellow Americans? What impact do the images have on you?
5. What is the tone of the paragraph? Why does Edelman use this tone?

## Writing Assignments

1. Do you agree or disagree with Edelman's argument that all responsible people need to be active in their communities and their nation? Write a persuasive paragraph on your answer.
2. Do you agree or disagree that children learn tolerance and empathy—or, for that matter, prejudice and hate—by the example of their parents? Write a paragraph in which you argue for or against that statement. Use examples and details to support your position.

# Flunking

## *Mary Sherry*

*Let's hope you never flunk a course, but if you do, you can try to look at that "F" the way the writer does: "an expression of confidence" that you "have the ability" to pass the course.*

**Word to Know**

**conspiracy**   plot

**Getting Started**

Do you agree or disagree with your school's policy regarding "F" and "incomplete" grades?

F lunking as a regular policy has just as much merit today as it did two generations ago. We must review the threat of flunking and see it as it really is—a positive teaching tool. It is an expression of confidence by both teachers and parents that the students have the ability to learn the material presented to them. However, making it work again would take a dedicated, caring conspiracy between teachers and parents. It would mean facing the tough reality that passing kids who haven't learned the material—while it might save them grief for the short term—dooms them to long-term illiteracy. It would mean that teachers would have to follow through on their threats, and parents would have to stand behind them, knowing their children's best interests are indeed at stake. This means no more doing Scott's assignments for him because he might fail. No more passing Jodi because she's such a nice kid.

## Questions About the Reading

1. What is the writer's opinion of the flunking grade?
2. What would it take to make the flunking grade be viewed as an "expression of confidence"?
3. What is the result of "passing kids who haven't learned the material"?
4. What would teachers and parents have to do to support the flunking grade?

## Questions About the Writer's Strategies

1. What is the main idea of the paragraph? Is it stated or implied? If stated, identify the sentences. If implied, state it in your own words.
2. What is the point of view of the paragraph? Is it consistent? If not, is the change justified?
3. Is the paragraph objective or subjective? Support your answer with sentences and words from the paragraph.
4. What is the tone of the paragraph?

## Writing Assignments

1. Write an argumentation or persuasion paragraph in which you agree or disagree with your school's policy on the "F" grade.
2. Write an argumentation or persuasion paragraph in which you agree or disagree with your school's policy related to grades as the criteria for sports eligibility.

# Hang It Up

*Jesse Scaccia*

*Imagine you are the teacher facing a classroom of students with cell phones at their ears or in their hands. Jesse Scaccia tells us how that feels.*

## Words to Know

**appendages**   attachments, add-ons
**confiscated**   taken away

## Getting Started

What is the policy of your school regarding having cell phones in the classroom?

---

You're a teacher in the New York City public school system. It's Sep- 1
tember, and you're lecturing the class on the structure of an essay. Your
students need to know this information to pass your class and the Regents
exam, and you, of course, hope that one day your talented students will
dazzle and amaze English professors all over the country.

You turn your back to write the definition of *thesis* on the chalkboard. 2
It takes about 15 seconds. You turn around to the class expecting to see
25 students scribbling the concept in their notebooks. Instead, you see a
group of students who have sprung appendages of technology.

Jose has grown an earphone. Maria's thumbs have sprouted a two-way. 3
Man Keung, recently arrived from China, is texting away on a cell phone
connected to his wrist. And Christina appears to be playing Mine Sweeper
on a Pocket PC on her lap.

Come the end of the term, a handful will fail the class. A number will 4
never pass the Regents exam. As we all know, far too many will drop out
of school. And I can tell you with no hint of pride that it isn't the teacher's
fault. As much as any other problem plaguing our schools, the onus for
failure should be placed on distractions in the classroom, specifically the
cell phone.

Though electronic devices have been banned in public schools for years, 5
the issue came to the forefront last month when Chancellor Joel Klein announced the random placement of metal detectors in schools. The result:
More than 800 cell phones have been confiscated.

Students and their parents, who say they rely on cell phones for safety  6
reasons, are outraged. There's even talk of a lawsuit arguing that the rule
should be struck down.

But as a former New York City public school teacher, I can tell you that  7
cell phones don't belong in the classroom. A student with a cell phone is
an uninterested student, one with a short attention span who cares more
about his social life than education.

Parents think of cell phones as a connection to their children in an  8
emergency. I have a few questions for those parents: First, when was the
last situation that genuinely called for immediate interaction with your
child? In most cases, the hospital or the police would seem more urgent.
Second, is phoning the main office and having it patch you through to
your child not quick enough? And third, do you know why your children
really want to take cell phones to school?

Because, just like the new Jordans and Rocawear they desire, cell  9
phones are status symbols. Because when their cell phone rings while
the teacher is talking, everyone laughs. Because playing video games
on their cell makes them look cool. Because text messaging their friend
in the next room is more fun than learning about the topic sentence. So
is listening to the new Three 6 Mafia song they just downloaded onto
their cell.

And saying students can store their phones in the locker is a joke. If  10
they have cell phones, they're going to bring them into class.

There are legitimate causes that parents should be taking on. Rally  11
against crowding in the classroom. Fight against the oppressive and culturally biased Regents tests. But you're wrong on this cell phone issue. In
this case, you are part of the problem, not the solution.

---

## Questions About the Reading

1. What is the teacher trying to teach?
2. What are the students doing?
3. What are the consequences, according to the writer, of the students'
   actions?

## Questions About the Writer's Strategies

1. What is the problem the writer addresses?
2. What is the writer's thesis or answer to the problem?

3. What evidence does the writer present to prove the thesis? Is the evidence adequate? Why or why not?
4. What modes of development does the writer use?

## Writing Assignments

1. *Working Together*   Join with some classmates to write an essay in which you argue for or against student use of laptop computers in the classroom.
2. Write an essay in which you argue for or against prohibiting cell phones in schools.

# Keep the Drinking Age at Twenty-One

*Robert Voas*

> *Robert Voas, a senior research scientist at the Pacific Institute for Research and Evaluation, counters Barrett Seaman's argument for lowering the drinking age.*

## Words to Know

**conjecture**   guess, inference
**glib**   easy, smooth, slick
**revanchist**   move to turn back or regain something lost

## Getting Started

When was eighteen made the legal age for voting?

A fter nearly four decades of exacting research on how to save lives and 1 reduce injuries by preventing drinking and driving, there is a revanchist attempt afoot to roll back one of the most successful laws in generations: the minimum legal drinking age of 21.

This is extremely frustrating. While public health researchers must pro- 2 duce painstaking evidence that's subjected to critical scholarly review, lower-drinking-age advocates seem to dash off remarks based on glib conjecture and self-selected facts.

It's startling that anybody—given the enormous bodies of research and 3 data—would consider lowering the drinking age. And yet, legislation is currently pending in New Hampshire and Wisconsin to lower the drinking age for military personnel and for all residents in Vermont.

I keep hearing the same refrains: "If you're old enough to go to war, 4 you should be old enough to drink," or "the drinking-age law just increases the desire for the forbidden fruit," or "lower crash rates are due to tougher enforcement, not the 21 law," or "Europeans let their kids drink, so they learn how to be more responsible," or finally, "I did it when I was a kid, and I'm OK."

First, I'm not sure what going to war and being allowed to drink have 5 in common. The 21 law is predicated on the fact that drinking is more dangerous for youth because they're still developing mentally and physically, and they lack experience and are more likely to take risks. Ask platoon leaders and unit commanders, and they'll tell you that the last thing they want is young soldiers drinking.

As for the forbidden-fruit argument, the opposite is true. Research shows 6 that back when some states still had a minimum drinking age of 18, youths in those states who were under 21 drank more and continued to drink more as adults in their early 20s. In states where the drinking age was 21, teenagers drank less and continue to drink less through their early 20s.

And the minimum 21 law, by itself, has most certainly resulted in 7 fewer accidents, because the decline occurred even when there was little enforcement and tougher penalties had not yet been enacted. According to the National Highway Traffic Safety Administration, the 21 law has saved 23,733 lives since states began raising drinking ages in 1975.

Do European countries really have fewer youth drinking problems? No, 8 that's a myth. Compared to [those for] American youth, binge drinking rates among young people are higher in every European country except Turkey. Intoxication rates are higher in most countries; in Britain, Denmark, and Ireland they're more than twice the U.S. level.

But you drank when you were a kid, and you're OK. Thank good- 9 ness, because many kids aren't OK. An average of 11 American teens die each day from alcohol-related crashes. Underage drinking leads to increased teen pregnancy, violent crime, sexual assault, and huge costs to our communities.

Among college students, it leads to 1,700 deaths, 500,000 injuries, 600,000 10 physical assaults, and 70,000 sexual assaults each year.

Recently, New Zealand lowered its drinking age, which gave researchers 11 a good opportunity to study the impact. The result was predictable: The rate of alcohol-related crashes among young people rose significantly compared to [the rate for] older drivers.

I've been studying drinking and driving for nearly 40 years and have 12 been involved in public health and behavioral health for 53 years. Believe me when I say that lowering the drinking age would be very dangerous; it would benefit no one except those who profit from alcohol sales.

If bars and liquor stores can freely provide alcohol to teenagers, par- 13 ents will be out of the loop when it comes to their children's decisions about drinking. Age 21 laws are designed to keep such decisions within the family where they belong. Our society, particularly our children and grandchildren, will be immeasurably better off if we not only leave the minimum drinking age law as it is, but enforce it better, too.

## Questions About the Reading

1. When was the drinking age raised to twenty-one?
2. At the time the essay was written, what states had legislation pending to lower the drinking age?
3. Why is drinking more dangerous for youth?
4. Who would profit, according to the writer, if the drinking age were lowered?

## Questions About the Writer's Strategies

1. What is the thesis of the essay? State it in your own words.
2. What are the false analogies in the essay that the writer refutes?
3. What modes of development does the writer use?

## Writing Assignments

1. *Working Together*   Join with some classmates to interview restaurant owners, health professionals, and others in your town to determine their opinion of the appropriate drinking age. Write an essay in which you argue for or against a drinking age of eighteen, twenty-one, or higher, based on the information from your interviews.

2. Use the Internet to determine the ages in the different states at which persons under eighteen are legally allowed to marry. Write an essay in which you argue for or against allowing marriage under age eighteen.
3. Write an essay in which you argue for or against allowing persons to vote at age eighteen.

# Banning Smoking

## *John Ruckdeschel*

*Dr. John Ruckdeschel argues that a ban on smoking in indoor workplaces should be adopted across the country.*

### Words to Know

**carcinogens**   cancer-causing agents
**emphysema**   respiratory disease caused by swelling in the lungs

### Getting Started

What is the smoking policy at your school?

---

**A**lthough lung cancer lacks the high public profile of breast or prostate  1
cancer, it's responsible for more deaths than these two cancers and colo-
rectal cancer combined. According to the American Cancer Society, 156,900
Americans died of lung cancer in 2000—28 percent of all cancer deaths.

Unlike some other serious diseases, we know the main cause of lung  2
cancer: cigarette smoking. Eighty percent of lung cancers are caused directly by smoking, which is also a major factor in heart disease, emphysema
and low-birth-weight babies. The American Lung Association estimates
that smoking results in $150 billion in annual health care costs and lost
productivity.

That's why Michigan should follow the lead of Florida, California,  3
New York and Massachusetts by restricting smoking in virtually all public
places.

Voters in Florida recently approved Amendment 6 to prohibit smok-  4
ing in all indoor workplaces, restaurants and other public places. Stand-
alone bars, tobacco stores, designated hotel rooms and private residences
(except those where health or day care is provided) are exempt from the
smoking ban.

This policy really should be the gold standard across the country. It  5
has been proved that banning smoking in public places such as restaurants is not as devastating to businesses as some would argue. People
will patronize these places despite a smoking ban.

Restricting the places where smoking is permitted would reduce expo-  6
sure to tobacco-related carcinogens for millions of people. The Florida law
is expected to cause a significant decline in tobacco sales, and of course,

nonsmokers will no longer inhale the secondhand smoke that permeates most buildings where smoking is permitted in designated areas. By 1999, almost 70 percent of workers in the U.S. worked at a site with a smoke-free policy. It's time to extend that privilege to everyone.

In addition, businesses should promote smoking-cessation programs 7 for their employees. Smoking is addictive, and relapses after quitting are common. However, today we have nicotine patches, gums, sprays, inhalers and pills, along with many forms of behavioral therapy and support groups to help people quit smoking. Unfortunately, smoking-cessation programs usually are not covered by health insurance.

Business leaders, provide these programs in the workplace or ensure 8 that they are part of your benefits. It's a good investment in better health for your employees and for your company's bottom line.

## Questions About the Reading

1. What is the annual estimated cost in health care and productivity due to smoking?
2. What places are exempt from Florida's smoking ban?
3. What was the percentage of workers, in 1999, who worked in smoke-free sites?
4. In addition to providing a smoke-free workplace, what else should businesses promote?

## Questions About the Writer's Strategies

1. What is the thesis of the essay? Is it stated or implied? If stated, identify the sentences. If implied, state the thesis in your own words.
2. Is the essay argumentation or persuasion?
3. If this essay is an argument, identify the elements. If persuasion, identify the persuasive sentences and words.
4. What other modes of development does the writer use?

## Writing Assignments

1. Determine your school's policy regarding smoking and write an argumentation or persuasion essay for or against the policy.
2. *Working Together*  Join with some classmates to write a formal argument for or against one of your school's policies.

# A Burning Issue

**Mary Boltz Chapman**

> Mary Boltz Chapman narrows the smoking issue to whether it should or
> should not be banned in restaurants.

### Words to Know
**constituency**  a group of supporters
**instituted**  started

### Getting Started
What is the smoking policy in the restaurants in your town?

---

There's a controversy blazing in several cities including Chicago, Dallas  1
and Denver: Should local government ban smoking in all city restaurants?
Politicians, restaurateurs, associations, lobbyists, health organizations,
smokers and nonsmokers have been lining up to give their opinions. I
submit that only one of those parties is entitled to an opinion. Restaurant
management.

## Where There's Smoke

Many existing and proposed regulations are confusing. A restaurant oper-  2
ator may have to decipher different rules set by the state, city and county.
In Pittsburgh, a ban on smoking in restaurants and bars failed because a
Pennsylvania state law, which actually restricts smoking, prohibits such
a local ban.

Others are unfair. In some localities, smoking is allowed in bars but  3
not restaurants. However, the line is blurry as many bars serve some
kind of food, ranging from a rack of chips to sophisticated tasting menus.
In California, the smoking ban instituted five years ago includes bars.
Strict but fair, right? Not necessarily fair to restaurants in the state's bor-
der towns.

Some feel that if politicians are going to legislate the issue, the only  4
fair way to do it would be on a national basis, to level the playing field.
In Massachusetts, the state restaurant association threw up its hands
over a potential statewide smoking ban. There, the differing laws make

it impossible to support their constituency one way or the other without hurting some of them.

Proponents call it a work-place issue; employees should not be sub-  5 jected to the health risks of secondhand smoke. But some servers are happy to work the smoking section. They say smokers linger over another drink or dessert, upping checks and tips. Others say they would rather the smoking customers not linger so they can turn the table. Often one section or another is busier, and servers vie for those tables. It depends on the restaurant.

For some operators, sales decline thanks to nonsmoking ordinances. For  6 others, profits increase.

At the end of the day, there is a difference between a public place where  7 a person goes because he has to, such as a courthouse, and a public place where he pays for the privilege, such as a restaurant. Each person can choose which eatery to patronize and is free to use the eatery's smoking policy as a barometer.

It should be left up to the restaurant management to decide that policy  8 based on their staff's and customers' needs.

## Questions About the Reading

1. What are the difficulties, according to the writer, in banning smoking in restaurants?
2. How do restaurant employees feel about a nonsmoking policy?
3. How does nonsmoking affect the profits of a restaurant?
4. Does the writer think there should be a difference between smoking policies in public places and restaurants? Why?

## Questions About the Writer's Strategies

1. What is the thesis of the essay? Is it stated or implied? If stated, identify the sentences. If implied, state the thesis in your own words.
2. Is the essay argumentation or persuasion? If it is an argument, identify the elements of the argument. If persuasion, identify the persuasive sentences and words.
3. What modes of development does the writer use?

4. Are the two essays—"Banning Smoking" by John Ruckdeschel and "A Burning Issue" by Mary Boltz Chapman—objective or subjective? Use the Internet to find information about the two writers to help you decide your answer.

## Writing Assignments

1. Determine the laws in your town regarding smoking and write an argumentation or persuasion essay for or against the laws.
2. *Working Together*   Join with some classmates to write a formal argument for or against the law banning the sale of cigarettes or liquor before age twenty-one or a bicycle helmet law.

# 11 Combining the Strategies

IN THIS CHAPTER, you will find some additional reading selections. Although some of the readings have one dominant **mode of development,** most of them illustrate combinations of the different modes.

As you read, keep in mind what we have stressed in earlier chapters. Determine the

- topic of each paragraph
- thesis of each essay
- structure of the reading (introduction, development, conclusion)
- supporting details
- modes of development
- point of view (person, time, tone)
- method of organization (time, space, order of importance)
- transitional words
- effective words and sentences

Then make use of these same strategies to write paragraphs and essays that are as clear and effective as those you have read.

# A Trip to Honduras

## Daniel Boehmer (student)

*A trip to Honduras convinced Daniel Boehmer that he wanted a career that would have a positive effect on other people's lives. He is realizing that desire as a student at George Washington University, majoring in international affairs.*

### Words to Know

**concurrently**   at the same time
**disparity**   difference
**docile**   obedient, accepting
**effervescent**   lively, high-spirited
**ensnare**   trap
**immersed**   absorbed, deeply involved

### Getting Started

Do you participate in some community or volunteer service?

---

It was a sizzling day in August as I stood watching the four-or-five- 1
year-old girl placidly eating the fly-covered, white-breaded peanut butter
and jelly sandwich I had just given her. As I watched, immersed in the
unfamiliar surroundings, I began to think about why I was there. What
had brought me to this impoverished Honduran community, Rincon de
Dolores, a village so strikingly named "Corner of Pain"? At first glance,
the little girl looked like any ordinary child her age. As I studied her more
closely, however, her frayed clothing, disheveled hair, and tiny shoeless
feet revealed her poverty to me. Though the exchange was undoubtedly
simple for her, for me it had a significantly deeper meaning. I began to
reconsider roles: Who was the giver and who was the receiver here?

I arrived in Honduras through my church, which was continuing its 2
tradition of sending a youth and medical team to this secluded nook of
Honduras to work with the people to improve their community in ways
that their government could or would not. That year we were assigned
to begin construction on a church in Rincon, and I jumped at the opportunity to go. I really had no idea what I was in for.

I presumed I was prepared to witness the widespread poverty that runs 3
rampant in the region. After all, I had seen documentaries, read articles
in *National Geographic,* and had been active in efforts of international aid

before, but no amount of mental preparation could prepare me for my surprising visit to this corner of the world.

At first I was greeted with what I had expected: a constant barrage of insects, bacterially infected water, the reality of life in a tin-roofed hut, and inescapable heat. As time went on, however, I began to see a side of Honduras I had not expected. Instead of seeing only the dramatic disparity in wealth between the Hondurans and me, I began to see the disparity in spirit between my comparatively rigid community back in the States and the Honduran community I experienced there. I was stunned by the undiscriminating kindness and the incredible work ethic of those people—the determination of a boy who woke at 4 A.M. every morning to trek several miles to school; the steadfast, vibrant piety of the Hondurans at their effervescent church services; and the sense of collective joy I saw in their faces when they greeted us to thank us for being there. Looking back, I wish I had been able to say how grateful I was for the inspiration they gave me. Honduras is very different from the relatively affluent Massachusetts community where I live. Though I had considered myself before my trip to Honduras to be a politically oriented and globally "aware" person, I soon realized that I had a great deal to learn about the nature of poverty—and the human spirit. I began to ask, "How had I intellectualized something as human as the daily struggle for life faced by 85 percent of our world's population?" Seeing was believing that summer of 2004.

My decision about the type of work I wanted to go into was a long and thoughtful process. That moment—looking into the little girl's docile and composed but concurrently resolute face—as well as my trip to Honduras as a whole, had a profound effect on my decision about what I want to accomplish in life. I saw the effort exerted just to stay alive—faced by so many—embodied by the girl. It has given me a definitive direction in ways that a high school education or a book of majors could only hope to give. I discovered that I would be unable to feel accomplished in any career without getting the sense that what I did would have a constructive effect on the lives of others. In the weeks and months following my trip to Honduras, I slowly realized that the world was smaller and humanity more universal than I had previously imagined by more than a hundred thousand fold.

Honduras was a turning point for me and will be a cornerstone for my future endeavors in life and vocation. Social action has moved me, and social action is my aim. International relations and government are areas of study that I know will allow me to have a constructive effect on the world. May I, throughout my life, ever be removed from the nets that ensnare those possessed by self-serving ambition, for success is truly fruitless unless it is in the conquest of helping one's fellow man.

# The Dare

## *Roger Hoffmann*

*Roger Hoffmann recounts an episode from his adolescence when approval from his peers was more important than his personal safety. No matter our age or particular adolescent experience, we are able to relate to the pressure Hoffmann felt as a child. The desire for acceptance by friends and colleagues is something we never outgrow.*

### Words to Know

**ambiguous**   not clear, having many interpretations
**escalated**   increased
**guerrilla act**   warfare carried out by an independent military force
**implicit**   understood although not directly stated
**provoke**   to cause anger or resentment
**silhouette**   an outline of something that appears dark against a
  light background, a shadow

### Getting Started

Have you ever taken a risk because of a dare?

---

T he secret to diving under a moving freight train and rolling out the   1
other side with all your parts attached lies in picking the right spot
between the tracks to hit with your back. Ideally, you want soft dirt or
pea gravel, clear of glass shards and railroad spikes that could cause you
instinctively, and fatally, to sit up. Today, at thirty-eight I couldn't be
threatened or baited enough to attempt that dive. But as a seventh grader
struggling to make the cut in a tough Atlanta grammar school, all it took
was a dare.

I coasted through my first years of school as a fussed-over smart kid, the   2
teacher's pet who finished his work first and then strutted around the room
tutoring other students. By the seventh grade, I had more A's than friends.
Even my old cronies, Dwayne and O.T., made it clear I'd never be one of
the guys in junior high if I didn't dirty up my act. They challenged me to
break the rules, and I did. The I-dare-you's escalated: shoplifting, sugaring
teachers' gas tanks, dropping lighted matches into public mailboxes. Each
guerrilla act won me the approval I never got for just being smart.

Walking home by the railroad tracks after school, we started playing   3
chicken with oncoming trains. O.T., who was failing that year, always
won. One afternoon he charged a boxcar from the side, stopping just

short of throwing himself between the wheels. I was stunned. After the train disappeared, we debated whether someone could dive under a moving car, stay put for a 10-count, then scramble out the other side. I thought it could be done and said so. O.T. immediately stepped in front of me and smiled. Not by me, I added quickly, I certainly didn't mean that I could do it. "A smart guy like you," he said, his smile evaporating, "you could figure it out easy." And then, squeezing each word for effect, "I . . . DARE . . . you." I'd just turned twelve. The monkey clawing my back was Teacher's Pet. And I'd been dared.

As an adult, I've been on both ends of life's implicit business and social  4
I-dare-you's, although adults don't use those words. We provoke with body language, tone of voice, ambiguous phrases. I dare you to: argue with the boss, tell Fred what you think of him, send the wine back. Only rarely are the risks physical. How we respond to dares when we are young may have something to do with which of the truly hazardous male inner dares—attacking mountains, tempting bulls at Pamplona—we embrace or ignore as men.

For two weeks, I scouted trains and tracks. I studied moving boxcars  5
close up, memorizing how they squatted on their axles, never getting used to the squeal or the way the air felt hot from the sides. I created an imaginary, friendly train and ran next to it. I mastered a shallow, head-first dive with a simple half-twist. I'd land on my back, count to ten, imagine wheels and, locking both hands on the rail to my left, heave myself over and out. Even under pure sky, though, I had to fight to keep my eyes open and my shoulders between the rails.

The next Saturday, O.T., Dwayne and three eighth graders met me  6
below the hill that backed up to the lumberyard. The track followed a slow bend there and opened to a straight, slightly uphill climb for a solid third of a mile. My run started two hundred yards after the bend. The train would have its tongue hanging out.

The other boys huddled off to one side, a circle on another planet, and  7
watched quietly as I double-knotted my shoelace. My hands trembled. O.T. broke the circle and came over to me. He kept his hands hidden in the pockets of his jacket. We looked at each other. BB's of sweat appeared beneath his nose. I stuffed my wallet in one of his pockets, rubbing it against his knuckles on the way in, and slid my house key, wired to a red-and-white fishing bobber, into the other. We backed away from each other, and he turned and ran to join the four already climbing up the hill.

I watched them all the way to the top. They clustered together as if I were  8
taking their picture. Their silhouette resembled a round shouldered tomb-stone. They waved down to me, and I dropped them from my mind and sat down on the rail. Immediately, I jumped back. The steel was vibrating.

The train sounded like a cow going short of breath. I pulled my shirttail 9
out and looked down at my spot, then up the incline of track ahead of
me. Suddenly the air went hot, and the engine was by me. I hadn't pic-
tured it moving that fast. A man's bare head leaned out and stared at me.
I waved to him with my left hand and turned into the train, burying my
face into the incredible noise. When I looked up, the head was gone.

I started running alongside the boxcars. Quickly, I found their pace, 10
held it, and then eased off, concentrating on each thick wheel that cut past
me. I slowed another notch. Over my shoulder, I picked my car as it came
off the bend, locking in the image of the white mountain goat painted on
its side. I waited, leaning forward like the anchor in a 440-relay, wishing
the baton up the track behind me. Then the big goat fired by me, and I
was flying and then tucking my shoulder as I dipped under the train.

A heavy blanket of red dust settled over me. I felt bolted to the earth. 11
Sheet-metal bellies thundered and shook above my face. Count to ten, a
voice said, watch the axles and look to your left for daylight. But I couldn't
count, and I couldn't find left if my life depended on it, which it did. The
colors overhead went from brown to red to black to red again. Finally, I
ripped my hands free, forced them to the rail, and, in one convulsive jerk,
threw myself into the blue light.

I lay there face down until there was no more noise, and I could feel 12
the sun against the back of my neck. I sat up. The last ribbon of train was
slipping away in the distance. Across the tracks, O.T. was leading a cavalry
charge down the hill, five very small, galloping boys, their fists whirling
above them. I pulled my knees to my chest. My corduroy pants puckered
wet across my thighs. I didn't care.

---

# Poetry

### Kirsten Bauman (student)

*That scary poetry assignment in an English class doesn't frighten Kirsten Bauman, a student at the University of Cincinnati Raymond Walters College in Blue Ash, Ohio. Here, she tells us about her good and bad poetry assignments.*

### Words to Know

**boundaries**   limits, confines
**confused**   lacking understanding
**self-conscious**   ill-at-ease

### Getting Started

What is your favorite poem? Have you ever written a poem?

---

Poetry is a form of free-thought expressed on paper. No boundaries or 1
limitations are set on the poet.

Many people think a poem has to rhyme or have a pattern, but that is 2
not the case. Poetry sets a mood or a tone by being humorous, sad, or
serious. Poetry lets readers make their own inferences about the meaning
of the poem. For that reason, a poem may be more meaningful or special
to one person than to another.

Many of my fellow students, as well as some adults, say they don't 3
like poetry. Maybe the reason I do is because of my early experiences
with poetry.

I can remember sitting on my bed with my Dad as he read aloud to me 4
from an old story book he had when he was a child. I remember that it
was a collection of children's poems that I loved, no matter how many
times my Dad read them to me. I liked the simple nature of the poems. I
liked the fact that I could memorize them so I could "read along" with my
Dad. I still remember what the book looked like. It was a tall, narrow book
with a wood cover. Because it looked different from all my other books, I
still remember it so clearly today.

I can also remember reading aloud from a wide, white poem book 5
called *A Light in the Attic* by Shel Silverstein. I remember liking the poems
because I could relate to them as a child, and they made me laugh.

Some of my later experiences with poetry weren't as pleasant. In ninth 6
grade English class, we read Shakespeare's *Romeo and Juliet*. I remember

having to read aloud and being confused by Shakespeare's use of words. I remember wondering why we were being tortured by reading something that everyone in the class clearly didn't understand.

In a later high school English class, we were divided into groups of  7 three. Our assignment was for each of us to write a poem that illustrated a different element of poetry. Our group was to illustrate the simile.

I had difficulty getting started on my poem; but once I had a begin-  8 ning place, thoughts and ideas just came naturally to me. I actually liked writing the poem. But we still had to present our poems in front of the class, and I was self-conscious about sharing my ideas with other people. It was hard to get in front of the class and read my poem aloud, but my turn was soon over. The class seemed to like my poem, so I decided that writing poetry was almost as pleasant as reading it.

# A Very Basic Decision

*Mary E. Mebane*

> *Mary E. Mebane discovered that prejudice can exist within as well as between races when she attended a North Carolina college for blacks in the 1950s. The light-skinned, urban, middle-class blacks who made up the faculty and most of the student body could not believe that a dark-skinned black girl from a poor rural family could be a superior student. In "A Very Basic Decision," a passage from* Mary: An Autobiography, *Mebane tells of two meetings she had with the wife of the English department's chairman, a light-skinned woman who was convinced that Mebane could not be as talented as her test scores and grades showed. But Mebane decided not to give up her quest for a college degree. She graduated at the top of her class and became a college English professor.*

## Words to Know

**appalled**   dismayed
**bolstered**   supported, propped up
**criteria**   standards
**defer**   submit, yield
**indistinguishable**   not able to be recognized or seen as different
**noncommittal**   to show no opinion or preference
**nonplussed**   confused, perplexed, baffled
**pinnacle**   peak, top
**recourse**   choice, option

## Getting Started

What experiences have influenced your choice of a school program?

N orth Carolina College at Durham (it used to carry the words "for 1 Negroes" in its official title—it said so on the sign right on the lawn) is located in the southern part of the town. Its immaculately groomed lawns and neat, squarish, redbrick classroom buildings and dormitories mark it as an oasis of privilege and ease. Looking at the postcard scenes through the low-hanging branches of the surrounding trees, one would not have believed that this was six minutes away from some of the worst slums in the South. The college hadn't forgotten their existence; it simply never acknowledged that they were there. The black dispossessed murmured against the "big dogs," and bided their time. I often thought that if and when "the revolution" came and the black masses in America awakened

from their long sleep, their first target was going to be the black professional class and it would be a horrendous bloodbath. . . .

During my first week of classes as a freshman, I was stopped one day  2
in the hall by the chairman's wife, who was indistinguishable in color
from a white woman. She wanted to see me, she said.

This woman had no official position on the faculty, except that she was  3
an instructor in English; nevertheless, her summons had to be obeyed. In
the segregated world there were (and remain) gross abuses of authority
because those at the pinnacle, and even their spouses, felt that the people
"under" them had no recourse except to submit—and they were right,
except that sometimes a black who got sick and tired of it would go to
the whites and complain. This course of action was severely condemned
by the blacks, but an interesting thing happened—such action always got
positive results. Power was thought of in negative terms: I can deny
someone something, I can strike at someone who can't strike back, I can
ride someone down; that proves I am powerful. The concept of power as
a force for good, for affirmative response to people or situations, was not
in evidence.

When I went to her office, she greeted me with a big smile. "You know,"  4
she said, "you made the highest mark on the verbal part of the examination." She was referring to the examination that the entire freshman class
took upon entering the college. I looked at her but I didn't feel warmth,
for in spite of her smile her eyes and tone of voice were saying, "How
could this black-skinned girl score higher on the verbal than some of the
students who've had more advantages than she? It must be some sort of
fluke. Let me talk to her." I felt it, but I managed to smile my thanks and
back off. For here at North Carolina College at Durham, as it had been
since the beginning, social class and color were the primary criteria used
in determining status on the campus.

First came the children of doctors, lawyers, and college teachers. Next  5
came the children of public-school teachers, businessmen, and anybody
else who had access to more money than the poor black working class.
After that came the bulk of the student population, the children of the
working class, most of whom were the first in their families to go beyond
high school. The attitude toward them was: You're here because we need
the numbers, but in all other things defer to your betters.

The faculty assumed that light-skinned students were more intelligent,  6
and they were always a bit nonplussed when a dark-skinned student did
well, especially if she was a girl. They had reason to be appalled when they
discovered that I planned to do not only well but better than my light-
skinned peers. . . .

When the grades for that first quarter came out, I had the highest aver-  7
age in the freshman class. The chairman's wife called me into her office

again. We did a replay of the same scene we had played during the first week of the term. She complimented me on my grades, but her eyes and voice were telling me something different. She asked me to sit down; then she reached into a drawer and pulled out a copy of the freshman English final examination. She asked me to take the exam over again.

At first I couldn't believe what she was saying. I had taken the course 8 under another teacher, and it was so incredible to her that I should have made the highest score in the class that she was trying to test me again personally. For a few moments I knew rage so intense that I wanted to take my fists and start punching her. I have seldom hated anyone so deeply. I handed the examination back to her and walked out.

She had felt quite safe in doing that to me. After all, she was the chair- 9 man's wife, and so didn't that give her the right to treat the black farm girl as she chose? (Life is strange. When in the mid-1960s the department started hiring native-born whites, it was she who most bitterly resented their presence.)

It was that incident which caused me to make a very basic decision. I 10 was in the world alone; no one bolstered my ambitions, fed my dreams. I could not quit now, for if I did I would have no future. . . . If I was going to get through college, I would have to be bland, noncommittal. I would simply hang on. I needed a degree and I would stay until I got it.

# Time to Look and Listen

### Magdoline Asfahani (student)

> Magdoline Asfahani, an Arab and a Muslim, gives us a sensitive and
> thoughtful account of the effect of discrimination on her life. Asfahani is
> a student at the University of Texas, El Paso.

### Words to Know

**alluding**   referring, suggesting
**incompatible**   not in agreement
**medley**   mixture, assortment
**monotheistic**   having a belief in one God
**nuances**   subtleties, slight variations or differences

### Getting Started

Do you feel that you discriminate against a group of people?

I love my country as many who have been here for generations cannot.  1
Perhaps that's because I'm the child of immigrants, raised with a conscious
respect for America that many people take for granted. My parents chose
this country because it offered them a new life, freedom and possibilities.
But I learned at a young age that the country we loved so much did not
feel the same way about us.

Discrimination is not unique to America. It occurs in any country that  2
allows immigration. Anyone who is unlike the majority is looked at a little
suspiciously, dealt with a little differently. The fact that I wasn't part of the
majority never occurred to me. I knew that I was an Arab and a Muslim.
This meant nothing to me. At school I stood up to say the Pledge of Al-
legiance every day. These things did not seem incompatible at all. Then
everything changed for me, suddenly and permanently, in 1985. I was only
in seventh grade, but that was the beginning of my political education.

That year a TWA plane originating in Athens was diverted to Beirut.  3
Two years earlier the U.S. Marine barracks in Beirut had been bombed. That
seemed to start a chain of events that would forever link Arabs with terrorism. After the hijacking, I faced classmates who taunted me with cruel
names, attacking my heritage and my religion. I became an outcast and
had to apologize for myself constantly.

After a while, I tried to forget my heritage. No matter what race, reli-  4
gion or ethnicity, a child who is attacked often retreats. I was the only Arab
I knew of in my class, so I had no one in my peer group as an ally. No

matter what my parents tried to tell me about my proud cultural history, I would ignore it. My classmates told me I came from an uncivilized, brutal place, that Arabs were by nature anti-American, and I believed them. They did not know the hours my parents spent studying, working, trying to preserve part of their old lives while embracing, willingly, the new.

I tried to forget the Arabic I knew, because if I didn't I'd be forever 5 linked to murderers. I stopped inviting friends over for dinner, because I thought the food we ate was "weird." I lied about where my parents had come from. Their accents (although they spoke English perfectly) humiliated me. Though Islam is a major monotheistic religion with many similarities to Judaism and Christianity, there were no holidays near Chanukah or Christmas, nothing to tie me to the "Judeo-Christian" tradition. I felt more excluded. I slowly began to turn into someone without a past.

Civil war was raging in Lebanon, and all that Americans saw of that 6 country was destruction and violence. Every other movie seemed to feature Arab terrorists. The most common questions I was asked were if I had ever ridden a camel or if my family lived in tents. I felt burdened with responsibility. Why should an adolescent be asked questions like "Is it true you hate Jews and you want Israel destroyed?" I didn't hate anybody. My parents had never said anything even alluding to such sentiments. I was confused and hurt.

As I grew older and began to form my own opinions, my embarrass- 7 ment lessened and my anger grew. The turning point came in high school. My grandmother had become very ill, and it was necessary for me to leave school a few days before Christmas vacation. My chemistry teacher was very sympathetic until I said I was going to the Middle East. "Don't come back in a body bag," he said cheerfully. The class laughed. Suddenly, those years of watching movies that mocked me and listening to others who knew nothing about Arabs and Muslims except what they saw on television seemed like a bad dream. I knew then that I would never be silent again.

I've tried to reclaim those lost years. I realize now that I come from a 8 culture that has a rich history. The Arab world is a medley of people of different religions; not every Arab is a Muslim, and vice versa. The Arabs brought tremendous advances in the sciences and mathematics, as well as creating a literary tradition that has never been surpassed. The language itself is flexible and beautiful, with nuances and shades of meaning unparalleled in any language. Though many find it hard to believe, Islam has made progress in women's rights. There is a specific provision in the Koran that permits women to own property and ensures that their inheritance is protected—although recent events have shown that interpretation of these laws can vary.

My youngest brother, who is 12, is now at the crossroads I faced. When  9
initial reports of the Oklahoma City bombing pointed to "Arab-looking
individuals" as the culprits, he came home from school crying. "Mom,
why do Muslims kill people? Why are the Arabs so bad?" She was angry
and brokenhearted, but tried to handle the situation in the best way possible: through education. She went to his class, armed with Arabic music,
pictures, traditional dress and cookies. She brought a chapter of the social-
studies book to life, and the children asked intelligent, thoughtful questions, even after the class was over. Some even asked if she was coming
back. When my brother came home, he was excited and proud instead
of ashamed.

I only recently told my mother about my past experience. Maybe if I  10
had told her then, I would have been better equipped to deal with the
thoughtless teasing. But, fortunately, the world is changing. Although
discrimination and stereotyping still exist, many people are trying to
lessen and end it. Teachers, schools and the media are showing greater
sensitivity to cultural issues. However, there is still much that needs to be
done, not for the sake of any particular ethnic or cultural group but for
the sake of our country.

The America that I love is one that values freedom and the differences 11
of its people. Education is the key to understanding. As Americans we
need to take a little time to look and listen carefully to what is around us
and not rush to judgment without knowing all the facts. And we must
never be ashamed of our pasts. It is our collective differences that unite
us and make us unique as a nation. It's what determines our present and
our future.

# Glossary

Various terms are used throughout this edition of *Patterns Plus* to explain the basic strategies of writing. These terms are boldfaced in the chapter introductions, and they are boldfaced and defined here in the following pages. Terms in bold type within the definitions are also defined in the Glossary.

**Alternating Method**   The alternating method of **comparison** and **contrast,** also called point-by-point method, compares and contrasts two subjects item by item. (See also **Block Method** and **Mixed Method.**)

**Antonym**   An antonym is a word that has a meaning *opposite* that of another word. For example, *pleasure* is an antonym of *pain*. Using an antonym is one method writers use to define an unfamiliar word.

**Argumentation**   Argumentation is a **mode of development** used to express a controversial idea. A classic or formal argument includes five elements: statement of the problem, solution, evidence, refutation, and conclusion. Argumentation may or may not include some persuasion, but should be rational, logical, and objective rather than emotional. (See also **Persuasion.**)

**Audience**   A reader or readers of a piece of writing. More specifically, an audience is that reader or group of readers toward which a particular piece of writing is aimed. (See also **Purpose** and **Occasion.**)

**Block Method**   In the block method of **comparison** and **contrast,** the writer first explains the characteristics of the first item in a block and then explains the characteristics of the second item in a block. (See also **Alternating Method** and **Mixed Method.**)

**Body**   The body is the development of the **thesis** in a group of related paragraphs in an **essay.** (See also **Introduction** and **Conclusion.**)

**Brainstorming**   A prewriting technique that many writers use to generate ideas for writing. In brainstorming, a writer jots down as many details and ideas on a subject as come to mind.

**Cause**   A cause is a reason why something happens or an explanation of why some **effect** occurs. Writers explain why an effect (or result) comes about by explaining its causes. See chapter 8, "Cause and Effect," for further discussion.

**Chronological Order**  See **Order.**

**Class**  In **classification** and **division,** a writer can classify or divide items if they are of the same type—that is, if they belong to the same class.

**Classification**  Classification is the process of sorting a group of items into categories on the basis of some characteristic or quality that the items have in common. As a **mode of development,** classification is used by writers to organize and develop information included in a **paragraph** or **essay.** Classification is sometimes combined with **division** to develop a **topic** or **thesis.** See chapter 5, "Classification and Division," for further discussion.

**Cliché**  Clichés are words or phrases that have become so overused they have lost their expressive power. Examples of clichés are "rosy red," "silly goose," "bull in a china shop," and "works like a horse."

**Coherence**  Coherence refers to the logical flow of a piece of writing. Writing is coherent when the **main idea** is clearly stated and the connections between the supporting **details** and the main idea are obvious. (See also **Unified/Unity.**)

**Collaboration/Collaborative Writing**  Collaboration or collaborative writing is the working together of two or more persons in developing and producing a piece of writing.

**Comparison/Compare**  When making a comparison, the writer discusses the similarities of objects or ideas. Writers sometimes combine comparison with contrast in developing their **main idea.** See chapter 6, "Comparison and Contrast," for further discussion.

**Conclusion**  In writing, the term *conclusion* is used to refer to the sentence or **paragraph** that completes the composition. Within the conclusion, the writer may restate the **main idea** of the composition or sum up its important points.

In reading, the term *conclusion* refers to the idea the reader can draw from the information in the reading selection. Drawing a conclusion involves making an **inference**—that is, deriving an idea that is **implied** by the information stated within a composition.

**Connotation**  Connotation refers to the feelings or qualities a reader associates with a word. In **persuasion,** writers often use the connotations of words to appeal to their readers. (See also **Denotation.**)

**Contrast**  When making a contrast, the writer discusses the differences among objects or ideas. Writers sometimes combine contrast with **comparison** in developing an idea. See chapter 6, "Comparison and Contrast," for further discussion.

**Deductive Order**  In deductive order—also called general-to-specific order—the writer presents the argument or discussion by beginning with a general statement, such as the **topic** of a paragraph or **thesis** of an essay, and proceeding to the specific information that supports the statement.

**Definition**  A definition explains the meaning of a word or term. Writers frequently use a variety of methods for defining the words and terms they use. They may use a dictionary definition, a **synonym,** or an **antonym.** They may also use any combination of the **modes of development** explained in this text.

An **extended definition** is one composed of several sentences or paragraphs. It is often used to define complex objects or concepts. See chapter 9, "Definition," for further discussion.

**Denotation**   Denotation refers to the exact definition, or dictionary definition, of a word. (See also **Connotation.**)

**Description**   In a description, the writer discusses the appearance of a person, place, or object. In descriptions, writers use words and details that appeal to the senses in order to create the **impression** they want the reader to have about what is being described.

**Details**   Details are specific pieces of information—examples, incidents, dates, and so forth—that explain and support the general ideas in a composition. Writers use details to make their general ideas clearer and more understandable to the reader.

**Development**   Development refers to the detailed explanation of the main—and usually more general—ideas in a composition. The **main idea** (or **topic**) of a paragraph is developed by providing specific information in the sentences within the paragraph. The main idea or **thesis** of an **essay** is explained or developed through **paragraphs.**

**Dialogue**   Dialogue is conversation, usually between two or more persons. It is used by writers to give the exact words spoken by people and is always set off by quotation marks. The writer usually uses a new paragraph to indicate a change of speaker. Dialogue is commonly found in **narration.**

**Division**   In division, the writer breaks down or sorts a single object or idea into its components or parts and then gives detailed information about each of the parts. Division is sometimes used in combination with **classification.** See chapter 5, "Classification and Division," for further discussion.

**Draft**   A draft is the first version of a piece of writing. Preparation of a draft follows prewriting in the writing process. A draft requires rewriting, revising, and editing. (See also **Edit, Prewriting, Revising,** and **Rewriting.**)

**Edit**   Editing is the final step in the writing process and involves checking the piece of writing for accuracy of spelling, sentence structure, grammar, and punctuation. (See also **Draft, Prewriting, Revising,** and **Rewriting.**)

**Effect**   An effect is the result of certain events or **causes.** An effect may be the result of one or more causes. Writers often combine cause and effect to explain why something happens. See chapter 8, "Cause and Effect," for further discussion.

**Essay**   An essay is a written composition based on an idea, which is called its **thesis.** An essay usually consists of at least three **paragraphs.** In the paragraphs, writers usually introduce and state the **thesis, develop** or explain the thesis, and **conclude** the essay. See chapter 1, "The Basics of Writing: Process and Strategies," for further discussion.

**Event**   An occurrence or happening that a writer wishes to portray, often as part of a **fictional** or **nonfictional narrative.**

**Example**   An example is a specific illustration of a general idea or statement. Writers may use one or more examples and may extend a single example over an entire essay in order to illustrate and support their ideas.

**Extended Definition**   See **Definition.**

**Extended Example**   An extended example is described in several sentences or paragraphs. It is used as a way of providing additional support for a **topic sentence** or **thesis statement.** See chapter 4, "Examples," for further discussion.

**Fact(s)**   Any thing or things known with certainty. Writers often present facts as a way of showing they are **objective** about a subject. (See also **Opinion.**)

**Fallacy**   A fallacy is an error in the writer's reasoning or logic. Types of fallacies include the post hoc (meaning "after this, therefore because of this"), hasty generalization, non sequitur (claiming an effect that does not follow from the cause), false analogy, circular argument, argument to the man (argument ad hominem), bandwagon, either-or, and begging the question. See chapters 8, "Cause and Effect," and 10, "Argumentation and Persuasion," for further discussion.

**Fiction/Fictional Narrative**   A **paragraph** or an **essay** that presents a story or event that did not occur or that differs significantly from a real or true event is called fiction. (By contrast, see **Nonfiction/Nonfictional Narrative.**)

**Figure of Speech**   A word or phrase used to compare unlike things to create an image or **impression.** Examples are "He fought like a tiger" and "A little girl is sugar and spice." (See also **Metaphor** and **Simile.**)

**First Person**   See **Person.**

**Formal Definition**   A formal definition assigns the word or term being defined to the **class** or **classification** of items to which it belongs and then describes the characteristics that distinguish it from other items in that class.

**Freewriting**   Freewriting is a **prewriting** exercise that involves writing without stopping for a set period of time, often five to ten minutes. Freewriting is an effective way to start writing and to generate ideas.

**General Idea/General Statement**   A general idea or statement is broad and sweeping and therefore must usually be explained with more specific information. The **main idea** of a **paragraph** or an **essay** is a relatively general idea, involving only the main features of the thought. In a paragraph or an essay, the general ideas and statements must be supported by more specific information.

**Hyperbole**   Hyperbole is a statement that is an exaggeration of a condition or situation.

**Image**   An image is a "vision" or impression created by descriptive or sensory details.

**Imply/Implied**  To imply is to hint at or indicate indirectly. Writers sometimes only imply their ideas rather than state them directly. An implied idea requires the reader to draw **conclusions** or make **inferences** in order to determine the idea.

**Impression**  The effect, feeling, or image that an author tries to create through **description.**

**Incidents**  Incidents are the more specific, detailed happenings that make up a particular event. The **narration** of an event will include an account of the specific incidents that occurred as part of the event.

**Inductive Order**  In inductive order—also called specific-to-general order—the writer presents the argument or discussion by beginning with specific supporting information and proceeding to the **general statement,** such as the **topic** of a **paragraph** or **thesis** of an **essay.**

**Infer/Inference**  An inference is a **conclusion** drawn by the reader based on information known or **implied.** Writers sometimes imply their ideas rather than state them. Readers must make inferences and use the information that is known or stated to determine the writer's ideas.

**Inform**  Inform means to relate or tell about something. Writers often use **process** as a **mode of development** to inform their readers, although any of the modes discussed in this text can be used to inform.

**Instruct**  Instruct means to teach or educate. Writers often use **process** as a **mode of development** to instruct their readers.

**Introduction**  The introduction of a **paragraph** or **essay** is at its beginning. The introduction of an essay is often where the writer places the **thesis statement.** (See also **Body** and **Conclusion.**)

**Irony**  The use of a relationship that is contradictory or unexpected. Writers often use irony to amuse, sadden, instruct, or anger their readers.

**Main Idea**  The main idea of a composition is the general concept, broad **opinion,** or argument on which the composition is based. The main idea of a **paragraph** is called the **topic.** The main idea of an **essay** is called the **thesis.**

**Metaphor**  A metaphor is a **figure of speech** that compares unlike items by attributing the qualities or characteristics of one item to the other. A metaphor compares the items without the use of the words *like* or *as*. (See also **Simile.**)

**Mixed Method**  The mixed method of **comparison** and **contrast** explains similarities and then differences, or differences first and then similarities. (See also **Alternating Method** and **Block Method.**)

**Mode of Development**  The mode of development refers to the kind of information used to **support** and explain the **main idea** of a paragraph or essay. Writers commonly use, either singly or in combination, the modes discussed in this text: **narration, description, examples, classification** and **division, comparison** and **contrast, process, cause and effect, definition,** and **argumentation** and **persuasion.**

**Narration/Narrative Writing**   Narration is a **mode of development** used by writers to tell a story or give an account of a historical or fictional event. See chapter 2, "Narration," for further discussion.

**Nonfiction/Nonfictional Narrative**   A paragraph or essay that presents a story or event that actually happened. (By contrast, see **Fiction/Fictional Narrative.**)

**Objective**   A paragraph or essay that presents the **facts** without including the writer's interpretation of those facts is said to be objective. (By contrast, see **Subjective.**)

**Occasion**   An occasion is a set of circumstances under which a particular piece of writing occurs. The writing assignments in this text are occasions for writing **paragraphs** and **essays.**

**Opinion**   An opinion is a belief or conclusion that may or may not be based on fact. Writers often use opinion as a way of presenting a subjective description of an event or object. (By contrast, see **Fact[s].**)

**Order**   Order refers to the sequence in which the information in a composition is organized or arranged. Information is commonly organized in chronological order, order of importance, or spatial order. In **chronological order,** the information is arranged according to time. In **order of importance,** the information may be arranged from the least to the most important—or from the most to the least important. In **spatial order,** the information is presented from a particular vantage point: the door to a room, front to back, floor to ceiling, and so forth.

**Order of Importance**   See **Order.**

**Paragraph**   A paragraph is usually a set of two or more sentences that help explain an idea. The major use of a paragraph is to mark a division of the information within a composition. Another use of the paragraph is to set off **dialogue.** In this text, a paragraph is considered as a unit. The first word of a paragraph is usually indented a few spaces from the left margin of the printed page.

**Parallelism**   Parallelism refers to the use of the same grammatical structure in successive sentences. Writers use parallel sentence structure to stress or emphasize the relation of or the connections among the pieces of information in the sentences.

**Person**   Person is indicated by the personal pronouns used in a composition. Writers use the **first person** (*I, we*) to represent themselves as participants or firsthand observers of their subject. They use the **second person** (*you*) to address the reader directly. They use the **third person** (*he, she, it, one, they*) to provide the reader with a less limited and more objective view of the subject than may be possible by using first or second person. (See also **Point of View.**)

**Personification**   Personification is a figure of speech that attributes human qualities or abilities to animals or objects.

**Persuasion**   Persuasion is a **mode of development** in which the writer appeals to the reader's emotions in an attempt to convince the reader to accept the writer's **opinion** or judgment. The writer's **thesis** may or may not be controversial. (See also **Argumentation.**)

**Point-by-Point Method**   See **Alternating Method.**

**Point of View**   Point of view refers to the way writers present their ideas. Point of view is determined by the **person, time,** and **tone** used in a composition. Person is indicated by personal pronouns. Time is determined by the words that indicate when the action discussed in the composition takes place (past, present, or future). Tone refers to the attitude that writers take toward their subjects. The tone may be serious, humorous, formal, informal, cynical, sarcastic, ironic, sympathetic, and so forth.

**Prewriting**   Prewriting may involve **freewriting** and **brainstorming.** The purpose of prewriting is to get the writer started on defining the **main idea.** (See also **Brainstorming, Draft,** and **Freewriting.**)

**Process**   Process is a **mode of development** used by writers to explain the method of performing a task, making or preparing something, or achieving a particular result. See chapter 7, "Process," for further discussion.

**Purpose**   Purpose refers to a writer's reason for writing. Writers usually want to **inform** and to **instruct.**

**Quotation Marks**   Quotation marks are a pair of punctuation marks (" ") used to indicate the beginning and end of **dialogue** or information cited verbatim from a source.

**Revising**   The process of evaluating, reworking, and **rewriting a draft,** keeping **audience, purpose, thesis, development,** and, finally, mechanics (sentence structure, punctuation) in mind.

**Rewriting**   Rewriting involves reworking and clarifying the **draft** of a piece of writing. (See also **Draft, Edit, Prewriting,** and **Revising.**)

**Rhetorical Question**   A rhetorical question is one that is not expected to be answered or to which the answer is obvious.

**Second Person**   See **Person.**

**Sentence**   A sentence is a group of words that expresses a thought. A sentence usually contains a word or words that express who is doing an action or is being acted upon (the subject of the sentence) and a word or words that express the action that is taking place (the *verb* of the sentence). The first word of a sentence begins with a capital letter. The end of a sentence is marked by a period (.), a question mark (?), or an exclamation point (!).

**Simile**   A simile is a **figure of speech** in which unlike items are compared. A simile is usually introduced by *like* or *as,* as in "He worked *like a horse* on the project" or "The chicken was as tasteless *as a piece of cardboard.*" (See also **Metaphor.**)

**Spatial Order**   See **Order.**

**Subjective**   Subjective writing is that in which the writer's own feelings about the topic are expressed. (By contrast, see **Objective.**)

**Support**   Support refers to the information—specific details, **examples,** and so forth—used to develop or explain the **general idea** in a composition.

**Symbol**   A symbol is a person, place, or object that represents something other than itself, usually something immaterial or abstract.

**Synonym**   A synonym is a word or phrase that has the same meaning as another word or phrase. Writers sometimes use a synonym to clarify an unfamiliar word or phrase used in their compositions.

**Thesis**   The thesis is the **main idea** of an essay. The thesis may be stated directly (see **Thesis Statement**) or only implied (see **Imply/Implied**).

**Thesis Statement**   The thesis statement is the sentence or sentences in which the **main idea** of an **essay** is stated. The thesis statement is generally placed at or near the beginning of an essay.

**Third Person**   See **Person.**

**Time**   Time refers to the period (past, present, future) when the action discussed in the composition took place. Time is indicated by action words (verbs) and such words as *tomorrow, yesterday, next week,* and so on. (See also **Point of View.**)

**Tone**   Tone refers to the attitude writers take toward their subjects. The attitude in a composition may be formal, informal, serious, humorous, and so forth. (See also **Point of View.**)

**Topic**   The **main idea** of a **paragraph** is called its topic. The topic of a paragraph may be stated directly (see **Topic Sentence**) or only implied (see **Imply/Implied**).

**Topic Sentence**   The topic sentence is the sentence (or sentences) in which the **main idea** of a **paragraph** is stated. The topic sentence is commonly placed at or near the beginning of a paragraph, but it may appear at any point in the paragraph.

**Transitions**   Transitions are words and phrases such as *for example, on the other hand, first, second,* or *to illustrate* that help the reader identify the relationships among ideas in a composition.

**Unified/Unity**   A **paragraph** or **essay** must be unified to be effective, which means each must deal with a single idea, and the information included in the paragraph or essay must be related to that idea. (See also **Main Idea** and **Coherence.**)

# Credits

**Chapter 2**

**John Updike:** "The Movie House" from *Five Boyhoods* (Doubleday) edited by Martin Levin, © 1962. Renewed © 1990 by Martin Levin. Reprinted by permission of Martin Levin. **Russell Baker:** "Learning to Write" from *Growing Up*. Copyright © 1982 by Russell Baker. Published by agreement with Congdon & Weed, Inc. **Sarah Smith:** "A Little Nebraska," *Plains Song Review*, Spring 2002, Vol. IV, pp. 24–25. Reprinted by permission of the Center for Great Plains Studies.

**Chapter 3**

**Richard Mack:** "The Wreck" excerpted from "A Sky of Rose and Quartz," p. 179, *South Dakota Review*, Spring/Summer 2005, Vol. 43. Reprinted by permission of Richard Mack, LaGrande, OR. **Kurt Anderson:** "Hush Timmy—This is Like a Church" *Time*, 4/15/85. © 1985 Time Inc. Reprinted by permission. **Lt. Nicole A. Elwell and Jeff Elwell:** "A Letter from the Desert," *Cleveland Plain Dealer*, 4/21/03, p. B7. Reprinted by permission of the author.

**Chapter 4**

**David Mazie:** Excerpted with permission from "Keep Your Teen-Age Driver Alive" *Reader's Digest* June 1991. Copyright © 1991 by The Reader's Digest Assn., Inc., pp. 85–86. **Peggy Robbins:** "The Kickapoo Indian Medicine Company," in *American History Illustrated*, Vol. XV, #2, May 1980. Reprinted through the courtesy of Cowles Magazine, publishers of *American History Illustrated*. **Jeff Glasser:** "Boomtown U.S.A.," *U.S. News & World Report*, June 25, 2001, Vol. 130, Issue 25, p. 16. Copyright 2001 U.S. News & World Report, L.P. Reprinted with permission. **Debra Aho Williamson:** "Foreign Flavors, Mainstream Taste." Reprinted with permission from the July 8, 2002 issue of *Advertising Age*. Copyright, Crain Communications Inc. 2002. **Kathryn VanSpanckeren:** "Chapter Six, Modernism and Experimentation: 1914–1945" in *Outline Of American Literature*. Manila (Philippines) United States Information Agency (presently U.S. Dept of State), 1994, pp. 60–61. Reprinted by permission of Kathryn VanSpanckeren. **Bonnie Smith-Yackel:** "My Mother Never Worked." Reprinted with permission from *Women: A Journal Of Liberation*, Vol. 4, No. 2, Spring 1975.

**Chapter 5**

**Lester C. Thurow:** "Brain Power" from "Brains Power Business Growth," *USA Today*, Monday, August 18, 1997, p. 13A. Reprinted by permission of the author. **Stephen King:** "Ever Et Raw Meat," *The New York Times Book Review*, December 6, 1987. Copyright © 1987. Reprinted with permission of Arthur B. Greene & Co. © Stephen King.

## Chapter 6

## Chapter 7

## Chapter 8

## Chapter 9

## Chapter 10

# Index

Ad hominem arguments, 249
Alternating method of comparison and
    contrast, 137–138
Anderson, Kurt, 59–62
Antonyms, 217
Argumentation and persuasion, 243–249
    audience for, 249
    circular, 249
    classic, 246–247
    implied, 247
    purposes of, 244, 246, 249
Argument to the man fallacy, 249
"Art of Making Fimo Beans, The" (Gifford),
    183–186
Asfahani, Magdoline, 282–284
Asimov, Isaac, 235–237
Audiences, 249
    writing for various, 1

Baker, Russell, 28–30
Bandwagon fallacy, 249
"Banning Smoking" (Ruckdeschel), 266–267
Bauman, Kirsten, 277–278
"Beekeeper, The" (Hubbell), 180–181
Begging the question, 249
Bernard, Sarah, 141–142
"Between Two Wars, 1913–1945"
    (VanSpanckeren), 94–97
Bishop, Elizabeth, 24–25
Block method of comparison and contrast, 138
Body of essays, 8
Boehmer, Daniel, 272–273
"Boomtown, U.S.A." (Glasser), 81–82
"Brain Power" (Thurow), 115–116
Brainstorming, 3–4, 47, 106
    for comparison and contrast, 136
    for examples, 76
"Brewing Beer" (Lichtenstein), 170–171
Britt, Suzanne, 149–151
"Burning Issue, A" (Chapman), 268–270

Capon, Robert, 222–223
Cause and effect, 9, 10, 189–194
    fallacies in, 193–194
    processes with, 191–193
    revising, 193
    thesis statements in, 189
    topic sentences in, 189
Chapman, Mary Boltz, 268–270

"Chili" (Kuralt), 107–108
Chronological order, 14
Classes, in definitions, 217
Classification, 4, 9–10
    in definitions, 217
    definitions with, 219
    purpose of, 103
Classification and division, 103–106
    category selection for, 103–105
    in comparison and contrast, 135
    purpose of, 103
    transitional words in, 105
Clichés, 216
Coherence, 105
Collaboration, 3–4
Comparison and contrast, 135–140
    brainstorming for, 136
    classification in, 135
    definitions with, 219
    irony in, 139–140
    objectivity in, 135–136
    organization of, 137–140
    transitional words in, 139–140
Conclusions, 246, 247
    of essays, 9
Concrete examples, 76
Connotations, 217, 243–244
Contrast, 135, 247–248. See also Comparison
    and contrast
"Conversational Ballgames" (Sakamoto),
    152–156
"Cook, The" (Lewis), 174–175
Cottle, Michelle, 195–196
Crane, Diana, 87–89
Credibility, 76

"Dare, The" (Hoffmann), 274–276
"Daughter's Doll Teaches Mom Lesson on
    Race" (Schultz), 32–34
Deductive order, 4–5
Definitions, 165, 217–219
    extended, 218
    formal, 217
    in processes, 165
    revising, 218
Denotations, 217, 243
Description, 14, 43–48
    definitions with, 218
    details in, 45–46

Description (*continued*)
   figures of speech in, 44–45
   organization of, 45–46
   processes and, 164
Descriptive essays, 10
Details
   in description, 45–47
   in narration, 14–15
Development, mode of, 271
Dialogue, 17
"Digital Revolution, The" (Wade), 79–80
"Distance Learning" (Lord), 77–78
Division, 104. *See also* Classification and
      division
Dog, The, 168–169
"Dogs and Cats" (Lorenz), 145–146
Drafting, 10
"Drinking—What Age?" (Seaman), 254–255

"Earning Their Pinstripes" (Reilly), 240–242
Edelman, Marian Wright, 256–257
Editing, 11
"Eggs, Twinkies, and Ethnic Stereotypes"
      (Park), 122–124
Either-or arguments, 249
Elwell, Jeff, 63–66
Elwell, Nicole A., 63–66
Essays, 1
   body of, 8
   conclusion of, 9
   developing, 7–11
   introduction of, 9
   objective, 16
   subjective, 16
Events, 13
"Ever Et Raw Meat?" (King), 117–121
Evidence, in argumentation, 247–248
Examples, 4, 9, 10
   in argumentation, 247–248
   concrete, 76
   definitions with, 219
   extended, 74–76
   order of, 73
   in processes, 165
   as support, 73–74
   uses of, 73
Extended examples, 74–76
"Eyewitness Account, An" (London),
      199–200

Facts, 16
   in argumentation, 247–248
Fallacies, 193–194, 249
   ad hominem, 249
   argument to the man, 249
   bandwagon, 249
   begging the question, 249
   false analogies, 249
False analogies, 249
"Fans" (Gallico), 113–114
Fiction, 17
Figures of speech, 44–45
First person, 16

Flores, Victor, 215–216
"Flunking" (Sherry), 258–259
"Folk Art in the Barrios" (Kroll), 83–84
"Foreign Flavors, Mainstream Taste"
      (Williamson), 90–93
Formal definitions, 217
Freewriting, 2–3
Friedman, Thomas L., 166–167
"Frightening and Fantastic" (Quindlen),
      252–253

Gallico, Paul, 113–114
Galvez, Ricardo, 85–86
Garrison, Gloria, 67–69
General-to-specific order, 4–5
"Geography" (Bishop), 24–25
Gifford, Julie, 185–188
"Giving In" (Cottle), 195–196
Glasser, Jeff, 81–82
"Global Warming in Canada" (Sinclair),
      205–208
"Good Girl, Bad Girl" (Quindlen), 143–144
"Grandparents" (Merrell), 228–229
Grogan, John, 49–50
"Guide to Proper Hand-Washing Technique,
      A" (Traig), 176–178

Hall, Heidi, 57–58
"Hang It Up" (Scaccia), 260–262
Hanley, Chris, 157–159
"Happy Returns" (Bernard), 141–142
Hasty generalizations, 194
Hayakawa, S. I., 226–227
Hills, L. Rust, 172–173
"Hiroshima Museum, The" (Kingsolver),
      51–52
Hoffmann, Roger, 274–276
"How to Bathe a Cat" (The Dog), 168–169
Hubbell, Sue, 178–179
"Hunt, The" (Stern), 20–21
"Hush, Timmy—This Is Like a Church"
      (Anderson), 59–62
Hyperbole, 45

Images, 48
Implied arguments, 247
Implied cause and effect, 194
Implied ideas, 6
Implied metaphors, 44–45
Impressions, 43–44
Incidents, 13
Inductive order, 5–6
"Indy 5000" (Hanley), 157–159
Inferences, 194
Inferred ideas, 6
Informing, 164
Instruction, 164
Introductions, of essays, 9
Irony, 139–140

Jackson, John L., 22–23
Jacobson, Michael F., 250–251
Jones, Mary Paumier, 147–148

Kary, Tiffany, 238–239
"Keep the Drinking Age at Twenty-One"
    (Voas), 263–265
King, Martin Luther, Jr., 201–202
King, Stephen, 117–121
Kingsolver, Barbara, 51–52
Kirn, Walter, 220–221
"Koto" (Yano), 182–184
Kroll, Eric, 83–84
Kuralt, Charles, 107–108

"Learning to Write" (Baker), 28–30
"Letter from the Desert, A" (Elwell & Elwell),
    63–66
Lewis, Barbara, 174–175
Lichtenstein, Grace, 170–171
"Limbo" (Lucas), 70–72
"Little Nebraska, A" (Smith), 38–42
Logical fallacies, 193–194, 249
London, Jack, 199–200
Lord, Mary, 77–78
Lorenz, Konrad, 145–146
Lucas, Rhonda S., 70–72

Mack, Richard, 55–56
"Mad Dog's Hair, The: Alcoholism" (Simons),
    111–112
Main ideas, 1
    in argumentation/persuasion, 246
    developing, 7–11
    finding, 2–4
    stating, 4–7
Malinowski, Christopher, 26–27
Manning, Brian, 211–214
"March of Science" (Page), 109–110
"Measure of Our Success, The" (Edelman),
    256–257
Mebane, Mary, 279–281
"Memorial Service, The" (Malinowski), 26–27
Mercier, Francine, 160–162
Merrell, Nancy, 228–229
Merriwether-deVries, Cynthia, 209–210
Metaphors, 44–45
Mixed method of comparison and contrast,
    138–139
Modes of development, 7, 9–10, 271
    argumentation and persuasion, 243–249
    cause and effect, 189–194
    classification and division, 103–106
    comparison and contrast, 135–140
    description, 43–48
    examples, 73–76
    narration, 13–17
"Momentous Arrest, A" (King), 201–202
"More Than Words" (Flores), 215–216
Morris, Desmond, 125–129
"Movie House, The" (Updike), 18–19
"My Mother Never Worked" (Smith-Yackel),
    98–102
"My Suit" (Galvez), 85–86

Narration, 10, 13–17
    chronological order in, 14

definitions with, 218
details in, 14–15
dialogue in, 17
point of view in, 15–16
processes and, 164
purpose of, 13
"Neat People vs. Sloppy People" (Britt),
    149–151
Nonfiction, 16–17
*Non sequiturs*, 194
"Nostalgia" (Shelton), 224–225

Objective essays, 16
Objective writing, 47, 136
    argumentation and, 246
Occasions, writing for various, 1
"On Being Unemployed" (Smith), 203–204
Order of importance, 45, 73
Organization
    chronological, 14
    in classification and division, 105–106
    for comparison and contrast, 137–140
    deductive, 4–5
    general-to-specific, 4–5
    inductive, 5–6
    by order of importance, 45
    of processes, 163–165
    by spatial order, 45
    specific-to-general, 5–6
    time, 14
"Overindulgence" (Hall), 57–58

Page, James K., Jr., 109–110
Paragraphs, 1
    developing, 7–8
Park, Jeanne, 122–124
Parker, Jo Goodwin, 230–234
"Perfect Dog, A" (Grogan), 49–50
Person, 15–16
Personification, 45
Persuasion, 9, 10. *See also* Argumentation and
    persuasion
    purposes of, 244–246
"Poetry" (Bauman), 277–278
Point-by-point method of comparison and
    contrast, 137–138
Point of view, 15–16
    in processes, 164, 165
*Post hoc* fallacy, 193–194
Prewriting, 10, 106
Problem statements, 246
Process writing, 163–165
    cause and effect with, 191–193
    combining with other types of writing,
        165
    definition of, 163
    definitions with, 218
    organization of, 163–164
    point of view in, 164, 165
    tone in, 164
Purposes of writing, 1
    in argumentation and persuasion, 244, 246,
        249

Purposes of writing (*continued*)
  in classification, 103
  in narration, 13

Questions
  begging the, 249
  rhetorical, 245
Quindlen, Anna, 143–144, 252–253
Quoted dialogue, 17

"Racial Stereotypes Go Underground"
    (Merriwether-deVries), 209–210
"Ravine, The" (Stott), 53–54
Reeves, Annie, 35–37
Refutation, 246
"Regular Customer" (Garrison), 67–69
Reilly, Rick, 240–242
Reimer, Courtney, 130–134
Revising, 11
  cause and effect writing, 193
  definitions, 218
  for order, 105–106
Rewriting, 11
Rhetorical questions, 245
"Right Way to Eat an Ice-Cream Cone, The"
    (Hills), 172–173
Ruckdeschel, John, 266–267
"Running with the Cardio-Bots" (Kirn),
    220–221

Sakamoto, Nancy Masterson, 152–156
Scaccia, Jesse, 260–262
Schultz, Connie, 32–34
Seaman, Barrett, 254–255
Second person, 16, 164, 165
"Secrets of Man's Unspoken Language"
    (Morris), 125–129
Shelton, Richard, 224–225
Sherry, Mary, 258–259
"Shopping in Pajamas" (Mercier), 160–162
Similes, 44
Simons, Gustave, 111–112
Sinclair, Liz, 205–207
Smith, Nelliejean, 203–204
Smith, Sarah, 38–42
Smith-Yackel, Bonnie, 98–102
"Social Meaning of T-Shirts, The" (Crane),
    87–89
Solutions, in argumentation, 246
Spatial order, 45
Specific-to-general order, 5–6
"Start Spreading the News: Seven Things You
    Should Know Before Moving to New
    York City" (Reimer), 130–134
Stern, Lesley, 20–21
"Story of My Ring, The" (Reeves), 35–37
Stott, Quincy, 53–54
Subjective essays, 16
Subjective writing, 47
"Supply Chain, The" (Friedman), 166–167
Support, 7
Synonyms, 217

"Tax Junk Food? Yes" (Jacobson), 250–251
Theses, 6, 243
  examples to support, 73–74
Thesis statements, 6–7
  in cause and effect, 189
  supporting with examples, 73–74
Third person, 16, 165
"Thirsty Animal, The" (Manning), 211–213
Thurow, Lester C., 115–116
Time, in point of view, 15–16
Time order, 14
"Time to Look and Listen" (Asfahani), 282–284
Tone, 15–16
  objective, 136
  in process writing, 164, 165
Topics, 4, 243
Topic sentences, 4
  in cause and effect, 189
  in classification and division, 105
"Total Eclipse of the Son" (Kary), 238–239
Traig, Jennifer, 176–178
Transitional words, 10
  in classification and division, 105
  in comparison and contrast, 139–140
"Trip to Honduras, A" (Boehmer), 272–273

"Ultimate Kitchen Gadget, The" (Capon),
    222–223
Unity, 105
Updike, John, 18–19

VanSpanckeren, Kathryn, 94–97
"Very Basic Decision, A" (Mebane), 279–281
Voas, Robert, 263–265

Wade, Ellen Cobb, 79–80
"What Does It Mean to Be Creative?"
    (Hayakawa), 226–227
"What Is Intelligence, Anyway?" (Asimov),
    235–237
"What Is Poverty?" (Parker), 230–234
"Why Eat Junk Food?" (Wurtman), 197–198
"Why Harlem Is Not Manhattan" (Jackson),
    22–23
Williamson, Debra Aho, 90–93
"Wreck, The" (Mack), 55–56
Writing
  argumentation/persuasion, 243–249
  cause and effect, 189–194
  classification and division, 103–106
  combining strategies in, 271
  comparison and contrast, 135–140
  definitions, 217–219
  descriptive, 43–47
  examples, 73–76
  process and strategies for, 1–11
  processes, 163–165
  purposes of, 1
Wurtman, Judith, 197–198

Yano, Edna, 182–184
"Yin and Yang" (Jones), 147–148